AN ECONOMIC AND SOCIAL HISTORY
OF BRITAIN
1066–1939

AN ECONOMIC AND SOCIAL HISTORY OF BRITAIN
1066-1939

BY

M. W. FLINN

PROFESSOR OF ECONOMIC HISTORY IN THE
UNIVERSITY OF EDINBURGH

MACMILLAN
London · Melbourne · Toronto

ST MARTIN'S PRESS
New York
1968

Published by
MACMILLAN AND CO LTD
Little Essex Street London WC2
and also at Bombay Calcutta and Madras
Macmillan South Africa (Publishers) Pty Ltd Johannesburg
The Macmillan Company of Australia Pty Ltd Melbourne
The Macmillan Company of Canada Ltd Toronto
St Martin's Press Inc New York

Printed in Great Britain by
ROBERT MACLEHOSE AND CO LTD
The University Press, Glasgow

PREFACE

Economic history is still a relative newcomer to the school curriculum, and the praiseworthy efforts of teachers to pioneer the subject have been impeded by the fact that most of the available textbooks were written primarily for older readers. Time has begun to remedy this deficiency; but there still appears to be a need for a book specifically designed to meet the requirements of the G.C.E. syllabus at the Ordinary Level. It is hoped that this book will go some way towards filling this gap. The task of preparing it has not been made easier by disparities between the syllabuses set by the different examining boards. Some syllabuses range from 1066 to the present day; others, less ambitiously, narrow the scope to the last two centuries. The framework of this book has been dictated partly by the need to effect a compromise between these disparities, though this purely material need has not been allowed entirely to swamp the author's own conception of a diet suitable for the delicate digestions of students at this level.

This, however, is not the only difficulty. The author has enjoyed the experience of teaching this subject in schools, of examining it for one of the larger boards, and of teaching it at the more academic levels of the universities. The attempt to balance these viewpoints, as well as to provide adequate material on each topic to meet the twin needs of the ablest students and the sternest examiners, may have led to the overloading of the book; but as few students may be expected to begin at the beginning and work steadily through to the end, this is probably to err in a safe direction. Clearly, students and teachers will select their topics. The author's intention throughout has been to explain adequately every topic judged suitable for inclusion, relating it where necessary to other cognate trends: some topics thus treated may accordingly be judged too difficult for the less able students, but it is hoped that the systematic explanations of all technical terms as they occur will help to make most of the material intelligible to all students at this level.

A subject so young as economic history inevitably moves swiftly; new interpretations and stresses come in quick succession to replace those of former generations. When so much is yet to be learnt about man's economic past this must remain so for many years to come. This book must therefore date, as others have done. All that can be said is that it tries conscientiously to present a survey of the subject as it is taught and understood by its specialists in the mid-twentieth century.

Not all the examining boards offer a clear lead on the upper time limits of their syllabuses, some of which stretch relentlessly to an ever-advancing 'present day'. History undoubtedly reaches up to yesterday; but, for the kind of students for whom this textbook is designed, at least, it should surely be available in a pre-digested form, and since time marches inexorably on, this can never be done. Before the second World War it was customary to call a halt at 1914. In the same way, for some years to come, it seems reasonable to draw the line at 1939. This terminal has been adopted for this book, though in some topics, where logical conclusions demand it, there are some brief excursions into the post-war field.

To supplement this textbook, the author has prepared a companion volume, *Readings in Economic and Social History*. These documents have been selected with a view to their readability and to their value in illustrating at first hand some of the movements and events discussed in the following pages.

My thanks are due to the following authors and publishers for permission to quote from the works mentioned:

E. Lamond (editor), *The Common Weal of this Realm of England* (Cambridge University Press, 1929); D. Read, *Peterloo: the Massacre and its Background* (Manchester University Press, 1958); A. E. Bland, P. A. Brown and R. H. Tawney, *English Economic History: Select Documents* (G. Bell & Sons Ltd., 1914); Friedrich Engels, *The Condition of the Working Class in England*, translated by W. H. Chaloner & W. O. Henderson (Blackwell, 1958); C. Morris (editor), *The Journeys of Celia Fiennes* (Cresset Press, 1947). I am also grateful to Mr. L. E. Morris, 99, Eastcote Road, Ruislip, Middlesex, for permission to reproduce the substantial quotation from his translation of the Ruislip Custumal (from his *History of Ruislip*, 1956) which appears on pp. 13–14.

ACKNOWLEDGMENTS

The publishers wish to acknowledge the help of the following, who have supplied illustrations on the pages quoted.

Aerofilms Ltd, pp. 337, 340.

M. W. Beresford (photograph by Clifford Farrar), p. 90.

P. J. Bowden, pp. 2, 72. (From *The Wool Trade in Tudor and Stuart England*.)

British Transport Commission, p. 250.

University of Cambridge (photographs by J. K. St. Joseph, Crown Copyright reserved), pp. 35, 38, 176 (both).

The Syndics of the University Press, Cambridge, pp. 21, 37, 122, 123. (From Darby: *An Historical Geography of England Before 1800*.)

The Syndics and Miss E. M. Carus-Wilson, p. 79. (From Postan and Rich: *The Cambridge Economic History of Europe, Volume II*.)

Central Office of Information, Crown copyright reserved, p. 25.

Harris Museum and Art Gallery, p. 210.

J. Harvey, p. 9.

Illustrated London News, p. 295 (both).

London County Council, p. 350 (both).

Longmans, Green, p. 227. (From Redford and Russell: *The History of Local Government in Manchester*); pp. 86, 158. (From Marshall: *English People in the Eighteenth Century*); pp. 15, 39, 41 (By permission of the Trustees of the British Museum); pp. 40, 76, 131, 138, 141, 160, 162, 215, 236–7, 249, 252, 287, 288, 355.

The Mansell Collection, pp. 153, 232, 318.

National Coal Board, p. 357.

Thomas Nelson & Sons, p. 152. (From Osborn: *The Story of the Mushets*.)

The Delegates to the Clarendon Press, Oxford, pp. 132, 133. (From Willan: *River Navigation in England*.)

Radio Times Hulton Picture Library, p. 326 (both).

G. D. Ramsey, pp. 84, 110, 114. (From *English Overseas Trade during the Centuries of Emergence*.)

Routledge & Kegan Paul, p. 80. (From Schubert: *History of the British Iron & Steel Industry*.)

Trinity College Library, Cambridge. (By courtesy of the College Council), p. 8.

Josiah Wedgwood & Sons Ltd, p. 166.

CONTENTS

MAPS

PART ONE

MEDIEVAL AND EARLY
MODERN TIMES

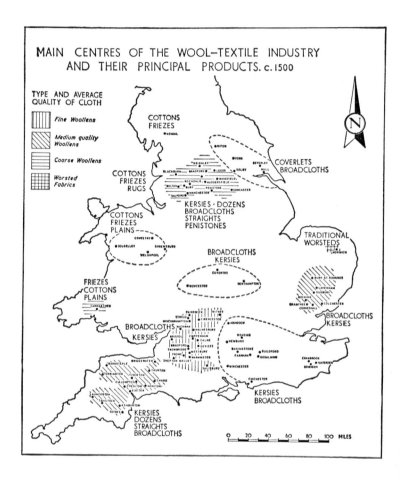

MAIN CENTRES OF THE WOOL–TEXTILE INDUSTRY AND THEIR PRINCIPAL PRODUCTS. c. 1500

TYPE AND AVERAGE QUALITY OF CLOTH

Fine Woollens

Medium quality Woollens

Coarse Woollens

Worsted Fabrics

CHAPTER I

THE MEDIEVAL VILLAGE

1. DOMESDAY ENGLAND

Twenty years after he had conquered England, William of Normandy dispatched a number of commissioners to all parts of his kingdom to make a detailed survey of the wealth of the country. The compilers of this *Domesday Book* of 1086 were to visit each town and village throughout the country, to enquire and record the details of land ownership, land values, farms, woodland, ploughs and stock. They were also to compare the present (1086) state in each town or village with the conditions immediately preceding the Norman Conquest in 1066 — 'in the time of King Edward' (the 'Confessor'). Though the surviving copies of Domesday Book are not quite complete (for example, there is no account of the city of London), there remains an extraordinarily detailed and informative picture of the wealth, institutions and feudal structure of England at the beginning of the Norman era.

Perhaps the most striking difference between Domesday England and modern England is that of population. England and Wales in the mid-twentieth century had a population of almost 44 million; estimates based on the Domesday survey show that the population in the late eleventh century was little more than one million. Nevertheless, this tiny population cultivated an area almost as great as that under the plough (not including permanent grassland) in the mid-twentieth century. The agricultural settlements which comprised probably nine-tenths of the early medieval population were small, scattered and frequently isolated. Much of England was covered by woodland and there were vast tracts of countryside where marsh or moorland discouraged any kind of settlement. There was little industry, and most of this was carried on by craftsmen in the village communities. Owing to the primitive means of transport, towns tended to serve fairly restricted local markets and were therefore numerous but small.

The Domesday Book also revealed in its full detail the feudal structure of English society. Feudalism was a system both of land tenure and of personal relationships. After his conquest of England in 1066, William I assumed the right to dispose of all the land in the kingdom as he thought fit. Some of it he allowed to remain in the hands of the former owners or occupiers; the rest he took into his own possession to grant to his followers or to retain to provide his own income. In general the *tenants-in-chief* to whom the king granted land were the great barons, his military chiefs, and religious foundations, the monasteries and priories. The feudal barons were under contract, as a condition of the holding of their estates, to raise a number of armed soldiers in proportion to the size of their holdings. The tenants-in-chief in their turn sub-let their estates in smaller parts, generally in units called *manors*, to sub-tenants who thus became lords of their respective manors.

At the level of the manors there were two classes of inhabitants. There were *free men* who owed little to the lords of their manors and were free to dispose of their property and to go and come as they wished. On the other hand were the *unfree men*, commonly called *serfs*. These men, their families, their land and their goods were legally the property of their lords. They had no rights except those that their lords chose to grant them. The principal economic advantage the lords secured from their serfs was their compulsory unpaid labour some days each week on the manorial *demesnes* (portions of manors not let out to tenants and farmed directly by the lords of the manors). A man born unfree endured the disability of serfdom throughout his life unless able to purchase his freedom from his lord; but once free, the man and his descendants remained free for all time.

Finally, Domesday Book revealed that the twenty years following the Norman Conquest had seen a diminution in population as well as in the value of manors in many parts of the country. This was the fruits of the Conqueror's ruthless suppression of the conquered English people. His reply to a rising against him in the North of England was 'the Harrying of the North', by which he burnt and laid waste whole counties. In many towns much valuable property was destroyed to make way for the castles by which William's authority was to be exerted. Twenty years was not sufficient to recover from these set-backs. The same period saw also a perceptible strengthening of the feudal relationships in manorial society.

But the Norman Conquest, by strengthening England's link with the Continent and by bringing to an end the long disruption of economic life associated with the Danish conquests of England, led in the long run to an era of economic expansion in England. For almost three hundred years after the Conquest there was a steady and fairly rapid growth of the population, which may have reached almost four million by the early fourteenth century. More people needed more land to cultivate and in the twelfth and thirteenth centuries much hitherto waste land was brought under the plough. Trading links with Europe were developed and the foundation of England's woollen industry was laid. This great medieval expansion slowed down during the fourteenth century; the growth of population may have been checked even before the great plague of 1348–9. The fifteenth century was largely one of stagnation in the economy. Only slowly was the land, abandoned after the Black Death, brought back into cultivation under the impulse of a gradually increasing population after about 1430. But in the last quarter of the fifteenth century there were stirrings of new forces which were to bring important changes: population began to grow more rapidly, the manufacture of woollen cloth began to emerge as a major industry, and changes in the demand for the products of agriculture put a pressure on the land that disturbed the traditional balance of English farming. Some of the forces underlying these conflicting trends in the medieval economy are discussed in this and the following chapters.

2. Open-field Farming

Though there were many different types of farming practised in early medieval England, over a wide area of the country arable farming was most commonly carried on in what were known as *open fields*. Arable farming consisted of the cultivation of crops, and in the medieval English village formed merely one part of the traditional system of farming. For English farming in the Middle Ages, where it was not specialized sheep farming (or other kinds of specialization), was basically mixed farming, involving cattle rearing (for draught animals, meat and dairy produce), poultry and pigs, as well as the usual range of arable crops.

Only a portion of the available land in any village could therefore be spared for arable cultivation. Since men needed the assistance of oxen and, later, horses for drawing the plough and the harrow, not to mention the need for milk, butter and cheese, grassland formed an important part of the farmland. And this grassland had to meet two needs — for grazing while the grass grew during the summer months, and for hay for winter feed. The latter was indispensable on the medieval farm; root crops were unknown and there were few alternative forms of winter foodstuff for the cattle. Thus the meadow, where the hay crop was grown, was often the richest and most valuable section of the farmland.

In the early Middle Ages good land for cultivation was only won slowly and at great expenditure of labour from the woodland, heath or marsh which formerly covered much of the land. There was no shortage of uncultivated land, which consequently became known as *waste land*. For this reason farmers could be allowed unlimited use of the waste land, much of which therefore became *common land*, or land shared by all. Some of this land consisted of quite good grassland which was accordingly valued for grazing cattle in the summer months. The woodland provided *pannage* (nuts, acorns, etc.,) for pigs as well as fuel for the villagers (*common of estover*), while the heath often provided peat or turf, the right to collect which was called *common of turbary*. Thousands of acres of upland England provided rough pasture for sheep and cattle which took the form of extensive commons between settlements. Where commons of this kind were shared by two or more villages, the practice was referred to as *intercommoning*.

The arable land must thus be seen against a background of mixed farming. In general it represented patient recovery of former waste land from woodland and heath. So great a labour of reclamation must inevitably have been shared by all the members of a community, and as each new area was added to the existing stock it had to be divided between those who had helped to win it. This led to the minute sub-division of land between the farmers in a village. The pattern of development of the arable area of a village might therefore take this form: initially two, three or four fields were brought under cultivation, each farmer having a share in each field; as time went on, additions were made to each field, each farmer once again taking his share of the new land; there remained the original number of fields — two, three or four, or multiples of those numbers — so that each farmer gradually acquired a large number of small holdings of land, equally distributed over the fields. The original fields became considerably magnified in size, and were made up of the irregularly shaped reclamations. These sub-divisions were called *furlongs*, *shots* or *selions*, and were, of course, sub-divided again into the separate portions of individual farmers. Since this was arable land, it follows that the shape of each of the individual holdings had to conform to the needs of the plough-team. The early medieval plough was heavy, was drawn by teams of four to eight oxen, and was therefore cumbrous — the longer the furrow without turning, the better. Accordingly, the individual holdings of the furlongs took the form of long, narrow strips. As the direction of the strips in each furlong was determined with a view to drainage by the lie of the land, each field gradually took on the appearance of a patchwork quilt. The irregular pattern of the furlongs in the open fields left many small *headlands* (spare land at the heads of strips giving access to them and allowing room to turn a plough-team) and *sikes* (grass tracks giving access to remoter parts of the fields) which provided a useful additional source of hay or grazing land for tethered cattle.

Each farmer cultivated his own strips, and since there were communal precautions to keep cattle off the arable fields, there was no need for any form of fencing between the strips. Indeed, when many operations were performed communally — ploughing and harvesting were often done this way — the fewer obstructions the better. Any form of fence or hedge was wasteful of land and the boundaries between strips were often marked by no more than stones or posts at each corner of the strip. Sometimes the boundaries were marked only in the detailed memories of the elders of the village. In other places a double furrow marked clearly the boundaries, while in a few instances an unploughed *baulk* of two or three feet, or even a raised bank, marked the boundaries.

The medieval peasant at work on the English Manor

The needs of man pressed perpetually on his very limited resources in the early Middle Ages, and every blade of grass was coveted. Hence, when the grain crop was harvested it was the custom to allow cattle to be turned to graze on the stubble before ploughing time when they could pick up a certain amount of nourishment and rest the common. This practice, together with the need for co-operation between the farmers in certain tasks, compelled the acceptance by all the farmers of a uniform farming calendar. When one of the fields was to be thrown open for common grazing on a given date after, say, the wheat harvest was home, a farmer who had chosen to plant an alternative crop which was harvested a month later would soon learn the wisdom of falling into line with his fellows. Hence each of the open fields tended to grow the same crop, regardless of the minute sub-division of the holdings in it. Another feature of medieval farming helped to determine the pattern of open-field

8

farming — the need to leave the land idle periodically in order that it might recover its goodness. Soil will not support repeated grain crops; grains exhaust land more rapidly than any other crops. The alternation of grain crops with root crops or clover will keep soil at a constant pitch of goodness, but in the Middle Ages this expedient was not known. Consequently every two, three or four years each field had to be left without any crop (*fallow*), though common grazing on the fallow field made some use of the otherwise idle land. Poor land, which needed to be rested in this way every second year in alternation with a grain crop, was said to be farmed on a *two-field* rotation; better land, where grain crops, say a winter-sown crop (wheat) and a spring-sown crop (barley) could be grown in successive years, leaving the land fallow in the third, was said to be farmed on a *three-field* rotation — this was probably the commonest method; the best land, which could sustain three years of cropping followed by a fourth fallow year, was said to be farmed on a *four-field* rotation.

An alternative to this open-field system of arable farming, called the *infield-outfield* or *run-rig* system, was practised in areas of poorer soil, particularly in north-western and south-western England. In this system, a part of the village or township's land,

Strips in the spring corn field — from a photograph of one of the few surviving open fields at Laxton, Nottinghamshire

the *infield*, was cultivated continuously for several years until the crop yield fell to uneconomically low levels; arable cultivation on it was then abandoned and another area taken into intensive cultivation in the same way. The remaining *outfield* was used for common pasture. In East Anglia and Kent, too, there were systems of cultivation which differed from both open-field and run-rig.

Thus, though the open-field system was probably the most usual form of arable cultivation in medieval England, it was far from being the only method of farming. Other systems operated in many parts of the north-west and the south-west, in East Anglia and Kent, while vast tracts of the North of England were covered by moorland or were so thinly populated that there was little intensive arable farming. In the fenlands and in parts of Somerset extensive marshland made arable farming impossible. In the main, therefore, the open-field system was practised in the 'Midland triangle' whose corners lay at the estuaries of the Thames, the Severn and the Humber. Outside this open-field area there is evidence that open-field cultivation was also practised in Devonshire, Cheshire and in the north-east as far north as County Durham.

3. THE MANOR

Outside the many small towns of early medieval England, most of the land occupied by farmers was divided into estates of varying sizes called *manors*. A manor was a unit of land ownership. In many cases it corresponded with the land farmed by the occupants of a particular village, but this was by no means invariably so. Some villages comprised two or more manors, while some manors included more than a single village, or parts of two or more villages. The village of Cottenham, Cambridgeshire, in the late thirteenth century, contained no fewer than six manors. A manor, in other words, did not necessarily correspond to a village, and must be considered simply as an estate owned by an individual or institution and farmed by those who lived on it. The manor was at one and the same time a legal and an administrative unit, and was often, in addition, a unit of agricultural organization. In so far as manorial organization was usually associated with farming there was a close relationship between the manor and the system of cultivation. The manor was held by the *lord of the manor* who was often a member of the aristocracy, but could be any individual or institution to whom the Crown had granted the manor or who could afford to purchase a grant. In this way manors often came into the hands of institutions like monasteries, cathedrals and colleges, which administered their property through a resident, salaried *steward* or *bailiff*.

Broadly speaking, there were three categories of land on the manor. The first, called the *demesne*, was retained in the occupation of the lord of the manor. The second part was the *freehold* land, farmed mostly by its *freemen* owners, but sometimes rented out by the freeholders to other cultivators. The third part, the *villenagium*, was occupied by the *unfree* of the manor. This land was held in return for specific services and payments. There was no regular pattern of combination of these three categories of land. Of the many thousands of manors in early medieval England, no two were the same. Many carried all three types of land; others consisted of two, and some of one only. All types of manors were subject to bewildering changes as manors changed hands or as the occupants bought or sold holdings or shifted their social status in response to ever-changing historical forces. It has already been shown that manors often did not coincide with villages: similarly, tenants or freeholders often held land in more than one manor. There was an unlimited variety of manors and none could be said to be typical.

But in spite of this diversity certain important features were common to most manors. These similarities rose out of two fundamental aspects of manorial organization — first, that manors were initially feudal in nature, and, second, that they were normally inseparable from the organization of farming. From the feudal point of view the fact that the demesne was a major source of revenue to the lord of a manor led to its exploitation in many districts by means of the unpaid labour of the unfree tenants of the manor. Without this servile labour force the demesne must often have gone uncultivated, for in the early Middle Ages there were few landless labourers available for weekly hire. Accordingly the unfree tenants were tied to their manors, not being free to leave without the consent of the lord, a consent, needless to say, seldom given without substantial payment. From the administrative point of view, the very nature of open-field farming as well as the need for farmers in a village community to pool their resources and help each other tended to turn the manor into an organization for regulating the seasonal routine of farming.

There was a great cleavage between the occupants of a manor — a cleavage between free and unfree. The freeman enjoyed virtually complete rights over his own land except in so far as he was bound in the communal interest to follow the agreed annual routine of cultivation. In some parts of England there existed a class of freemen called *sokemen*, free in all respects except that they were not free to sell their land and were thus tied to their manors, and that they were obliged to seek justice in the lord's court, not the King's.

The burdens of the more numerous groups of unfree tenants offered a marked contrast to the condition of the freemen. The unfree men were known collectively as *serfs* and their unfree or *servile* status as *serfdom*. Among the serfs, the *villeins* held the larger farms, and the *cottars* or *bordars* the smaller; but all serfs owed the same kind of obligations to the lord which were usually in direct proportion to the size of their holding of land. From the twelfth century a further class of landless labourer — the *famulus* — was emerging. In some districts this class became fairly numerous in later centuries.

Holdings of all classes of farmers, whether free or unfree, freeholders or tenants, varied considerably. In the early Middle Ages a holding by a villein of about twenty-five to forty acres, known as a *virgate* or a *yardland*, was common, but sub-division of holdings, on the one hand, arising out of divided inheritance between two or more sons, and consolidation of holdings by purchase and marriage on the other hand, destroyed any regular patterns there might once have been. Half and quarter virgate holdings in villeinage became quite common, while at the other extreme both freemen and villeins sometimes accumulated holdings of several hundred acres. Cottars or bordars commonly held less than ten acres and in many parts cottar holdings of under two or three acres predominated.

The most onerous of the serf's obligations was to work for the lord on the demesne. This labour service took two main forms — a full day's work by one man from the family to be performed two, three or four days a week according to the size of the serf's holding or the custom of the manor (*week work*), and extra work by all members of his household at harvest time (*boon work*). Week work was unpaid and may be regarded as the way in which the serf paid his rent for his land. Boon work was partly rewarded — food and drink were provided for all who worked to bring in the harvest on the demesne. Week work took many forms — ploughing, hoeing, mowing, carting, malt-making, sheep-shearing or a host of other routine farming tasks. The variety of the labour services owed by a typical villein may be judged from the following entry in a description of the manor of Ruislip in the County of Middlesex of the year 1248:

'Item from the feast of St. Peter ad Vincula to Michaelmas he must reap three days a week, with one man, wherever required, or do whatever else other work the lord wishes him to do, without maintenance. And if he carries for his work from the fields beyond the grange of Bourne he must carry a waggonload of corn or two cartloads, and if from the fields on this side of the said grange two waggonloads or four cartloads. He must also at the first boon day of harvest find one man to reap and (he shall) have maintenance. And so at the second boon he must reap with all his family, except his wife and his herdsman. And he himself shall be present the whole day with a rod of authority to see that his family work well, and they shall have maintenance twice in the day, namely, about the hour of nine, corn bread, cheese, ale or cider, and in the even corn bread, pottage . . . or ale or cider. Item, at the third boon day he must reap with one man, at his own payment, and about the hour of nine and in the evening have . . . in common in the midst of the fields in . . . two full pots of ale or cider and three tubs full of apples if the lord should have apples. Item, if it happens that the lord shall wish to send hams or other produce to Bec (the manor of Ruislip was held by the Abbey of Bec in Normandy at this time) he has to find carriage to the Thames for that purpose. Item, if he should have pigs of his own rearing he must pay pannage for them, namely a pig of over a year old a penny, and less than a year old a halfpenny and in the same way he must pay pannage for all his pigs that are separated from the mother. Item, in Lent he must harrow for one day, if required, and have maintenance and carry for one day at harvest time and have maintenance. Item, in a year in which full work is worked he must work from Michaelmas to the feast of St. Peter ad Vincula three days a week wherever required, at whatever kind of work the lord may require, with one man, and for feast days falling within the aforesaid term he must make good the work on succeeding working days and in the same way must plough just as he ploughs when not fully working, but on the days on which he ploughs for the accustomed service of herdage two works must be remitted to him. He must also prepare a load of malt for Christmas and have fodder or firewood ready dried, with remittance of one work; and for Easter all in the same manner. Item, he must do carrying service to the neighbouring market, namely half a quarter of corn, and in the meantime be quit of one work, and if he goes to London he must collect a waggonload and be quit of one work, and if to St. Neots quit of three days, likewise if to North Stoke of three days, likewise if to Swyncombe of two days. Item, if the monks go to distant parts he must find a baggage wagon for them and their equipment and other necessities and then three of his works must be remitted, and he must have maintenance for the journey, and if to near places so that it is possible to return the same day he must be quit of a single work only. Item, he must harrow as often as he may be instructed to, in such wise that when the ploughs of the lord begin to plough he must harrow to the hour when they cease. He must also do sheep washing and shearing right up to the completion of the shearing, and he must scythe the meadows, make the hay, cart it and put it into cocks, until all is complete, and all alike shall receive a ram or twelvepence, and he must carry letters, drive animals, load manure and spread it on the fields, carry the folds of the lord from one place to another, prepare and mend the wattles, cut up wood for fencing and make it into fences, and he shall ditch and dig. And if he brews he shall give a penny of toll for one sester. Item, he is not to sell a horse or an ox of his own rearing without the licence of the lord, nor give his daughter in marriage. Item, for all dues and aid he must pay scot and lot (i.e. in entirety), and after his death the lord shall have the best beast as a heriot, and if he dies intestate all his goods and chattels shall be at the disposal and will of the lord. And he must be reeve if the lord wishes it, and pay a toll on all things sold within the boundaries of the manor.'

But week work was by no means universal on medieval manors. It depended on the existence of a manorial demesne, and there were many manors without demesnes. Manors in which the demesnes were cultivated wholly or partly by paid labourers (*famuli*) were by no means uncommon. On some ecclesiastical manors in Leicestershire in the fourteenth century only a small proportion of the unfree tenants owed week work

Taking corn to be ground at the lord's mill
(from the Luttrell Psalter)

(though all owed boon work) and those that owed week work seldom worked on the demesne more than one day a week.

In addition to week work and boon work, the serf often owed contributions to the lord in money or in the produce of his farm — eggs, chickens, grain or honey. The uncertainty of the *tallage* — a money tax levied at will by the lord — could be particularly burdensome. When a serf's daughter married, a fine known as *merchet* was exacted by the lord. On the death of a serf custom usually decreed that the holding passed to his heir, but the lord gave his approval to the inheritance only in return for another payment, the *heriot*, consisting usually of the best beast from the holding. A serf was subject to many other restrictions on his freedom. He was obliged to have his corn ground at the lord's mill at a price fixed by the lord. He was not free to leave the manor and, if he deserted, could be brought back again by the lord: medieval society made it very difficult for a serf to acquire personal freedom. He could plead for justice only in his lord's court. Finally, his land was held *at the will of the lord* — that is to say that the lord could, if he wished, alter the terms of the tenure or even end it. In practice, the *custom of the manor*, accepted in the Middle Ages by both lord and tenant, mostly regulated tenures in such a way as to protect the tenant. When a holding changed hands or was passed by inheritance to a new tenant, the terms of the tenure were inscribed in a *court roll* of the manor and the tenant given a copy. Land held in this way in the later Middle Ages accordingly became known as *copyhold* land.

Servile or *villein* tenure appears at first sight to have operated exclusively in the interest of the lord and to have imposed considerable hardship on the unfree tenant. But there were compensations. In the lawless society of early medieval England the protection of a powerful feudal magnate as lord of the manor was no small attraction. Life then was a struggle for survival and a villein's holding provided the means of an adequate, sometimes ample, existence. The holding of strips in the arable open fields carried with it the whole range of common rights, providing the villein with pasture for his sheep, cattle, pigs and poultry, with peat or wood for his hearth and building material for his cottage. In the course of time some villeins became wealthy men. But it remains true that as they advanced in wealth, the first object of most villeins was to buy their freedom from the lords — the shackles of villeinage were increasingly resented. The forces that led to the gradual disappearance of serfdom are analysed more fully in the last section of this chapter.

It was possible, however, for the feudal elements in the manor to decay, leaving the manor still thriving as a unit of agricultural organization. Open-field cultivation, by its very nature, called for some degree of co-operation. The strips of all farmers, whether freemen or serfs, were intermixed in the great fields, while the extensive use of common pastures raised many problems of regulation. To handle these questions of communal farming, each manor was subject to the control of the manorial court in which a jury of freemen and tenants, under the supervision of the lord or his bailiff, determined farming routine and punished offenders against the rules governing the use of the common or the straying of animals. It was necessary for the court to determine precisely the dates when the open fields should be thrown open for grazing on the stubble, when they should be closed again for ploughing, how many beasts each farmer should be allowed to put on the common or how much should be charged for the sale of hay from the sikes which gave access to all parts of the fields. Some idea of the work of these courts may be gained from the following regulations for the

commons and open fields of the manor of Wimeswould (Leicestershire) in the year 1425:

> 'For neat (cattle) pasture we ordain Orrow and Breches,
> Woldsyke and Wyloughbybroke, for to be broken (thrown open for
> grazing) on Crowchemesseday (Crouchmas was the feast of the
> Invention of the Cross, and fell on 3 May); and whoso break this,
> every man shall pay for each beast that may be taken in any other
> several pasture a penny to the church; therefor to go a seven night
> day (i.e. to endure for a week).
>
> 'Also, for the neat pasture, after that be eaten, all the wheat-
> field, to wit, Hardacre field namely, save Strete headlands, where
> they may not go for destroying of corn; this for to endure another
> sevennightday under the pain before said. . . .
>
> 'Also, if any man tie his horse or reach on any headlands or by
> brookside into any man's corn, he shall make amends to him that
> has the harm, and for each foot that is within the corn pay a penny
> to the church.'

So long as open-field farming or common pastures remained,
some remnants of manorial organization survived. Laxton, in
Nottinghamshire, the sole surviving open-field village in the
mid-twentieth century, still retains its *Court Leet*, which carries
on its traditional functions though all feudal relationships
disappeared many centuries ago.

4. THE DECLINE OF SERFDOM

The growth of population in the three centuries following the
Norman Conquest led to continuous extension of the arable
area. The clearance of woodland, the draining of marshes and
the embankment of coastal plains added more and more
cultivable land. Romney Marsh, for example, was drained
during the thirteenth century, while extensive reclamations of
sea marshes around the Wash were made in the twelfth and
thirteenth centuries. Many new villages appeared in this process. Nearly all these intakes of new land were farmed by freemen. In this way, though the number of villein holdings might
remain unaltered, the proportions of free holdings in the whole
was raised.

From the twelfth century, however, other forces were at work
which tended to reduce the unfree element in the population so

that by the end of the fifteenth century serfdom had virtually died out. Freedom from serfdom, or *manumission*, could only be achieved with the consent of the lord of the manor, and so long as it remained in the interest of the lord to retain his tenants in serfdom it was very difficult for the villein or cottar to change his legal status. There was no lack of motives for the serf to want his freedom. The very increase of freemen around him served only to emphasize the inferiority of his position. The time given to labour services on the lord's demesne detracted seriously from his ability to farm his own land efficiently and thwarted any ambition he might have to extend his holding. More important, as towns grew, so did the opportunity to sell farm produce in the new urban markets. This steady growth in trade between country and town put more money into the hands of the farmer who previously had achieved little more than the satisfaction of the needs of his own family, and increased his incentive to grow more food. Labour services stood in his way, but the sale of his products in the nearest town would give him money with which to buy his freedom. Moreover, a steady rate of *enclosure* (taking a portion of common land into private ownership and fencing it in) was slowly whittling away some common rights during the twelfth to fourteenth centuries with the result that the economic position of many tenants declined. Further diminution of the common land resulted from the encroachments of settlers on the waste.

In the early Middle Ages payments at a great many levels were made in the form of labour or in kind. The barons and knights to whom the King had granted manors paid for these by military service, while they in their turn farmed their demesnes with the aid of the labour services of their servile tenants. But already by the twelfth century the inconvenience of this method of raising an army had become apparent and the practice of hiring paid mercenary soldiers substituted. On the manors the lords themselves were conscious that labour services unwillingly performed were perfunctory and inefficient. The sale of the produce of the demesne in the rising urban markets gave the lords, too, an incentive to more efficient farming. The writer of a thirteenth-century treatise on husbandry, Walter of Henley, observed that villeins 'neglect their work and it is necessary to guard against their fraud'. Given an alternative supply of labourers available for daily and weekly hire, wage labour was a more satisfactory answer to the problem of cultivating the demesne than were the labour services of the unfree tenants. The increase of population in the twelfth and thirteenth centuries contributed to the increase of this labour force through the younger sons of villeins and cottars who inherited no land. In part, also, this growing class of landless labourers was recruited from those who had secured freedom by flight from their own lords as well as from a not very numerous group who were granted manumission in order that they might join the Crusades of the twelfth and thirteenth centuries.

In the long run, however, it was the abandonment of demesne farming by the lords themselves that proved to be the most decisive factor in the decline of labour services. The supervision of villein labour services made demesne farming tiresome and expensive, and from the twelfth century it became increasingly common for lords to *lease* the whole demesne to a single farmer. A lease was an agreement to rent a piece of land for a fixed number of years at a fixed money rent. To the money rent from the leasing of the demesne was added the money rents now paid by the villeins whose labour services had been *commuted*, and many lords found this to be a more profitable arrangement. In particular the leasing of the demesne appealed to non-resident lords who were often monasteries or colleges.

By the mid-fourteenth century *commutation* had made considerable progress, though less in some regions than in others. In the north and west of England, for example, commutation appears to have abolished labour services almost completely by 1348, but in the south and east, with the exception of Kent where labour services had never been exacted, commutation had made less headway. One historian has estimated that villeins performed all the work on the demesnes of about half the manors in the country in the mid-fourteenth century. Villeinage, therefore, was still very much a reality, but a class known as *molmen* — tenants who retained all the marks of villeinage but who paid money rents instead of labour services — was becoming increasingly common. While population was growing there tended to be more prospective tenants than there was good land, a situation which played into the hands of the lords. But in the mid-fourteenth century a major catastrophe over-whelmed England. In 1348 the *Black Death* — the bubonic plague — struck England. For over a year it swept the country leaving a trail of death behind it. Its incidence varied in different localities, but its general effect was to reduce the population of the country at a single blow by almost one fifth. In some parts the effect was more drastic, as many as one half of the popula-tion succumbing to the plague. Plagues, of course, were frequent visitors to the shores of this country in the early Middle Ages and exercised a constant check on population. The rate of growth of population in the three centuries after the Norman Conquest was accordingly slow, and the country's population had probably not reached four million in 1348. Population may have begun to decline even before 1348, but the Black Death, besides causing an immediate sharp fall in the population, initiated a period of declining population which lasted until about 1430.

The immediate effect of the Black Death on manors was to convert the shortage of land into a shortage of labour. Wages rose steeply, from 3d. or 4d. a day to 5d. or 6d. a day. Lords faced the prospect of drastic losses of income unless they could succeed in attracting new tenants. Economic forces swung in favour of tenants whose power of bargaining to secure manumission and commutation of labour services was doubled overnight. In an effort to stabilize wages the government, acting needless to say in the interests of the lords rather than of the common people, issued first an *Ordinance of Labourers* in 1349, and later a *Statute of Labourers* in 1351. These new laws forbade the payment of wage rates in excess of those paid between 1325 and 1331 and required the compulsory service in employment of all able-bodied men and women under sixty not already engaged in trade or industry. Though vigorous attempts were made to enforce these laws, they fought a losing battle against the superior forces of economic pressure. Lords competed against each other for labour to till their demesnes: higher wages were the inevitable response to the drastic shortage of labour.

The Black Death, therefore, provided lords of manors with an incentive to retain labour services rather than to pay inflated wages for scarce labour. But here too their attempt to check

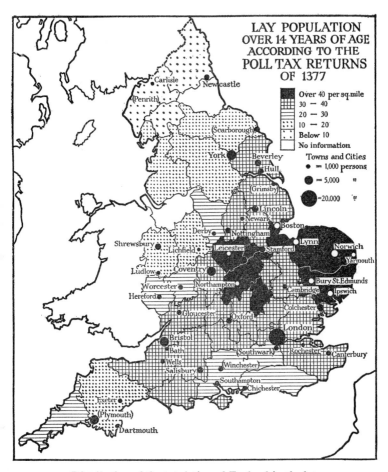

Distribution of the population of England in the late
fourteenth century

the progress of commutation had to take account of the much
stronger economic position of the tenants since the Black Death.
The struggle between lords and serfs ultimately came to a head
in the *Peasant's Revolt* of 1381. The immediate cause of this great
rising of serfs which affected mainly south-eastern England and
East Anglia was the unfairness of poll taxes levied in 1377 and
1381, but the rising was really an expression of the growing
resentment of the unfree people of England against the burdens
imposed by their inferior status. The rebels demanded princi-

pally the cancellation of the Statute of Labourers of 1351 and the abolition of serfdom. Though the young king Richard II, to secure the dispersal of the rebels who had converged on London, promised careful consideration of their demands, none was conceded and the rebel leaders were executed. But the failure of the revolt did not check the progress of commutation. Labour remained the scarce factor, and lords continued to abandon the direct cultivation of their demesnes or were forced to concede the commutation of villein labour services for money rents in response to the various economic forces described above.

Commutation, once granted, was not irrevocable. On the estates of the Priory of Burton in Staffordshire the majority of tenants owed full labour services in the early twelfth century. By the mid-twelfth century most of the demesnes on the Priory's manors were leased to the former villeins. But in the thirteenth century the tenants were forced back to villein status and obliged to perform labour services once again. There appears to have been a widespread movement in many parts of the country towards commutation in the twelfth century, followed by some recovery of labour services in the thirteenth century. In the fourteenth century the pendulum swung back in the direction of freedom, and by the end of the fifteenth century labour services and the stigma of serfdom had virtually disappeared.

The fundamental changes in the structure of English rural society described above were accompanied by some modifications of the basic pattern of open-field farming. These changes arose mainly out of two trends — the extension of the area of arable cultivation, called by historians the *colonization of the waste*, or *assarting*, and the process of *enclosure*. Most of the new land recovered from the waste after the twelfth century was not divided into strips, but was farmed in separate enclosed holdings; most of it, too, was held as free land, that is, was not subject to the obligations of villein tenure. Thus the effect of the colonization of the waste was to diminish both the proportion of land farmed in open fields and the proportion of unfree tenants. *Enclosure* of open-field land involved the gathering by one or more farmers in an open-field community of their scattered strips into consolidated holdings which could then be withdrawn from the open-field system, fenced off and farmed according to the ideas of the individual farmers. There was also some enclosure of commons, mainly by lords of manors, most frequently in response to the growing demand for wool in the later Middle Ages. Before 1235 it was apparently not possible for lords to enclose a common without the consent of their free tenants, but in that year the *Statute of Merton* recognized the lord's right to enclose on condition that he left sufficient grazing land for his free tenants. The statute did not define what was meant by 'sufficient', and its effect was to facilitate enclosure by lords of the commons and wastes.

Enclosures, therefore, contributed to the disappearance of both the open fields and of the common rights of manorial tenants. No reliable estimate has been made of the extent of enclosures during the Middle Ages. Even at the end of the fifteenth century most of the land which had been cultivated under the open-field system in the eleventh century was still unenclosed, but enclosure had made changes that were significant in some areas.

CHAPTER 2

THE MEDIEVAL TOWN

1. The Growth of Towns

In the early Middle Ages a town was distinguished from a village in a number of ways. Firstly, its occupants were all free men not subject to any lord; secondly, many medieval towns from the twelfth century were self-governing through their own elected councils; thirdly, its inhabitants were engaged, directly or indirectly, principally in industry and trade; and, fourthly, most towns held regular markets. Villages did not possess these characteristics.

Most towns owed their origins to trade. Seaports, particularly those facing France and the Low Countries across the Channel or those facing Scandinavia across the North Sea, naturally attracted merchants. Inland, the focal points were the lowest bridge points of rivers. Merchants carrying goods, perhaps from their place of growth or manufacture to the capital or to a seaport, naturally met at these bridge points. Chester, Gloucester, London, Exeter, York and Newcastle all originated for this reason. Away from the rivers the need for local markets led to the growth of towns at important road junctions. Even in the early Middle Ages, when England's population was so small, many towns were already a thousand years old, having their origin in Roman civil or military centres. Some Roman towns like Wroxeter in Shropshire, or Silchester in Hampshire, failed to survive owing to their remoteness from trade routes in later centuries. Others, like Colchester and Cirencester, survived to become small market towns in the Middle Ages. Other towns, again, had grown up as a result of the protection given to traders by a castle of the king or a powerful feudal lord, or through the trade arising out of a great church shrine or monastery.

Not all the towns that grew up in this way in the Middle Ages retained their importance into modern times. In the early

Middle Ages, Thetford in Norfolk, for example, was one of the largest towns in the country, while King's Lynn and Boston were two of the country's major ports: these centres have subsequently declined in importance. Ravenserod, a thriving seaport at the tip of Spurn Head, which guards the entrance to the Humber, was gradually overwhelmed by the sea in the mid-fourteenth century and its site now lies under the waves. Another East Riding seaport, Hedon, decayed in the late Middle Ages and much of its harbour can be traced today only by some humps in fields near a medieval church, the only one of four in the town to survive. In this instance, however, part of the medieval town survived to become the nucleus of a lively modern town.

The greater medieval towns were walled for defence, but the whole area inside the walls was not necessarily covered by buildings. Most towns made use of fields both inside and outside the walls on which the townsmen's cattle grazed, indicating that it was a long time before the divorce between town and country was completed. Within the walls a town was subdivided into parishes, each with its parish church. Though the

Weavers' cottages of the fifteenth and sixteenth centuries at Lavenham, Suffolk

population of medieval towns was not numerous, all people were churchgoers, so that there were a great many parish churches in a medieval town. There were well over one hundred in the City of London, and about fifty in medieval York. In addition to parish churches many medieval towns boasted a cathedral, and most possessed one or more abbeys or priories. There were frequently other religious foundations like hospitals and alms-houses. There were even a few schools. Most medieval towns had a castle, many, like that of York, of the early Norman *motte and bailey* type. In addition to the houses, shops and warehouses of the town's businessmen, there were many splendid halls of the various merchant groups and gilds. The Merchant Venturers' Hall, the headquarters of the overseas traders, was often the most magnificent of these in towns which, like York, Bristol or Exeter, served as centres for overseas trade. Each craft gild had its own headquarters, and in London, where the gilds of merchants developed into the wealthy Livery Companies, these halls were substantial and sumptuously decorated.

Medieval towns were usually extremely small by modern standards — only London, in the Middle Ages, boasted a population of much over 5,000 — but they were rich in fine buildings, both ecclesiastical and civil, and fostered an extremely active corporate life. They harboured, of course, immense discrepancies of wealth, for trade and industry have always generated wealth more rapidly than agriculture, while the concentration of employment and charitable institutions has always attracted those in search of work or relief of their poverty.

2. TOWN GOVERNMENT

Though towns from the earliest days have always sheltered a great diversity of occupations — traders, manufacturers, craftsmen, domestic servants, seamen, clergymen and officials — one group, the merchants, have invariably become the most powerful by virtue of their greater wealth. Nor have they hesitated to use this power to protect and further their own interests, an action which took the form from the early Middle Ages of an association of traders in each town. Associations of this kind in the Middle Ages were known as *gilds*, and the earliest form of gild to emerge was a general association of all traders in a town, known as the *Gild Merchant*. Loose forms of gilds of this type appeared in England shortly after the Norman Conquest, and more highly organized gilds emerged during the twelfth and thirteenth centuries. By the thirteenth century about one-third of all English towns had Gilds Merchant. They never became universal and London and the Cinque Ports (the Channel trading ports) never had this type of gild.

Competition in trade or production has always been welcomed by the consumer but disliked by the trader or producer. Not surprisingly, then, the primary aim of the Gild Merchant was to restrict competition. This took the form of restricting the right to buy or sell within the town. Gild ordinances gave to gildsmen the exclusive right of selling wholesale or retail within the town, with exemption from *toll*, a tax levied by the town government on goods sold in the town. Non-gildsmen were permitted to sell wholesale to members of the Gild Merchant only and then only on payment of the toll. Even then there were certain commodities — wool, grain and unfinished cloth, in most towns — in which non-gildsmen were prohibited from dealing.

Having taken these precautions to retain the advantage in the local market, the Gild Merchant then endeavoured to ensure that no member should have an unfair advantage over any other member. The gild established what was called the right of *lot* which required that, if a gildsman made a purchase, any other member who had been present at the transaction was entitled to a share in the purchase at the original price. Similarly, the gild itself bought collectively in order to strengthen the merchants' bargaining power against strangers, and in order to present members with equal opportunities for favourable purchases.

Membership of a Gild Merchant was not easily obtained. There were three ways of securing entry — by patrimony (the right of a father to introduce his son to membership), by redemption (the payment of a heavy entry fine), or by apprenticeship. A town's right to possess a Gild Merchant, granted to it by charter, automatically carried with it the right of the gildsmen to elect their own governing body, which consisted of an alderman at its head, other officials, an elected court of twelve or twenty-four, and a common council of all members. The substantial entry fees filled the 'gild purse' and made it possible for the gild to assist in the provision of social services in the town. Gilds frequently helped the sick and the poor of the town with money payments or by the maintenance of hospitals and alms-houses. They contributed, too, to the defence of the town. This sort of activity, however, was subsidiary to the gild's main purpose which was the defence of the economic interests of the merchants of the town.

The interests of the merchants, however, were not necessarily those of the town as a whole. There were, broadly speaking, three aspects of town life in the Middle Ages which fell outside the narrower interests of the trading community — those of royal taxation, those of the personal status of the citizens (important in an age of feudalism), and those of town government. The history of the royal taxation of towns is long and complex, and it must suffice here to observe that after the Norman Conquest the Crown looked to the towns as a major source of revenue and imposed taxation on them which was collected by the King's official in each county, the shire-reeve, or *sheriff*. The growing desire of towns to collect the tax themselves to transmit directly to the Exchequer, and the willingness of the Crown to accede to this desire, is evidence of the desire of these towns for independence as well as of the inefficiency of the sheriffs.

From quite early in the twelfth century grants of local self-government were made by the King to towns. The first known grant was made to Lincoln in 1130 and was followed by another to London within a few years. These grants were made by royal charter and gave to a town the status of a borough. The charters endowed boroughs with the right to collect and remit the royal taxation directly, a privilege known as the *farm of the borough* (to 'farm' was to collect and remit taxation). The borough charter also established the form of government within the borough — who should have the right to participate in elections and how many councillors and higher officials there should be, for example. Charters conveyed many other subsidiary privileges upon boroughs and their citizens — the right, for example, to hold fairs or markets, the right to have a Gild Merchant, the right to hold a court for the transaction of legal business or the settlement of disputes between traders in the borough, the right to levy *tolls* on goods sold or to collect *stallage* (rents on stalls or booths in the market), and the guarantee of the personal freedom of all citizens. Many other duties fell on boroughs, such as the regulation through what were known as the *assizes of bread and ale* of the quality of these articles produced in the town. These privileges satisfied the pride of citizens as well as created the conditions in which trade might flourish. The citizens of most towns accordingly exerted every effort to secure such a charter, offering the King large sums for them. Kings like John (1199–1216), who suffered more than most kings from financial difficulties, were only too ready to supplement their inadequate revenues by the sale of charters.

Needless to say the wealthy merchants who normally put up the money to secure the charter claimed the first rights to participate in the government of the new borough. In this way a close link was established between the Gild Merchant and the Borough Council. Though they were distinct bodies, the borough tended to owe its existence to the energies of the gildsmen, while the gild continued to exist by virtue of a clause in the borough charter; and in many instances the membership of both bodies was similar if not identical — the same group of wealthy merchants dominated both. In this way borough councils eventually supplanted the Gilds Merchant in the general government of towns.

Normally the right to participate in a borough election or to be eligible for election as a councillor was reserved for *freemen* or *burgesses*. Freedom of a borough might be acquired in many different ways — by the payment of tax, by the occupation of certain burgages or properties existing in the borough at the time of its grant of charter, or by outright purchase. All too commonly the wealthier citizens did all in their power to restrict the number of freemen, and in many towns the body of freemen remained a small, close oligarchy, governing the town in the exclusive interest of the merchant body. Whether numerous or few, the freemen elected the borough *council* or *common council* which consisted usually of twelve or twenty-four councillors drawn from the body of freemen. The council elected a mayor. As well as presiding over the meetings of the council the mayor acted as chief magistrate in the borough court.

The shape of borough government determined in the early Middle Ages has persisted until today. The ability of the wealthy merchants to restrict the entry of new freemen succeeded in retaining both political and economic power in the boroughs in the hands of this small but rich minority until the nineteenth century. Not until the Municipal Corporations Act of 1835 was the right to participate in borough government thrown open to all householders, and the policy of borough councils accordingly diverted from the protection of the interests of a small minority to the improvement of urban conditions for the general benefit of the whole body of citizens.

3. THE CRAFT GILDS

The Gild Merchant was a general association of all kinds of traders in the town. With the expansion of trade and manufacture in the twelfth and thirteenth centuries there gradually began to appear fairly substantial groups of gildsmen occupied in particular crafts or trades. These, in their turn, began to organize themselves into separate gilds for their own crafts. The earliest *craft gilds* which may be distinguished from the Gilds Merchant appeared in the eleventh century, but there is little evidence that these early craft gilds took permanent forms or were very numerous. They really became important in the thirteenth and fourteenth centuries, and by the end of the latter century they had virtually displaced the old Gilds Merchant. In the later Middle Ages each town possessed a wide range of craft gilds covering all the principal trades practised in the town. There was a gild for each craft in each town. Gilds did not operate outside the towns and they exercised no control over craftsmen who worked in the countryside.

The craft gilds were concerned to regulate the organization of their trade in the interests of their members. As in the Gild Merchant this was achieved primarily through restriction of entry to the craft. But the craft gilds had wider aims than these. Recognizing that in the long run their interests were best served by the maintenance of a high quality of production, they directed many of their regulations to the preservation of high standards of workmanship. This was achieved by insisting on the thorough training of all who wished to practise the craft, by reserving to specially appointed officials (*wardens* or *searchers*) the right to inspect the workmanship of members, and by the occasional prohibition of work by artificial light by members. In some gilds an aspiring member was required to present a 'master-piece' as proof of his workmanship before he could be admitted to full membership. Occasionally the craft used its local mono-poly to fix prices at a higher level than free competition would have determined, while some gilds also regulated the wages that might be paid to workers.

These purely economic aims were supplemented by social and religious aims, for though the craft gilds existed primarily to protect the interests of the producers, they filled a wider role in medieval urban society. Gilds were essentially brotherhoods of craftsmen with common interests, and one of their main pur-poses was to provide an organization to bring together the men of a craft occasionally for purely social and convivial purposes. Hence they were commonly called *fraternities*.

Craft gilds normally had strong religious connections, associating themselves with particular religious festivals or saints from whom they sometimes took their names. The King's charter of 1448 to the London Haberdashers, for example, stressed their association with St. Catherine:

'Know ye that of our especial grace and the inspiration of charity, and for the especial devotion which we bear and have towards the Blessed Virgin Catherine, we have granted and given licence . . . to the men of the mistery (craft) of Haberdashers within our City of London, that they may begin, unite, found, create, erect and establish a gild or fraternity in honour of the same Virgin. . . .'

It was generally part of the purpose of a gild either to endow a chantry or provide for a priest to say masses in honour of the gild's patron saint.

Gilds operated, in varying degrees, a kind of insurance scheme, using their funds to make payments to members in time of sickness, to members' widows, or to pay funeral ex-penses. The White Tawyers (leather makers) of London, for example, in their regulations of 1346, provided for payment of 7d. per week 'if by chance any one of the said trade shall fall into poverty, whether through old age, or because he cannot labour or work and have nothing with which to help himself'. Their widows were to receive a similar weekly pension of 7d., and costs of members' funerals were to be defrayed by 'the common box'. It was not uncommon for gilds to be bequeathed sums of money by wealthier members to be used for lending, interest-free, to young members to enable them to establish themselves as masters in their trades.

In their attempts to restrict competition within their trades, craft gilds exercised rigid control over entry. As with the Gilds Merchant, there were commonly only three ways by which entry might be obtained — by patrimony, a recognition of a father's right to be followed in his trade by his son; by redemption, which served the dual purpose of allowing entry to the occasional outsider and of providing a useful source of income, particularly in the trading gilds where entry fines were often extremely high; and by apprenticeship, the most common way. Apprenticeship served a double purpose, for not only did it ensure that a thorough training was given to all who intended to practise the craft, but it also provided a source of cheap labour. This latter aspect of the system of apprenticeship is often overlooked, but craftsmen themselves, as well as borough government and the state, were deeply concerned at times with the exploitation of apprentice labour and took steps to restrict the number of apprentices a master craftsman might employ at any one time.

Apprenticeship, then, was both an education and an initiation into the 'mystery' of the craft. It took the form of several years' training of a young man by a master of a craft. Youths were commonly apprenticed at about the age of thirteen to fifteen and apprenticeships varied in length from five to ten or even twelve years; the commonest duration was seven years. Clearly many trades could be learned and skills acquired in less time than this; other trades, on the other hand, required the full period for training. The apprentice was 'bound' by contract signed by his master as well as by the apprentice or his father, and during the years of training he always lived with his master, who accepted full responsibility for clothing and feeding as well as training him. A typical contract or *indenture* of apprenticeship is the one by which John Goffe of Penzance was apprenticed to a master of 'the craft of fishing' in 1459:

'This indenture made between John Gibbs of Penzance in the County of Cornwall of the one part and John Goffe, Spaniard, of the other part, witnesses that the aforesaid John Goffe has put himself to the aforesaid John Gibbs to learn the craft of fishing, and to stay with him as apprentice and to serve from the Feast of Philip and James next to come after the date of these presents until the end of eight years then next ensuing and fully complete; throughout which term the aforesaid John Goffe shall well and faithfully serve the aforesaid John Gibbs and Agnes his wife as his masters and lords, shall keep their secrets, shall everywhere willingly do their lawful and honourable commands, shall do his masters no injury nor see injury done to them by others, but prevent the same as far as he can, shall not waste his master's goods nor lend them to any man without his special command. And the aforesaid John Gibbs and Agnes his wife shall teach, train and inform or cause the aforesaid John Goffe, their apprentice, to be informed in the craft of fishing in the best way they know, chastising him duly and finding for the same John, their apprentice, food, clothing linen and woollen, and shoes, sufficiently, as befits such an apprentice to be found, during the term aforesaid.'

For the advantages of instruction and board, a cash payment was normally paid to the master when an apprentice was bound. This was regarded as an investment rather than a payment for services since it opened the door to a career and source of livelihood to which the other doors of patrimony and redemption were less accessible for many.

On completion of his apprenticeship the young craftsman, now in his early twenties, was free to marry and become a master. Few, however, possessed the necessary capital to set themselves up as masters immediately on the termination of their apprenticeships. Accordingly they had to find a master who would employ them as labourers, to be paid by the day or week. For this reason this class of worker was called *journeymen* (from the French *journée*, day). In the early Middle Ages, when the scale of manufacture remained small, few masters employed more than one or two apprentices or journeymen, and most journeymen enjoyed a prospect of eventually becoming masters. But as the scale of industry increased the proportion of journeymen to masters became greater, so that more and more journeymen had to face the likelihood of remaining journeymen permanently. Their interests began to diverge from those of the masters and the problem of labour relations in industry was born. How this process led to the formation of separate gilds for journeymen is discussed more fully in Chapter 5, section 3.

The masters were the only full members of the craft gilds. They alone had power to elect or become officials and to assist in the making of gild regulations. Following the traditional pattern of medieval corporate organization already established by the Gild Merchant and the borough council, the masters of the craft gilds elected usually twelve or twenty-four councillors. Smaller gilds — some had as few as a dozen members — elected two, three or four wardens. The principal officer, holding office usually for a year, was known either as Master or Warden. It was usual to appoint officials, again, confusingly, sometimes called 'wardens' or 'searchers', who were charged with the inspection of the goods produced by members.

In these ways the effective power in the gilds was kept in the hands of the masters who, as time went on, became an increasingly small proportion of all those occupied in any craft. It is true, of course, that gilds owed their existence to the borough council, and that their regulations commonly had to be approved by the borough council and were issued with the Mayor's authority, but the borough council itself consisted mainly of the same wealthy master craftsmen who dominated the gilds. The craft gilds, like the borough council and the Gild Merchant, proved to be all too frequently merely the means by which the wealthy employers legalized and perpetuated their already strong economic grip on the medieval urban community.

4. THE WOOLLEN INDUSTRY

Medieval England boasted only a single major industry — that of the manufacture of woollen cloth. There were, of course, other industries — some ironmaking, coal-mining, shipbuilding and the mining of lead, copper and tin, but these remained on the smallest of scales throughout the Middle Ages. Of these industries, the various branches of mining were probably the most important. Cornish tin, important as a constituent of pewter, was famous throughout Europe both before and during the Roman occupation of Britain, and the metal continued to be

Medieval iron pits at Bentley Grange, West Riding of Yorkshire

an export of some importance throughout the Middle Ages. Lead was mined in the Mendips of Somerset, and in the Pennines of Derbyshire and Cumberland. Together with coal-mining, which seldom penetrated more than a few feet into the ground and was limited therefore to outcropping seams, these extractive industries, alone of the lesser industries, provided any kind of concentrations of industry. Building, shipbuilding and ironworking tended to be widely dispersed in small units.

The manufacture of woollen cloth, on the other hand, as old as civilization itself, was well established in this country at the time of the Norman Conquest. The existence of gilds of weavers in places as widely separated as London, York, Winchester, Oxford, Nottingham, Lincoln and Huntingdon as early as the twelfth and thirteenth centuries testifies to a well developed industry. After a period of steady expansion in the twelfth and early thirteenth centuries, there followed a period of stagnation and even decline in the late thirteenth and early fourteenth centuries. Edward III (1327–77) took a series of important steps which helped materially to revive the decaying industry. By offering protection and special privileges, he attracted to England large numbers of skilled woollen workers from the Low Countries where political disturbance was destroying the industry; he forbade the importation of foreign cloth, and compelled the wearing of English cloth in this country by law. The latter measures were only temporary, but they provided a useful stimulus to recovery. As a result of these measures the second half of the fourteenth century witnessed a major expansion in the industry; during the forty years between 1355 and 1395 the export of woollen cloth more than trebled. There was some set-back to the growing industry in the third quarter of the fifteenth century owing to civil war in England and trade quarrels with European countries, which reduced exports. An important revival in the last quarter of the fifteenth century initiated the great sixteenth-century expansion of the industry which is discussed more fully in Chapter 5, section 2.

The woollen industry was regarded as a major source of wealth in the Middle Ages — 'the chief wealth of this nation', as a Venetian ambassador described it. It provided employment for the poor — Parliament commented in the fifteenth century that it was 'the greatest occupation and living of the poor commons (common people) of this land' — as well as being the foundation of the wealth of the great clothiers and cloth merchants, and providing, through taxation, a valuable source of revenue to the Crown. For these reasons it was the constant care of both Crown and Parliament to protect and foster the industry, though it has to be admitted that the methods they chose to achieve this end were not always well-advised or even effectively enforced. The gilds, of course, were the principal channel through which it was intended to regulate the manufacture and to maintain the quality and reputation of English cloth. Until the sixteenth century the government persisted in its efforts to retain the gilds' authority over all branches of woollen manufacture. But the use of the fulling-mill, by drawing the industry out of the old towns into the countryside, nullified these attempts. In the event, however, freedom from gild control was probably beneficial rather than harmful to the industry. The value of Edward III's policy of attracting skilled foreign workers to this country has already been noticed. With a view to insisting on universal high standards of production, the famous *Assize of Cloth* of 1197 regulated the widths of various types of cloth and established officials in all wool-making towns for its enforcement. Later, in the fourteenth century, an officer called the *Aulnager* was appointed to inspect the measurements and quality of every piece of cloth, stamping it with his seal if satisfied.

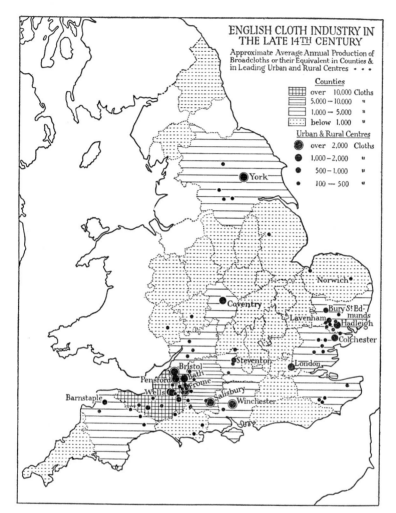

ENGLISH CLOTH INDUSTRY IN
THE LATE 14TH CENTURY
Approximate Average Annual Production of
Broadcloths or their Equivalent in Counties &
in Leading Urban and Rural Centres • • •

Counties
over 10,000 Cloths
5,000 — 10,000 "
1,000 — 5,000 "
below 1,000 "

Urban & Rural Centres
over 2,000 Cloths
1,000 — 2,000 "
500 — 1,000 "
100 — 500 "

Though there were few, if any, counties in medieval England in which the manufacture of woollen cloth was not carried on, there were certain areas in which there were particular concentrations of the industry and which developed specializations of their own, as well as certain towns which became the major commercial centres of the industry. East Anglia, Yorkshire and a wide area of south-west England embracing Gloucestershire, Wiltshire, Somerset and Devon, attracted the greatest concentrations of cloth workers. East Anglia was the principal centre

37

Lavenham: a wool-manufacturing town of the later Middle Ages

for the production of *worsted*, a type of cloth which took its name from the industrial village in Norfolk where its manufacture originated. Though the village of Kersey in Suffolk is not far from Worstead, the manufacture of *kerseys*, narrow woollen cloths, brought fame and wealth to the Devonshire weavers. For the rest, the famous English *broadcloth* proved to be the backbone of the medieval industry.

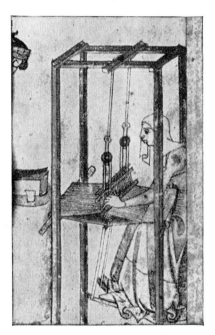

Medieval weaving

The manufacture of cloth in the Middle Ages was a complex business involving many processes. After the raw wool had been scoured to remove dirt and other impurities, the fibres had to be aligned in preparation for spinning. This was achieved either by carding or combing, laborious and unpleasant processes, since the cards and combs required to be heated in open charcoal fires. Spinning was done mainly by women, at first on the distaff, and later on the spinning wheel. The spun yarn was then woven at the loom by the weaver, usually a man, assisted in the case of the broader cloths by a boy. The loom was operated by the feet and hands of the weaver until the very end of the eighteenth century, and until the invention of the knitting frame in the sixteenth century was probably the most complex piece of machinery in general use. Cloth from the loom still required many finishing processes — dyeing or bleaching; fulling, by which the fibres were felted together to give strength and rigidity to the fabric; teazling, or raising the nap by the use of teazles; and shearing to remove the long fibres which teazling had raised and to give an even surface to the finished cloth. Of these finishing processes only one — fulling — was mechanized during the Middle Ages. The invention of the water-powered fulling-mill in the twelfth century proved to be an innovation of the highest significance in the history of the industry. In addition to reducing the cost of the finishing process, it drew first cloth-

Medieval dyeing

Spinning and carding wool (from the Luttrell Psalter)

finishing, and later other processes, out of the towns, where the industry had been subject to strict gild regulation, into the countryside (in search of sources of water-power), where it escaped both gild and borough control.

Each of these diverse processes involved distinct skills, so that the large-scale manufacture of cloth demanded a complex and fairly advanced form of organization capable of passing the semi-finished material from one set of workers to another and marketing the finished product both at home and overseas. For the most part the actual processes of manufacture were carried on in the worker's home. In industries in which the craftsman manufactured an article from start to finish himself it was usual for him to own the machinery or equipment as well as the raw materials on which he worked, a system which gave him complete independence and which gave rise to the gild system as described in earlier sections of this chapter. But the complexity of the cloth industry made it impracticable for each craftsman to buy and re-sell the article on which he was merely performing one of many processes; it was more convenient for a single merchant to provide the initial supply of raw wool, to organize the transmission of the semi-finished article from one process worker to another, and to pay each worker in proportion to the work he put in at his own process.

This type of merchant was known as a *clothier*, from the cloth whose production he managed, and the method of organization has been called by historians the *domestic system*, because it involved manufacture in the worker's home, or the *putting-out system*, because the clothier 'put out' the raw or semi-finished material to the workers in their homes. The clothiers tended initially to be drawn from the finishing trades, acquiring their power by extending their control backwards through successive processes of manufacture until, by entering the market for the raw wool, they closed their grip over the whole range of production. Not unnaturally, the clothiers became extremely wealthy. Sometimes the power this wealth brought to them was put to good use. The beautiful 'perpendicular' churches of the fifteenth century testify to the good taste of many medieval clothiers. The great church at Lavenham, built by the Suffolk clothier, Thomas Spring, or the wonderful stained-glass of Fairford in Gloucestershire, presented by the clothier John Tame, will stand for ever as monuments to the culture and piety of these medieval wool manufacturers. But their power for good was matched by their power for evil, and the working of the domestic system of industry has unfortunately always been marred by the exploitation of the domestic workers by the capitalist clothiers or their equivalents in other industries. This exploitation has taken the form of using the power gained by the extensive grants of credit to the workers to force down the rates of pay. For these reasons the domestic system has always involved extremely long hours of work which too frequently yielded the poorest of livings for the workers. Consequently, to strengthen the economic position of the domestic worker, woollen manufacture was frequently combined with agriculture in a family unit with a small holding.

CHAPTER 3

MEDIEVAL TRADE

1. Overseas Trade Routes

Because Britain is a small island there are severe limits to the range of commodities she can produce herself, and though the island is richly endowed with certain raw materials, it is wholly deficient in others. These circumstances have always given an unusually high importance to overseas trade in Britain's history. In recent times, for example, between one-fifth and one-quarter of the goods consumed in this country have been imported, and a similar proportion of the goods produced in the country have been exported. The economic history of Britain must therefore concern itself closely with the development of so important a sector of the economy.

In the early Middle Ages, of course, the techniques of production in both agriculture and industry did not leave a very great surplus available for export after the needs of the producers and the home market generally had been met. Foreign trade was accordingly of less significance. Nevertheless English wool, iron, grain and dairy produce were exported overseas in exchange for the products of other foreign countries. For the most part these foreign markets were European. Some of the produce of Asia — silk, cotton and spices — was brought to this country, but not directly.

There were four main routes for English medieval trade. Two of these linked England with the nearest part of the Continent — the Low Countries — and through this area passed the great bulk of English overseas trade. In the early Middle Ages the principal route to the Continent from England was through the ports of the Netherlands, from Bruges and Ghent to the ports of the Zuider Zee. Through these ports the great rivers of the Rhine, Meuse and Scheldt gave access to the vast hinterland of north-west and central Europe. In Flanders and Brabant there was the greatest concentration of industry in medieval Europe, and English wool enjoyed its principal market in the cloth manufacturers of the Low Countries. The industrial and trading towns of this area became the great commercial centres of north-west Europe, and merchants from all over Europe gathered at the great fairs to buy and sell, to grant credit and settle their financial transactions. The other trade route to north-west Europe led to Calais and assumed considerable importance in the mid-fourteenth century when this port, which, it must be remembered, remained an English possession until the sixteenth century, was selected to be the staple or principal channel of trade to north-west Europe in several important commodities including wool. The practice of confining a trade to a staple port, which was enforced by the authority of both Crown and Parliament, proved to be particularly advantageous to the Crown when it came to collecting export duties.

These two principal channels were, of course, supplemented by trade through innumerable smaller ports. Altogether the trade with north-western Europe accounted probably for three-quarters of England's total overseas trade. Wool dominated this export trade; in the fourteenth century, however, exports of woollen cloth began to assume some importance, and by the end of the fifteenth century cloth exports, the outcome of the rise of the native cloth manufacturing industry, had taken pride of place from those of raw wool. Together these exports probably accounted consistently for not less than three-quarters in value of all exports. In 1421, for example, the tax on wool exports produced 74% of all the customs revenue for both imports and exports. Of the remaining exports to north-west Europe, corn was probably the most important, followed by various metals and dairy products. These exports were exchanged for French wines, woad for dyeing, salt, building stone, linen and herrings.

The third major trade route was through the straits between Denmark and Sweden to the Baltic countries, and across the North Sea to Scandinavia. These countries were valuable markets in the later Middle Ages for English woollen cloth and were almost the sole source of essential raw materials for shipbuilding — hemp (for rope), flax (for sailcloth), tar and masts.

The fourth main route was through the Straits of Gibraltar

to the Mediterranean. Throughout the Middle Ages the Italians dominated the trade of Europe; the great galleys of Florence and Venice carried the produce of the Mediterranean and the luxuries of the East — spices, costly textiles and wines — to all parts of Europe. The towns of northern Italy housed a concentration of industry rivalled in importance only by that of Flanders. The Italians had carried the arts of commerce and banking to a far higher stage of development than other nations, and their strategic position between the Asiatic and European markets gave them command over some lucrative trades. Venice was the leading Mediterranean mercantile power and used her position to profit from the Crusades of the twelfth and thirteenth centuries.

2. Fairs and Markets

Most internal trade in medieval England was transacted at fairs or markets. They provided the periodic occasions which brought buyers and sellers together. Markets were local affairs at which the inhabitants of a town or village were able to buy goods directly once or twice a week. The goods sold were, therefore, the everyday needs of ordinary people — food, clothing and household utensils. Markets provided supplies of retail goods under competitive conditions as well as an opening for traders and manufacturers to sell their wares. All sections of the medieval town benefited, therefore, from its markets, and the right to hold such a market was much sought after. Borough charters normally granted the right to hold a weekly market.

Fairs, on the other hand, were national occasions. They were attended by merchants and manufacturers from all parts of the country and even from overseas. Though there were many fairs in England, each fair was normally held once a year only, and lasted a week or more. A wide range of goods was handled, mostly in wholesale transactions. Goods like semi-finished metals, salt in bulk, horses, cloth and luxuries from abroad were sold. Some fairs specialized in certain types of commodities, others handled anything and everything. By bringing together merchants and manufacturers they promoted the goodwill so essential to commerce, and provided occasions for the settlement of debts. Many transactions in the Middle Ages involved the use of credit and the fairs helped to bridge the gap filled today by banks.

To meet the needs of trade and to settle the inevitable disputes arising from it, each fair held its own court, called, after the dusty feet of the merchants who had often travelled long distances to attend, the *Court of Piepowder* (from the French 'pieds poudrés'). The court was presided over by the Mayor of the borough and provided the immediate justice essential to merchants who only met once a year. It handled cases arising out of debts, contracts and contraventions of the assizes of bread and ale.

The fair was opened by a proclamation from the Mayor in which those taking part were enjoined to keep the peace, give honest measure, preserve the sanctity of the Sabbath and abide by the rulings of the court. The fairs were normally held in open country outside the towns. The booths or stalls were arranged in long rows which often took their names from the traders who were grouped for the convenience of buyers. Stallage had to be paid for the right to set up a stall, and a *toll* or tax on each commodity sold was sometimes exacted. These taxes went to the borough or lord of the manor and provided a valuable source of revenue, which explains why the right to hold a fair or market was so jealously guarded.

To say that fairs and markets came into being to meet the needs of trade is to state the obvious. But many other factors contributed to their growth and influenced their subsequent development. Most fairs and markets may be traced to religious origins. Feast days, saints' days and annual pilgrimages to famous shrines, by bringing together large numbers of people, naturally gave rise to commerce. The great concourse which came annually to celebrate the feast of St. Cuthbert in Durham, for example led to the growth of a great fair even before the Norman Conquest. The greatest of the English fairs, at Stourbridge in East Anglia, was founded by King John (1199–1216) in order that the revenue might support the Hospital of St. Mary Magdalene.

Once established, fairs were perpetuated and multiplied because they provided both the conditions under which trade could flourish and the revenue which encouraged the Crown, the boroughs and the lords of manors to give them their protection. The 'peace of the fair' provided all who attended (except outlaws) with immunity from arrest. Even escaping serfs could not be recovered while the fair lasted. Concentration of trade in fairs and markets facilitated the collection of royal revenues, while townsmen and any other privileged groups naturally preferred set fairs and markets, where their privileges could be safeguarded, to unregulated transactions.

In the fifteenth century the importance of the fairs began to decline. Complaints from many fairs recorded serious diminutions in the numbers of buyers attending them. The decline continued in the sixteenth century and very few fairs survived into the seventeenth century, though the famous Stourbridge fair could still be described by Defoe in the early eighteenth century as 'not merely the greatest in the whole nation but in the world'. The causes of this decline may only be guessed, but are certainly associated with the growth in size of towns, which, as they grew, were able to cater more fully for their own needs of trade and commerce. In particular, as the cloth manufacture in this country grew in the fifteenth century, it tended to develop its own complex marketing system, both in the home and in the overseas markets, which became less and less dependent upon the old fairs.

3. FOREIGN TRADERS

In the early Middle Ages Englishmen showed little inclination to participate in overseas trade. The earliest English merchants were drawn from the lowest ranks of society, frequently from the younger sons of villeins. England's foreign trade was, as a result, allowed to fall preponderantly into the hands of foreign merchants. This is not to say that foreign merchants monopolized overseas trade; until the fourteenth century Englishmen simply held a smaller share of the trade than did foreigners. In 1273, for example, English merchants handled only one-third of the export trade in wool. The alien merchants were never popular with the English trading community who resented their competition and frequently greater wealth. In the early Middle Ages towns normally required that visiting foreign traders should reside with an English *host* who would witness all his deals (a practice called *hosting*) and that their stay should be limited to forty days in the town in any one year. But the Crown, on the whole, favoured the foreign merchants. The King was concerned with relations with foreign countries and good relations often hinged on the treatment given to foreign traders in a country. Foreign traders, too, were a source of revenue. Most important, however, the foreign traders were often the wealthiest body in the country and were a valuable source of loans to the Crown, albeit at high rates of interest. For these reasons the Crown willingly conceded privileges to foreign merchants, and even when Parliament attempted to destroy their privileged position, the Crown granted exemptions from these enactments.

The first group of foreign merchants to establish a footing in English commercial circles was the Jews. They were established in the 'Jewries' of several English towns in the twelfth century and used the profits gained by trade to lend extensively to the Crown, to the Church for the building of monasteries and cathedrals, and to private traders. The Jews acquired great unpopularity, since interest rates were very high in those uncertain times, and they became the object of universal hatred. This unpopularity stemmed also from the exceptional privileges granted to them by the Crown. Because of their need for loans, successive kings extended their protection to the Jews. Eventually, after a generation of persecution, Edward I (1272–1307), with popular approval, drove them out of this country.

In the thirteenth century, the place formerly held by the Jews was taken by the Italians. Italian merchants dominated the commerce of London in the late thirteenth and fourteenth centuries, when they performed a variety of functions. They were extensive traders, bringing to England the produce of the East and the Mediterranean and exchanging it for English wool, cloth and staple foodstuffs. They made use of the channels of commerce thus established to remit the revenues owed by the English Church to the Papacy in Rome or the income derived from English manors owned by the great monastic houses of Europe. Their financial strength and their skill in accounting enabled them to bid for and secure the 'farm of the customs' — a method used by the Crown to facilitate the collection of customs duties; the 'farmer' paid over an agreed sum, rather less than the anticipated yield of the tax, and hoped by efficient or grasping tax collection to collect more than he had paid for the 'farm'. Like the Jews, too, as the wealthiest section of the commercial community they engaged in extensive money-lending, particularly to the Crown.

The Italians' banking and trading activities in this country aroused great hostility on several scores. They imported largely luxury goods which were generally felt to be very poor returns for the export of wool. They had a reputation for unscrupulous dealing and did not hesitate to take what was often felt to be immoral advantage of temporary shortages. Most of all, their money-lending activities offended against the principles of the medieval Church, which condemned *usury* or money-lending at interest. However, the Church's general opposition to usury was subject to so many qualifications that money-lending and other capitalistic practices could be carried on and even justified by Italians and others throughout the Middle Ages. The Crown, though continuing to borrow heavily from the Italians through-out the fourteenth century, shared the general dislike of them; but their loans were indispensable until, by the end of the four-teenth century, the growing wealth of the king's subjects made it possible to dispense with the money-lending services of the Italians. Nevertheless, even in the face of hostility which reached the pitch of a popular rising against them in 1436, the Italian merchants continued to lend to the English traders. But their importance was declining, and in the fifteenth century the most powerful body of foreign merchants in England was German.

The independent trading cities of north Germany had formed a confederation in the early Middle Ages, known as the *Hanseatic League*. The cumulative power of these great commercial centres which controlled the routes into central Europe — Cologne, Bremen, Hamburg, Lübeck, Stettin, Rostock and Danzig — en-abled the *Hansards*, as the members of the league were called, to extract valuable trading privileges from other European countries. In England the Hansards were established with important liberties and privileges by the end of the thirteenth century. The most important of their privileges was a special rate of customs duty on exported English cloth, which was not only lower than that paid by other foreigners, but lower even than that payable by English merchants. The London head-quarters of the Hansards was known as the *Steelyard* (its site is occupied today by Cannon Street Station) where they were established as early as 1320. As the manufacture and export of woollen cloth expanded in the fifteenth century and was matched by England's growing need for the shipbuilding materials of the Baltic, so the importance of the Hansards in this country grew.

From the late fourteenth century there was a growing body of English merchants who were becoming increasingly jealous of the power, wealth and privileged position of foreign merchants. This hostility had succeeded in the previous century in driving the Jews from these shores as well as in diminishing the influence of the Italian traders, and in the fifteenth century the English merchants determined not merely to destroy the privilege of the Hansards in England, but to capture their valuable trade for themselves. Confident in the strength of their established position in the trade, the Hansards refused to concede to English merchants in their cities the same privileges they demanded and received in London. The struggle raged throughout the first three-quarters of the fifteenth century. It was both indecisive and damaging to the trade of both parties. It took the form of piracy by both sides on each other's commerce, of naval warfare, of the confiscation of the goods of merchants abroad, and of attempts to regulate shipping between England and the Baltic by control of the Sound, the narrow straits between Denmark and southern Sweden. A compromise agreement was finally reached at Utrecht in 1474 which brought peace, though it did not diminish the resolution of the English merchants. The Hansards were to retain their full privileges in England in return for very vague concessions to the English merchants, whose share of the Baltic trade remained low until the renewal of the struggle in the sixteenth century. (See section 5 of this chapter.)

4. The Wool Trade and the Merchants of the Staple

In the fourteenth and fifteenth centuries the export of wool dominated English overseas trade. Though the trade was shared by merchants of many nations, by the fourteenth century more than half of it was in English hands. The Italian merchants mostly carried their purchases of wool directly by sea to Italy and sold it to Mediterranean manufacturers. There was also a certain amount of trade in the inferior wools of the North from the north-east ports to Scandinavia and Holland, but the great bulk of the trade took the short Channel passage to the industrial towns of the Low Countries. This trade was mainly, though not exclusively, in English hands.

Wool was produced in most parts of England in the Middle Ages, though its quality varied enormously. The best wool, for example, grown in Shropshire and Herefordshire, sold for 14 marks a sack (one mark was 6s. 8d.), while the inferior wool of East Anglia fetched less than 4 marks. The wool passed from the grower to the exporting merchants through a variety of channels. Some merchants bought it directly, the merchants or their representatives travelling round the wool-growing districts on regular buying trips once or twice each year. Others bought it through middlemen, known in the Middle Ages as *wool-mongers* or *broggers*. The Italians, though they sometimes bought direct from the growers, purchased much of their wool from monasteries. Some of the monastic orders — the Cistercians, the Premonstratensians and the Gilbertines in particular — employed the demesnes of their manors for grazing huge flocks of sheep, and they customarily contracted for the sale of their wool two or three years in advance to Italian buyers. After shearing, the wool had to be sorted and packed in canvas sarplers or wrappers. These were skilled jobs performed by the *wool-packers* who formed crafts gilds of their own. The bulky woolpacks were carried by packhorse to the ports of export. The merchants who exported the wool sold it at fairs or markets in Continental towns to the manufacturers of woollen cloth. Most of these stages in the trade involved the use of credit on which interest was charged.

The merchants who conducted the principal trade across the Channel to the Low Countries soon found it to their advantage to form a trading association. For several reasons it was advantageous to all parties — exporters, buyers and Crown — to canalize the trade to the Low Countries through a single town or *staple*. Hence the association of merchants engaged in this trade was known as the *Merchants of the Staple*. The Staple originated in the thirteenth century, but its organization was not perfected until the fourteenth century. The *Ordinance of the Staple* of 1313 regulated the trade through the Staple and gave the full backing of law to the institution. It is quite clear that the Merchants of the Staple were already a well-organized body by this date, though it was not until the fifteenth century that the organization of the Merchants of the Staple as a company was explicitly confirmed by grants of charters from the Crown. Many places were tried during the fourteenth century as locations for the Staple both in England and abroad, but by 1390 it was settled permanently at Calais, where it remained until the loss of that town to the French in 1558, by which time the trade in wool had almost completely died out.

The 'Fellowship of the Merchants of the Staple' was a *regulated company*. It was, that is to say, an association of individual traders or partnerships of traders each carrying on their own trade under a common set of regulations. It was a large body of between 300 and 400 members and it controlled roughly four-fifths of the total wool trade of the country. Most of the members traded from London, but a few shipped wool to the Staple from Boston, Ipswich and Hull. The various ordinances and charters from 1313 gave the Staplers a monopoly of the export trade in wool to the Low Countries so that only members could participate in that trade. The Staplers' Company, presided over by its Mayor, was one of the most powerful and influential bodies in later medieval England. Its functions reached into spheres far wider than merely the regulation of the wool export trade. It was instrumental, for example, in administering, through its own courts in the staple towns, the commercial law arising out of one of Europe's busiest trades. In its efforts to preserve its monopoly over the wool trade it maintained an extensive inspection of wool and a watch against smugglers who sought to evade the Staple. It collected for the Crown the customs on the export of wool, and advanced money to the Crown in anticipation of these revenues. Finally, the Staplers were made responsible for financing the defence of Calais, the seat of the Staple throughout the fifteenth century.

The Staplers enjoyed a long hey-day, but in the later fifteenth century their trade was dwindling. England was expanding her manufacture of woollen cloth, and an increasing proportion of the wool crop was being consumed at home. The Flemish manufacturers were drawing more of their raw wool from Spain. As the export of wool declined, that of woollen cloth rose. The annual trade of the Merchant Adventurers' Company in woollen cloth surpassed that of the Staplers by the middle of the fifteenth century. The Staplers tried unsuccessfully to assert their rights over the growing cloth trade. By the end of the fifteenth century the trade in wool, though still substantial, was declining steadily. By the mid-sixteenth century exports of wool, which had averaged 35,000 sacks yearly in the early fourteenth century and 8,000 sacks in the mid-fifteenth century, had fallen to about 3,000 sacks a year, and by the 1580's to a mere hundred or two sacks each year. The Staplers had conceded their leadership of English foreign trade to the Merchant Adventurers.

5. THE MERCHANT ADVENTURERS

In the Middle Ages the name *adventurer* or *venturer* denoted any merchant who risked his capital trading overseas, but the name Merchant Adventurers was given to two particular groups of merchants in medieval England. The first of these were the associations of exporters in a number of provincial trading ports — Bristol, Ipswich, Hull, Newcastle and York. The second, much more important group was the merchants of London exporting woollen cloth to the Low Countries, who handled the greater part of England's export trade in cloth.

There were loose associations of so-called 'merchant adventurers' trading on the Continent as early as the thirteenth century, but the real history of the Merchant Adventurers only began in the fifteenth century with the rise of the English manufacture of woollen cloth. Until the mid-fifteenth century the cloth merchants of London tended to group themselves according to their livery companies — Mercers, Grocers, Haberdashers, Drapers and Skinners. Of these groups, that associated with the Mercers appears to have been the most important and became the nucleus around which the other cloth merchants gathered. As the cloth trade expanded, the advantages of closer association between merchants engaged in the same trade became more apparent, while the King, too, had learnt by his experience with the Staplers that a single

C

organization in a trade facilitated the collection of taxes. By the 1470's these various forces had conspired to weld the London cloth merchants together into a single group, though it was not until 1486 that the fellowship of Merchant Adventurers in London received formal recognition. The company's first charter came in 1505, though its most comprehensive grants were received in a later charter of 1564.

The Merchant Adventurers' Company, like the Merchants of the Staple, was a *regulated* company. Each member traded individually but the company chartered the ships in which the cloth was carried across the Channel and fixed the times of sailings of convoys. Admission to the company might be gained by any of the three traditional medieval methods — by apprenticeship, which in this company was for eight years; by redemption, for substantial fees (in the early seventeenth century the fees had reached the very large sum of £200); and by patrimony, by which a young man whose father had been a member at the time of his son's birth might enter at the age of twenty. The quantity of cloths members might ship each year was restricted, the *stint* or allocation increasing with the length of membership. New members were permitted to export a maximum of 400 pieces for their first three years; thereafter the stint was increased by 50 pieces each year up to a maximum of 1000 pieces. But many merchants did not use their stint to the full, while some, on the other hand, exported far more, suggesting that the stint was not enforced very keenly. Though the company concentrated on the export of woollen cloth, its members were general traders also, shipping lead, tin, leather and corn to the same markets.

In London the company was administered by a Governor, a Deputy-Governor and a Court of twenty-four Assistants, twelve of whom had to be drawn from the livery companies. Meetings of the General Court of all the members were held either in London or in one of the overseas centres at which the company concentrated its selling activities. The charters of 1505 and 1564 conferred on the company extensive trading privileges. Its members were to have exclusive trading rights to the coast of Europe from the mouth of the Somme in north-east France to the north of Denmark, an area which included the principal European markets for cloth in the Low Countries as well as access to Central European markets up the valleys of the Meuse, the Rhine and the Elbe. Members were required to export their goods to a specified *mart town*. Here the activities of members could be supervised and taxes collected, and the Governor of the Company frequently passed most of his term of office in residence at the mart town. Though the company generally tried to maintain a single mart town, political difficulties on the Continent did not always permit this. Consequently the mart town was shifted frequently to places as widely separated as Antwerp and Hamburg and there were times when more than one mart town was employed.

During the first seventy-five years of the existence of the Merchant Adventurers' Company the export trade expanded immensely, bringing great wealth to the members of the company. From the mid-sixteenth century, however, the company ran into a great deal of opposition. This came from three main sources — the Hanseatic League, the provincial companies of Merchant Adventurers, and from *interlopers* (independent traders who infringed the company's monopoly). Interloping was a permanent problem for monopoly trading companies. The extremely high entrance fees demanded by the Merchant Adventurers kept out all but the wealthiest traders, and there was always a body of smaller merchants excluded from the trade who were prepared to risk the penalties of interloping. Occasionally the voices of the excluded merchants were raised in vociferous protest against the monopoly. In the early seventeenth century this opposition, led by Alderman Cockayne, succeeded in persuading the King to revoke the company's charter. The disastrous results of Cockayne's scheme are discussed more fully in Chapter 5, section 2. The relationship between the Merchant Adventurers' Company in London and the provincial companies is obscure; some provincial companies appear to have been branches of the London company, others not. It is quite clear, however, that the London company resented the outports' share of the trade and did everything in their power to prevent these smaller groups trading in their area of north-west Europe.

In the mid-sixteenth century the struggle between English merchants (now represented by the Merchant Adventurers) and the Hanseatic League was resumed. In 1552, acting on the advice of the economist Sir Thomas Gresham, Edward VI's government withdrew the trading privileges of the Hanseatic League on the ground that they were being abused by the League. Queen Mary restored the Hansards' privileges when she came to the throne in the following year, but when in 1557 a new tariff of customs duties was declared which no longer gave the Hansards preferential rates, they broke off trading relations with England. Trade was re-opened three years later, but relations remained uneasy. The struggle was one between rival monopolies — the Merchant Adventurers and the League — both seeking to capture the valuable trade between England and the north German ports. The Merchant Adventurers scored a triumph in 1567 when one of the Hanseatic cities, Hamburg, rebelling against the League, allowed the Merchant Adventurers to set up their mart there. Ten years later the League persuaded Hamburg to withdraw the privileges it had conceded to the English company. The company moved to Emden, only to be driven from there in the same manner after a three years' stay. From Emden the Merchant Adventurers moved to Stade, and when in 1598 the League succeeded in driving them from that city, the English government retaliated by revoking all the Hansards' privileges in England. The Steelyard was closed after serving for nearly three hundred years as the Hansards' headquarters in London. The Merchant Adventurers moved their mart to Holland, but the long conflict between the two trading giants had damaged the trade.

In spite of these embarrassments, the Merchant Adventurers emerged at the end of the sixteenth century relatively unscathed, their monopoly of the valuable cloth trade still firmly in their hands. The Germans could not easily forego the trade with England and were forced to re-admit the Merchant Adventurers early in the seventeenth century, though the Hansards did not return to London. Just as, in the history of English overseas trade, the fifteenth century belonged to the Merchants of the Staple, so the sixteenth century belonged to the Merchant Adventurers. But the spirit of the seventeenth century grew hostile to monopolies and, though woollen cloth continued to be the mainstay of England's overseas trade, the 'Fellowship of Merchant Adventurers' decayed rapidly in the new century.

CHAPTER 4

THE EXPANSION OF TRADE

1. VOYAGES OF DISCOVERY

During the Middle Ages mariners seldom ventured great distances from the coast, not because, as is sometimes said, they feared that as the earth was flat they were in danger of sailing over the edge of it, but because their primitive navigational instruments combined with a very inadequate knowledge of geography made voyages out of sight of land perilous. For the most part there had been little urge to travel beyond the well-known routes of north-western Europe and the Mediterranean; what little trade there was with the East used the centuries-old overland route to the eastern Mediterranean, whence Venetian traders made the links with the lands of western and northern Europe.

Since about 1400, however, the Portuguese, the first European sailors to venture far from the customary trade routes, had explored southwards down the west coast of Africa. Prince Henry the Navigator organised many voyages in the first half of the fifteenth century which opened up the African coast to Portuguese trade as far as Guinea by the middle of the fifteenth century, and as far as the mouth of the Niger by 1470. Finally, in 1486, Bartholomew Diaz reached the southernmost tip of Africa only to be prevented by contrary winds from entering the Indian Ocean. These were the first true voyages of exploration of modern times, partly inspired as they were by little more than the desire for knowledge characteristic of this period of the Renaissance. Later, however, the main spirit behind the many voyages of discovery from the 1490's onwards was the desire to find a sea route to China and the Indies. The silks and spices of these countries found ready markets in Western Europe and provided compact and valuable cargoes suitable for the long-distance trade.

By the end of the fifteenth century the fact that the world was spherical was well established. The Portuguese voyages of Prince Henry's sailors had established the existence of the apparently limitless land mass of Africa barring the eastward passage to China; and as yet sailors were not prepared to risk the ice and storms of the difficult route round northern Europe. Columbus, a Genoese mariner, was not alone in concluding that China could most easily be approached by sea by striking west across the Atlantic, but till 1492 no one had had the courage to undertake such an immense voyage into the unknown. Columbus's voyage of that year, under the King of Spain's flag, established the existence of land three months' sailing distance across the Atlantic which his optimism and ignorance led him to think at first to be one of the islands of the East Indies. When, in the course of subsequent voyages westwards in 1493, 1498 and 1502, the mainland of the American continent was revealed, Columbus demonstrated that the quest for a sea route to China was going to be a long one. A new and hitherto unknown obstacle blocked the westerly route to Cathay.

It was no longer a question of a direct ocean passage to China; the land masses of Africa and America had first to be circumnavigated. Thus the last years of the fifteenth century saw two attempts being made in new directions to find a sea passage to the East. In 1497 a Genoese sailor who had settled in England, John Cabot, set out from Bristol across the Atlantic with the aim of avoiding the mainland of America by striking to the north. Not realizing the extent of North America, he made land at Newfoundland, and was obliged to return without discovering a north-west passage. In the same year, Vasco da Gama, another Portuguese adventurer, followed up Bartholomew Diaz' important discovery of the route to the Indian Ocean round the Cape of Good Hope. Between 1497 and 1500, he traced the coast of East Africa northwards to Zanzibar, where Indian pilots familiar with the trade routes of the Indian Ocean showed him the route to the Malabar Coast of India. The seaway to China was now open, though because of the immense distances involved, it was a long time before regular use was made of this route for trade with the East. After Vasco da Gama's voyage, many Portuguese sailors, amongst whom Albuquerque was the most famous, explored the coasts of the

Indian Ocean, reaching China and the many islands of the East Indies.

Apart from the voyages of Cabot, Englishmen had not joined the Spanish and the Portuguese in these voyages of exploration. By their conquests of Mexico and Peru in the 1520's and '30's, the Spaniards laid claim to all the known parts of Central America, while the Portuguese claimed exclusive trading rights over the whole of the Indian Ocean and the western Pacific. In the middle years of the sixteenth century, however, a serious decline in the European demand for woollen cloth caused some English merchants to begin to take an interest in some of the newly discovered lands as possible new markets for English manufactures to make good the decline in the European market. With this aim in view an expedition was equipped in 1553 under Sir Hugh Willoughby and Richard Chancellor to attempt to trace a new passage to China round the north of Europe and Asia — the ' north-east passage '. Of the three ships in this expedition, two came to grief and their crews, including Sir Hugh Willoughby, 'for lack of knowledge were frozen to deathe'. The remaining vessel, the *Edward Bonaventure*, reached the White Sea, and Chancellor landed in northern Russia (then known as Muscovy). He made his way overland to Moscow on the invitation of the Czar, Ivan IV, with whom he succeeded in negotiating a trade treaty giving valuable privileges to the English merchants. Chancellor returned home safely, and though he had failed to discover a new sea route to China, a useful new market for English cloth was opened up.

The voyage of Willoughby and Chancellor had clearly demonstrated the hazards of the northern sea route to China, and no more attempts were made by Englishmen in that direction. Realizing that the route round Africa could only lead to conflict with the Portuguese, and that the route to the Pacific round South America, taken by Magellan on his voyage round the world in 1519–22, was too long and difficult to be practicable, as well as involving conflict with the Spaniards, English attempts to find a route to China in the later sixteenth century concentrated on the 'north-west passage'. In 1576, Frobisher reached the shores of Baffin Island, and ten years later Davis entered the straits now named after him between Greenland and Baffin Island, but none of the Elizabethan sailors did more than skirt the fringe of the icy vastness of the Arctic Ocean that closed the north-west passage to explorers until the nineteenth century. The most determined efforts to penetrate the ice-floes towards China were made in the course of three voyages by Henry Hudson. On his last voyage, in 1610, Hudson found his way into the great bay which now bears his name. Believing that the southward turn of the coastline would lead him to the open waters of the Pacific, he traced the coast of the bay southwards into St. James' Bay. Here once again the coast turned westwards, then northwards, and it was clear that the north-west passage did not lie through the great bay. Hudson, however, determined to persevere with his quest for another season, but his now mutinous crew would not willingly bear the intense hardships of cold, hunger and illness any longer. Hudson, his young son, and a few supporters were cast adrift in a longboat to perish in the ice, while the remaining crew, more dead than alive, brought the ship back home. The tragic end to the efforts of Hudson discouraged any further attempts to find a north-west passage to China. In any case, by the beginning of the seventeenth century, Vasco da Gama's route to the East round Africa had become well established and was being used by the newly founded English East India Company.

Many of the other voyages which contributed to establishing the seafaring repute of the Elizabethan sailors were voyages of buccaneering rather than of exploration. From the 1540's onwards, the Spaniards were drawing immense quantities of silver from the mines of South America and this bullion was brought from Panama across the Atlantic in treasure fleets heavily escorted by men-of-war. The capture of even a single silver-laden galleon produced a fortune for the lucky crew, and when Anglo-Spanish relations deteriorated into war in the 1580's, these hitherto illegal acts of piracy were legalized as warfare. The names of Sir Francis Drake and Sir Walter Raleigh are popularly associated with these activities. In 1577 Drake, attempting to go one better than his rivals, sailed through the Magellan Straits in order to attack the Spanish ships carrying silver from the mines in Peru for trans-shipment at Panama. Unable, owing to the prevailing winds to return the same way, he explored the Californian coast as far north as Vancouver Island before turning west to cross the Pacific and so became the first Englishman to circumnavigate the globe. After returning from this epic voyage in 1580 he was knighted by Queen Elizabeth on board the *Golden Hind* at Deptford.

2. THE JOINT-STOCK COMPANY

In the Middle Ages the principal overseas markets for English goods were near at hand — in France and Spain, the Netherlands, Germany and Scandinavia. When, in the fifteenth and early sixteenth centuries, English traders began to enter some more distant markets in the Mediterranean and Baltic areas, these were still over well-established routes and with countries accustomed to western trading methods. The voyages of discovery of the sixteenth century, on the other hand, opened up to English merchants markets in distant countries where the trading risks were great and where the costs of initiating trade were high. Amongst the new markets were the Levant (the coasts of the eastern Mediterranean), Russia, the West African coast and the Far East. With these countries the methods of trading customarily used in the established trades were not suitable. The trade to north-western Europe, for example, was controlled by the Merchant Adventurers, an organisation of merchants which did not itself carry on business, but simply laid down regulations governing the manner in which individual merchants (who were obliged to become members of the company if they wished to trade with these markets) should do business. In this and other *regulated companies*, the fact that the trade was with neighbouring countries where risks were slight gave the merchant a quick turnover for his capital and permitted trade to be carried on with the limited resources of a single merchant or of a small group of partners.

The new markets called for expensive expeditions, larger ships, long voyages (tying up large sums of capital for long periods of up to three years at a time), expenses in building warehouses and maintaining officials in foreign countries, as well as expensive bribes and presents to the rulers and officials of foreign countries to obtain secure conditions of trade. These demands on capital far exceeded the resources of individual merchants and were heaviest at the initiation of a new trade. Almost £50,000 (a very large sum in the sixteenth century) was needed to open the trade with Russia, and it was claimed that of this, £30,000 was 'dispended and lost' merely in establishing the trade.

Thus the new trade routes called into existence a new type of trading company — the *joint-stock company* — in which a large number of individuals pooled their capital ('stock' simply meant money capital at that time), and traded, not individually as hitherto, but as a group, employing managers and a clerical staff. This new kind of trading organization was powerful enough to negotiate directly with the rulers of foreign countries, could bring together the large sums of money necessary to finance the long voyages, reduced the danger of loss by spreading the risks over a large number of share-holders, and, by its ability to outlive individual merchants, provided a permanent and enduring basis for trade. Joint-stock companies were normally created by Royal Charter, and in compensation for the heavy risks attached to their ventures, were commonly given exclusive or *monopoly* trading rights in their chosen areas.

Joint-stock companies often attracted large numbers of shareholders, in marked contrast to earlier forms of commercial organization, which seldom comprised more than three or four partners. The Muscovy Company brought together 201 share-holders in 1555, while the East India Company began its long history in 1600 with 218 shareholders. This numerous body of proprietors could not conveniently administer a business calling for minute attention to detail as well as for a consistent general policy, and it was customary for the *General Court* of all the shareholders to elect from their own number a governor, a deputy-governor and a court of twenty-four assistants who were charged with the control of the trade. These, in their turn, appointed a staff of clerks and mariners to carry on the company's business.

3. The Trading Companies of the Sixteenth and Seventeenth Centuries

The first of the newly-opened markets to attract English traders was Russia, and, after the return of Chancellor, the Russia Company was chartered in 1555, with the monopoly of trade with Russia and all areas lying 'northwards, northeastwards or north-westwards of the British Isles, unknowen, or by our merchants and subjects by the seas not heretofore commonly frequented'. Because Willoughby and Chancellor had set out in 1553 to discover the north-east passage to China, the port through which Chancellor eventually opened the trade with Russia was St. Nicholas in the White Sea. Not only was the voyage long and frequently stormy (the Russian Ambassador who came to England on the company's second return voyage to England in 1556 was wrecked off the north coast of Scotland), but St. Nicholas on the Arctic coast was hundreds of miles north of Moscow, and it is hard to conceive a more arduous and expensive trade route. Nevertheless, the Russia Company, at great initial cost, succeeded in establishing a regular, though small, trade. English woollen cloth was particularly suited to the needs of the Russian market, while Russia supplied furs, wax, tallow, flax and hemp rope.

Three years after the establishment of the Russia Company, the Russians captured the port of Narva at the extreme eastern end of the Baltic. This, of course, provided a far easier route to trade, but it was by no means clear whether the charter of 1555 gave the Company the monopoly of trade to Russia through the Baltic, for this was not 'unknowen or . . . not heretofore commonly frequented'. The Company ran the risk of having to share the trade with independent traders, who would reap all the advantage of the Company's heavy initial expenditure in opening up the Russian market, without bearing any of the charge of this. The Company chose, therefore, to neglect the route through Narva, and to continue to use the more hazardous northern route, relying on its grant from the Czar of exclusive trading privileges to keep out the *interlopers* (independent merchants attempting to infringe the Company's monopoly). In this they were never entirely successful, and the history of the Russia Company in the later sixteenth century is a long story of disputes with interlopers over the exact nature of the Company's monopoly rights.

Believing that the great rivers and inland seas of Russia would enable them to extend their trade easily from Russia southwards towards India, the Russia Company initiated some of the most astounding trading expeditions in the whole history of English commerce. Not content with the long voyage through Arctic seas to St. Nicholas and the wearisome overland march to Moscow, in 1557 and 1561–3 Antony Jenkinson undertook two immense journeys in search of new markets. Armed with a permit from the Czar and some samples of English cloth, in 1557 Jenkinson traced the Volga to the Caspian Sea and reached Bokhara, one of the great trading depots of central Asia on the ancient caravan route to China. Four years later he followed the same route to the Caspian, but this time, crossing the Caspian to the south, he reached Kasvin, the capital of Persia, where he succeeded in obtaining trading privileges from the Shah of Persia. The company followed up Jenkinson's enterprising journeys with further expeditions, but losses through piracy on the Caspian, and other difficulties associated with organizing a regular trade over such a formidable distance, soon discouraged the company and the Persian venture was discontinued.

While the Russia Company was struggling in the face of such severe difficulties to consolidate the new trade, other groups of English merchants were forming companies for trade with other new markets. Broadly speaking, there were two types of markets concerned, each presenting rather different problems. There were markets well-known to European traders in the sixteenth century, but which English traders had not previously succeeded in penetrating; and there were markets in the newly-discovered distant lands to the east and west.

Two areas nearer to hand which English merchants succeeded in opening to direct trade were the southern shores of the Baltic — the north coasts of Germany and Poland known to the English in the sixteenth century as *Eastland* — and the extreme eastern end of the Mediterranean where the coasts of Turkey, Syria and Egypt were known as the *Levant*. In 1579 and 1581 respectively, the Eastland and Levant Companies were chartered by Queen Elizabeth, with monopoly trading rights in their respective areas. The Eastland Company, was, in fact, taking over a flourishing trade which had formerly been in the hands of the Hanseatic merchants. The hostility to foreign traders, which has been mentioned already in Chapter 3, section 3, had continued to grow, until in 1552 the special privileges of the Hansards in England were suspended (they were partly restored later), and in 1598 the Steelyard, the

Hansards' trading depot in London, was finally closed. The Eastland Company stepped into the position vacated by the Hansards and maintained the lucrative trade with the Baltic countries. These parts were valuable markets for English cloth, but, more important, supplied the masts, hemp, tar and flax which were essential materials for a maritime nation. The Eastland Company was a *regulated company*, for its trade was not one that called for large resources of capital, and the voyage out and back could be accomplished in a single year.

English merchants penetrated the Mediterranean in the last quarter of the century and rapidly captured much of the trade formerly carried on by the merchants of Genoa, Leghorn and Venice. English traders were welcomed to Leghorn in the early 1570's, and the defeat of the Turks by the Christian powers in the great naval battle of Lepanto in 1571, by destroying the Turkish naval hold over the Mediterranean, gave renewed access to European traders. This opportunity was grasped by the group of London merchants who formed the Levant Company in 1581. Once again, the distance to the Levant was great, and the diplomacy necessary to acquire and retain trading rights with the Turkish lands was a continuous expense. Thus the Levant Company started as a *joint-stock* company, though after the period of inauguration of the trade was completed the company turned to a *regulated* form of organization. The Levant Company was the means of bringing to England the silks and spices of the East which continued to reach Europe by the overland route until the close of the sixteenth century.

The expense of this overland route, however, was the cause of many of the voyages of exploration of the sixteenth century, and after the discovery of the sea route to the East, it was only a matter of time before the old land route would be superseded by the new sea route. At the end of the sixteenth century, England's trade with the Indies and China was handled by the Levant Company, and it was this group of merchants who were largely responsible, in 1600, for founding the new company that aimed to inaugurate the sea route to the Indies.

On the last day of the year 1600 a charter was granted to the East India Company. Some 218 merchants together subscribed £30,000 into the *joint stock* of the new company. Four ships — the first fleet of the company — left London in February 1601 under the experienced East Indian explorer James Lancaster, and a trade was inaugurated that was to bring great wealth to this country, found a vast empire and raise an institution more powerful than any other in the country, second only to Parliament. The four vessels all returned safely a little more than two years later, bringing profitable cargoes of pepper and other spices. The cargoes and vessels were sold, and the original capital, plus profit or *interest*, returned to the subscribers, who were then invited to subscribe anew for a second voyage. This method of finance is known as a *terminable joint stock*, but it was discarded by the Company in 1657 because of difficulties of accounting when two or more voyages overlapped.

In the East, the Company aimed to trade at first with the East Indian islands, the main sources of spices, but this only led to conflicts with the Dutch, who had prior rights of trade there. When, in 1623, the Dutch massacred the English traders on the island of Amboyna, the English withdrew from the Indies, and concentrated their attention on the Asian mainland. In India, after some initial encounters with the Portuguese, the East India Company laid the foundations of a permanent trade by the establishment of *factories*, or warehouses, from which its servants sold English goods and bought Indian produce to await shipment by the Company's ships round the Cape of Good Hope to England. The collapse of the great Mogul Empire of central and northern India early in the eighteenth century led to a prolonged period of political disturbances when wars between the petty princes of minor provinces threatened to bring peaceful trading to a stop. To make matters worse, there was a tendency for the European nations to play off one native prince against another in the hopes of disposing of the influence of the other European nations there.

Throughout the seventeenth century the Company ran the gauntlet of a powerful opposition at home. The Company's enemies pointed out that, because the climate of the Indies discouraged the sale of England's main export — woollen cloth — the immense imports of spices, silks and calicoes were paid for by the Company in bullion (gold and silver). The trade was unfavourably balanced, and, by reducing the country's stock of the precious metals, ran contrary to what many merchants and statesmen believed to be desirable. The company, in answer to this objection, was able to claim that a high proportion of the goods brought by them from the East was re-exported to Europe, yielding bullion in return which replaced that shipped to the East. Nevertheless, opposition continued, though its principal source was the desire of merchants outside the company to share the substantial profits won by the company. *Interloping* in the distant waters of the Indian Ocean was less attractive than in more accessible markets. By the end of the century, aided by a government hostile to the company, a rival company, formed by the principal opponents and interlopers, was chartered, and for eleven acrimonious years the two companies, the Old and the New, traded side by side. The undesirable nature of this arrangement rapidly became clear, and in 1709 the monopoly of English trade with the East was restored to the original company through the amalgamation of the rival concerns.

One feature of the East India Company deserves particular mention. So strong and reliable did the company become by the later seventeenth century, that its shares were looked upon as one of the safest investments available, with the result that the company was able to borrow money at lower rates of interest than even the government.

There were other trading companies of a similar nature, but they traded on a smaller scale and did not achieve the fame of the greater institutions like the East India Company. A Barbary Company, founded in 1588 to trade with the west coast of Africa, enjoyed only a very short existence owing to the opposition of merchants excluded from the trade by the company's monopoly. Better known was the Hudson's Bay Company, chartered in 1670 to handle the fur trade of Canada. At first this company suffered through conflict with the French, who had colonized the St. Lawrence valley of Canada and resented the intrusion of the English in the north. But the Company persevered with the fur trade and is still thriving today, the only survivor of the old joint-stock chartered companies.

The joint-stock companies described so far were all formed for the purpose of trade. In the early seventeenth century this form of organization was employed also for another purpose — to develop newly-founded colonies in North America. Two attempts had been made in Elizabeth's reign to establish a colony in Virginia, but these had failed. In 1609, however, a large company was chartered, known as the Virginia Company, to finance the establishment of the colony. In ten years £100,000 was raised, but the results at first were hardly commensurate with the expense. The small group of colonists only survived owing to the energy and resourcefulness of their leader, Captain John Smith. Though the colony survived and ultimately contributed much to the prosperity of North America through its tobacco plantations, this was the fruit of individual enterprise rather than that of the company which ceased to exist after a mere sixteen years. Similarly, the Massachusetts Bay Company of 1628 was instrumental in establishing a thriving group of colonists in New England, though its subsequent activities were of little importance.

The history of English overseas trade in the century after 1550 is dominated by the great joint-stock and regulated trading companies. They played a notable part in the extension of overseas trade. With the exceptions of the East India and Hudson's Bay companies their principal role was limited, however, to the *initiation* of trade. Once established, company control of the trade tended to wither away. Thus the importance of the trading companies in the history of English trade is that they opened up new markets for English manufactures and made available to the English consumer new sources of raw materials and manufactures. Many of these new markets were distant, and to open up the trade required heavy capital expenditure. Long trade routes locked up capital in ships and merchandise for long periods, and in the sixteenth and seventeenth centuries involved considerable risk from the hazards of the sea, war and pirates. By bringing together the savings of large numbers of investors and spreading the risk widely, joint-stock enterprise made possible trade on many routes which otherwise would have remained closed.

The pattern and organization of English trade in the mid-seventeenth century differed, therefore, in some important respects from that of a century earlier. It would be wrong, however, to assume that trading companies were the sole medium of overseas trade at the later date. Though some important markets were reserved by monopoly grants to trading

companies, others remained open, while even in the monopolized markets the interloper was seldom absent. Much of the
trade from London fell into the hands of the companies, but
very little of the trade from other ports was restricted in this
way. The individual merchant handled an increasing proportion of the overseas trade of this country as the seventeenth
century progressed.

4. THE EARLY HISTORY OF BANKING

A banker may be defined as one who performs two main
functions — he accepts deposits, using this cash to make loans
to other customers; and he facilitates the circulation of money
by the provision of cheques or notes. Merchants who performed
both these functions did not emerge in England until the second
half of the seventeenth century. But before this time scriveners
were known to have accepted deposits and made loans. A
scrivener was normally employed to draft financial documents
and his specialized knowledge of financial matters led him, from
the late sixteenth century and throughout the seventeenth
century, to profit as a banker from the opportunities for this
kind of trade that came his way.

After 1650, however, a much more important group of
London goldsmiths began to enter the business of banking.
The goldsmith bankers not only accepted deposits (which they
encouraged by the payment of interest) and made loans (which
earned a higher rate of interest); they also initiated the practice
of issuing paper money and, by giving credit to the government
in a variety of forms, they established the close relationship
between banking and government finance which has been an
important characteristic of the London money market throughout its history.

A number of these London goldsmith bankers became known
for their wealth and integrity, so that the receipts which they
issued against deposits soon became acceptable as a means of
making payments between the depositors and other persons.
For greater convenience the goldsmiths evolved several forms of
paper money of which the most useful were the earliest forms of
cheques and banknotes, both of which were essentially means of
facilitating the transfer of a bank deposit from one person to

another. The attraction of a safe deposit for cash which earned interest, coupled with the convenience of the new forms of paper money, soon brought to the goldsmith bankers a vigorous clientele which included the great majority of the London and many provincial merchants.

In their relations with the Exchequer, the goldsmith bankers were on less sure ground. The revenue of the Crown was insecure and frequently inadequate. From the early Middle Ages the king had made a practice of borrowing money in anticipation of revenue, but as revenue so often failed to come up to expectations, lending to the Crown involved risk at least of delay in repayment. Attractive rates of interest, however, compensated for the risk, and in most periods there were bodies of merchants in London willing to invest their wealth in this type of loan. The goldsmith bankers naturally fell into this role and, for the most part, found it a profitable business. Their fingers were seriously burned, however, in 1672, when Charles II, whose political entanglements involved him in extraordinary financial difficulties, was obliged to call a *Stop of the Exchequer*, or a temporary suspension of repayments of loans. Five goldsmith bankers were bankrupted and the businesses of several others were severely weakened by the Stop of the Exchequer. The Stop of the Exchequer was a step on the road to a sounder financial system, but the pioneers of banking acquired their experience in a hard school.

The rise of banking was thus closely associated with Crown borrowing, and a further step in this direction was taken in 1694, when the demands of war called for borrowing by the government on a larger scale than hitherto. In that year a newly-formed joint-stock company — the Bank of England — was chartered. A capital of £1·2 million was raised which was immediately lent to the government at 8%. This initial loan was quickly followed by others. The Bank's loans to the government fell into two categories — short-term loans (repayable by the government within a few weeks or months and financed out of deposits), and long-term loans financed by additions to the Bank's capital. The latter have never been repaid and proved to be the foundation of the permanent *national debt*. Apart from this aspect of its operations, the Bank of England functioned in all other respects like any other bank, accepting deposits, making loans and issuing notes. The Bank was a chartered company from the start with a constitution similar to that of the other joint-stock companies. In 1708 an important extension of the Bank's privileges was enacted which affected the whole course of English banking history for over a century. An act of that year prohibited the establishment of any bank (other than the Bank of England) having more than six partners or subscribers. By preventing the extension of joint-stock banking this act ensured that only small (and hence often unstable) banks could function.

The Bank of England remained throughout the eighteenth century essentially an ordinary commercial bank, but it possessed certain functions which distinguished it from the many other banks which appeared during that century. It remained, of course, the only joint-stock bank in England; it lent the major part of its capital to the government; it managed all the government's borrowing operations; it held the accounts of government departments; it held the principal reserve of gold bullion in the country (a function which was to give the Bank's operations a special significance in the early nineteenth century); and it soon became the only London bank to issue notes.

Whilst the Bank of England was acquiring these special functions, private bankers, limited since the act of 1708 to not more than six partners, continued to extend their operations. The goldsmith bankers, concentrating their business entirely on banking, became known in the eighteenth century as the *London private bankers*. They dropped their issues of banknotes but added to their normal business of commercial banking the important role of acting as agents for the growing number of small provincial bankers. The latter, known as *country banks*, began to emerge in the early eighteenth century, but there were still less than a dozen in existence by 1750. Thereafter their numbers increased rapidly: there were 119 in 1784 and over 350 by the end of the century. The country bankers often combined banking with other industrial and commercial activities. They issued banknotes which circulated locally. By facilitating commercial payments between traders in different parts of the country and by their finance of commercial credit, the country banks made possible the important developments in industry and commerce of the late eighteenth century.

The foundation of the Bank of England was followed within a year by the establishment of a similar chartered bank in Scotland — the Bank of Scotland of 1695. But the subsequent course of Scottish banking history diverged from that south of the border. The Bank of Scotland did not achieve a monopoly comparable with that of the Bank of England, and within fifty years it had two rivals. The Scottish chartered banks, unlike banks in England, turned to branch banking quite early in their histories. After 1750 they were joined by a large number of smaller private bankers with businesses similar to those of the English country bankers.

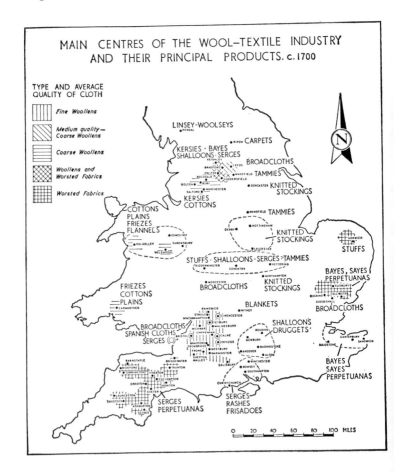

MAIN CENTRES OF THE WOOL–TEXTILE INDUSTRY AND THEIR PRINCIPAL PRODUCTS. c. 1700

CHAPTER 5

THE EXPANSION OF INDUSTRY

1. THE GREAT PRICE RISE

The economic history of England in the sixteenth century was dominated by a persistent rise in the prices of almost all commodities. This *inflation* was not gradual, but was marked by sudden spurts separated sometimes by long periods of fairly steady prices. More important, the rise in prices was much more pronounced in some commodities than in others. In England the inflation began about 1540 and continued for a century, by which time prices had multiplied, on the average, some four or five times. Similar inflations were occurring in the currencies of other European countries.

Historians have not yet succeeded in explaining satisfactorily why this inflation occurred. So far as the price of grain for food-stuffs is concerned, the most plausible explanation is that, at a time of a rapid increase of sheep and cattle farming, corn-growing did not expand sufficiently to meet the needs of the steadily growing population. The development of many impor-tant new fuel-consuming industries after 1540 created an immense pressure on the supplies of wood which may well explain the drastic rise in its price during this period. But the price rise was too general to be explained piecemeal in this way. The *debasement of the coinage* in the 1540's by Henry VIII, by which, in order to make a temporary gain out of the Mint for the Crown, the king put less silver into the coinage than hitherto, undoubtedly contributed; but the silver content of the coinage was subsequently restored by Queen Elizabeth I, so that the century-long inflation cannot be explained solely in these terms. After about 1540 the silver mines of the New World vastly augmented the supply of metal for coinage. But we can-not too readily assume that the increase in the supply of money drove up prices; the sharp rise in all forms of economic activity in the sixteenth century called for a much greater supply of

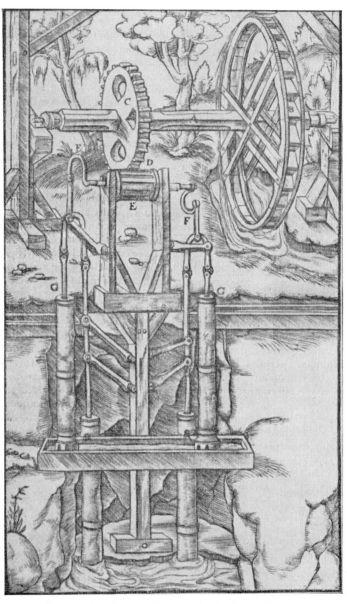

Water power for mine drainage in the sixteenth century

money, which the flow from the New World may merely have met. Undoubtedly the faster rate of growth of population, the immense increase in trade and manufacturing activity, the rise in demand for certain important commodities, the debasement of the coinage, and the flow of American silver all contributed, though in what proportions it is hardly possible yet to say.

The effects of such a drastic and prolonged inflation on an economy are many, and in the sixteenth century they combined to produce some fundamental changes in the organization of trade, industry and agriculture. When standards of living are low, as they were in sixteenth-century England, changes of this kind tend to increase poverty and generate social unrest. Hence it is that Tudor England was characterized at one and the same time by increasing wealth on the one hand, and by the spread of pauperism on the other; for when the prices of goods rose, the labourer and craftsman found that their wages bought fewer goods. Ultimately, wages rose to meet the higher prices, but they seldom rose as much as did prices and there was always a time-lag. In the meantime the growing discrepancy between rising prices and stationary wages brought greater profits to manufacturers and traders: what brought hardship to one group of people gave profit to another. This fortuitous rise in the profits of those already wealthy increased the amount of capital available for investment. The impetus this gave to industry is discussed in the next section, together with the results of the increased profitability of overseas trade. In the sphere of agriculture, the effects of the price rise must be considered in relation to other developments which were occurring at about the same time, and a fuller discussion of this aspect will be found in Chapter 6, section 1.

2. INDUSTRY IN THE SIXTEENTH AND SEVENTEENTH CENTURIES

The progress of English industry in the period 1540 to 1640 was so rapid compared with its very slow expansion in earlier centuries that one modern historian has been tempted with some exaggeration to speak of an 'industrial revolution' in this century. In comparison with the more widely recognized industrial revolution of the eighteenth century, the changes of the sixteenth century were on a far smaller scale; nevertheless this century witnessed the beginnings of several new large-scale industries as rivals of the older woollen cloth industry.

Minting coins in the second half of the sixteenth century

A number of factors were responsible for this important new turn in the English economy. The discovery of new routes to the markets of the East has been mentioned in the preceding chapter. In the sixteenth century new outlets for English manufactured exports were also found in the Baltic and the Mediterranean, while the seventeenth century saw the beginnings of colonization in North America and the West Indies, which provided new markets to add to those opened up by the East India Company. These new markets were potential sources of wealth in the sixteenth century, rather than immediate openings. At that time, the countries of north-west Europe were far the most important consumers of English goods, and it was the decline of manufacturing industry in some of these, owing to war and its resulting interruption to trade, that accounted for the most valuable increases in English exports. The way in which the price rise made industrial investment more attractive to those with capital has already been mentioned in the previous section.

Water power for mine drainage and winding in the sixteenth century

The religious changes of the Reformation had, surprisingly enough, important repercussions on industry. In England, the confiscation by Henry VIII in 1536–9 of the lands and properties of the many hundreds of monasteries transferred their vast estates to new owners. Many of these new owners were primarily concerned with the economic development of their new estates. In particular, much of the coal-bearing land in the northeast on which monastic control had discouraged mining during the Middle Ages now came into the hands of civil landlords anxious to exploit this valuable new source of wealth. Perhaps more important was the altered approach, at least in official circles, to the morals of business. It has been argued by one group of historians, for example, that the new ideas of the Protestants encouraged just those qualities in men which made for success in business — sobriety, integrity and hard work.

The frequency of wars on the Continent, combined with the relative peacefulness and security of England in the sixteenth century, attracted to England both foreign industrial capital and foreign labour. Many of the important new processes which provided the impulse to the industrial progress of this century were brought to this country and taught to English workers by skilled immigrants from France, the Low Countries, Germany and Italy. Another pre-requisite of rapid industrial development is a highly mobile supply of cheap labour. Some of the agricultural changes in the sixteenth century may have contributed to the supply of labour for industry, and there is evidence that there was an unusually high degree of labour mobility at this time.

Industrial growth came first to England's oldest established industry — woollen cloth manufacture. In the first half of the century, mainly owing to the growth of export markets, there was a very great increase in the manufacture of this commodity. The number of short-cloths exported from the port of London rose from 50,000 in 1500 to 133,000 in 1550. An important factor in the expansion of the industry in the late sixteenth and early seventeenth centuries was the introduction from the Continent of new types of cloth. These *New Draperies*, as they were called, were mostly lighter and more attractive cloths than the traditional English *broad cloth*, and were manufactured at first mainly in East Anglia, where many of the refugees from

Early sixteenth-century lights in the cloth makers' window at
Semur-en-Auxois
left: Raising with teazles; right: Shearing

religious persecution in France and the Low Countries settled. Only in one respect did the English woollen industry continue to be unable to compete with its continental rivals, and that was in the finishing branches of the industry — principally in bleaching and dyeing. An attempt was made in 1613, through a scheme organized by Alderman Cockayne, to encourage the finishing of woollen cloth in this country by prohibiting the export of *white* (unfinished) cloth. The effects of this scheme were disastrous: it simply encouraged the continental manufacture of cloth at the expense of the home industry. The scheme was abandoned after four years, but the renewal of widespread war on the Continent (the Thirty Years' War, 1618–48), followed by the disturbances of the English Civil War (1642–49), delayed the recovery of the English industry until the later seventeenth century.

Two other old-established English industries benefited from the expansion of the sixteenth century. These were shipbuilding and housebuilding. It is well known that the early Tudor monarchs founded the English navy, and this, combined with a demand for the big ships needed for the new trades to distant countries, led to the establishment in the late sixteenth and early seventeenth centuries of large shipyards, mainly in the Thames estuary and on the south coast. The survival of so many Elizabethan houses both large and small is sufficient testimony to the vast building activity that was an important feature of the sixteenth-century economy. It also indicates that

a great deal more wealth was becoming available to the upper
and middle classes in English society in this period.

Plentiful supplies of coal in many parts of the country were
the means by which the later industrial growth of the country
was made possible. The real beginnings of the modern coal
industry can be traced to the sixteenth century. The growth of
towns and of wood-consuming industries such as iron-making,
brewing and salt-making caused a sharp rise in the price of
wood for fuel. Not unnaturally this led to an increased consumption of coal for domestic purposes, as well as attempts by
wood-consuming industries to turn to the use of coal fuel. The
most important domestic market for coal was London, and the
sixteenth century saw the beginning of the Newcastle-London
east coast coal trade which proved to be such an important
nursery for our seamen. Among the industries which took to
coal for fuel in the sixteenth century were salt- and soap-making,
dyeing, and brewing. Attempts were made to substitute coal
for charcoal in the growing iron industry, but these were not
successful until the eighteenth century.

Perhaps the most important of the new industries to arise in
England in the sixteenth century was the iron industry. Here
again, the importation of both skilled workers and new processes was the key to development. The blast furnace, in which

Charcoal-making in the seventeenth century

Water-powered blast furnace bellows in the sixteenth century

molten metal was produced from the ore with charcoal aided by a bellows-operated blast, had been used in Belgium as early as the fourteenth century, but the first known furnace in this country was constructed in the late 1490's. Only slight progress was made until the 1540's, but the next thirty years saw the growth of an important industry. In 1540 there were probably not more than six blast furnaces; by 1600 there were more than 120, half of which were in the Weald district of Sussex and Surrey. Some of the iron was cast directly from the furnace into cannons and cannon-balls, fire-backs, grave-slabs and pots, but most of it was forged into *bar iron* to be distributed to innumerable forges and smithies up and down the country for the manufacture of nails, brackets and iron implements.

Another important metallurgical industry to be introduced into this country by foreign capital and skill was copper-making. In 1564, Daniel Hochstetter, a member of an Augsburg (Germany) mining firm, secured rights to search for copper in England. As a result of his discoveries, in 1568 two joint-stock companies were chartered in which his firm was joined by English investors. The *Mines Royal* was given the monopoly of copper-mining in several counties and began large-scale operations at Keswick in Westmorland. The *Mineral and Battery Works*, with the monopoly of brass and wire-making, set up works at Tintern in Monmouthshire. These linked undertakings never really thrived, but the art of making copper and brass remained in this country to expand into an important industry in the eighteenth century.

The significant industrial expansion begun in the sixteenth century continued into the seventeenth century. It is true that it was to be a long time before industry in England became as important as agriculture, yet the industrial production of England in these two centuries was sufficiently important to influence the nation's destiny. Industry produced a surplus for export, and the desire for sure markets was an important element in the growth of an empire. Exports must be carried in ships, and England's maritime traditions grew largely from her vast merchant navy. Perhaps most important of all, however, large-scale industry demanded greater accumulation of capital and new forms of organization. The sixteenth and seventeenth centuries produced many interesting experiments in the forms of industrial organization. Most of all, these developments made possible the giant strides in industrial growth of the eighteenth and nineteenth centuries.

3. CHANGES IN INDUSTRIAL ORGANIZATION

The changes in industry discussed in the previous section made several departures from the long-established medieval forms of industrial organization. In the early Middle Ages most industry had existed in towns where it came under the control of borough and gild regulations discussed in Chapter 2. Only after the thirteenth century, when first fulling, then other branches of the woollen industry migrated to the countryside in search of water-power, did some branches of industry become free from gild control. But in the sixteenth century some entirely new industries grew up, and these, because they were never subject to gild or borough regulation, were free to develop forms of organization suitable to their scale of operation. Some of the older industries shifted their location as a result of new techniques of manufacture, and others increased the scale of their operations so that they outgrew the usefulness of the older forms of gild regulation. Thus it is no coincidence that the sixteenth and seventeenth centuries, in which the beginnings of English heavy industry may be discerned, also witnessed a decline in the power and influence of the medieval craft gilds.

There were probably more gilds with more members in the sixteenth century than ever before, but their usefulness had largely been outlived. They now seldom provided the ladder by which the young apprentice climbed to a position of equality with his former master. For the masters had by now emerged as a class of their own, recruiting their ranks largely from their own sons or from the sons of those wealthy enough to buy their way in. An apprentice lacking wealth or influence became a journeyman — a skilled labourer — and remained a journeyman. In some cases the journeymen formed gilds of their own (*journeymen gilds*), but these could do little to replace the spirit and purpose of the old craft gilds. Mostly they concerned themselves with little more than small insurance schemes of the type run by benefit societies in later periods. (For the development of journeymen gilds into trade unions, see Chapter 13, section 5.)

In London, where the gilds had consistently played an

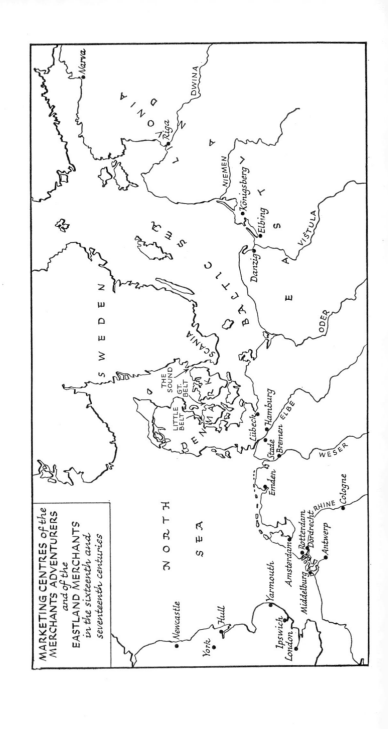

MARKETING CENTRES *of the*
MERCHANTS ADVENTURERS
and of the
EASTLAND MERCHANTS
*in the sixteenth and
seventeenth centuries*

Narva

LIVONIA

DWINA

Riga

NIEMEN

Königsberg

Elbing

Danzig

VISTULA

PRUSSIA

BALTIC SEA

ODER

SWEDEN

SCANIA

THE SOUND

GT. BELT

DENMARK

LITTLE BELT

Lübeck

Hamburg

Stade

Bremen

ELBE

WESER

Emden

Cologne

RHINE

Rotterdam

Dordrecht

Antwerp

Amsterdam

Middelburg

NORTH SEA

Yarmouth

Ipswich

London

Hull

York

Newcastle

important part in City government from the early Middle Ages, the masters of the wealthier gilds had gradually raised themselves above their own journeymen and apprentices, leaving a gap between themselves and their workers that only the wealthy could span; but they had in addition raised their gilds above those of the less wealthy trades. Most of these rich gilds were those that had been in a position to develop the merchanting aspect of their trade at the expense of manufacture. As London was not only by far the largest market for internal trade in the country but also the chief exporting centre, this trend was all the more rapid. Thus the Merchant Taylors, the Haberdashers, the Drapers, the Ironmongers and the Fishmongers divorced themselves from production and concentrated on trade. The liveries — the ceremonial uniforms of these wealthy merchant gilds — were hardly accessible to the journeymen. Spurning the humble title of gilds, these trades now became known as the *Livery Companies*. They assumed immense influence in City politics, and to this day the twelve livery companies of London retain the right to elect London's Lord Mayor. By the eighteenth century the names of gilds and livery companies bore little or no relation to the occupations of their members; there were ironmongers in the Drapers' Company and drapers in the Ironmongers' Company.

In the provincial gilds, too, by the mid-eighteenth century, the idea of 'one craft — one gild' had long since been forgotten. Though both boroughs and gilds were still able, to some extent, to insist on gild membership as a pre-requisite to the pursuit of any occupation or trade in a borough, for the most part it mattered little which gild a man belonged to. Indeed, from the sixteenth century on, gilds for new crafts were almost unheard of, and with the passage of time new trades and industries replaced the older ones. Industries like iron-making and coal-mining, which had never had gilds, became more important than others that had always been closely controlled by gilds. New industries like cotton and glass manufacture arose, in which gild control was quite unknown. The peculiar conditions of the medieval town which had given birth to the gilds no longer existed by the seventeenth century, and the gilds, dying slowly since the sixteenth century, had very little life left in them by 1700.

But though the gild system which had dominated all urban

industry for more than five hundred years was no longer a living force, small-scale industry persisted. The unit of production, for the most part, remained the home. The factory, though not unknown, was the exception rather than the rule. The *domestic system of industry* prevailed until the nineteenth century. Under this system, the worker worked up his raw material into the finished article in his own home with the aid of his own family, an apprentice and a journeyman or two. There were many variants to this basic pattern, depending mainly on who owned the raw material and means of production. In the purest form of the domestic system, the worker bought (sometimes on credit) his raw material each week, and manufactured the product with his own machines or implements. At the week's end he carried the finished article to market, sold it, and with the proceeds bought his raw material for the next week. Too often this system permitted the worker to get into debt with his supplier of raw material, and it was easy for him to find himself permanently working on raw material belonging to a merchant, who, retaining ownership of the material all the time, merely put it out to be worked on by the domestic worker. In the nail industry of the Black Country, where this form of organization prevailed in the seventeenth and eighteenth centuries, the

Domestic woollen spinning in Yorkshire in the eighteenth century

nailers, as a result of debts, fell under the control of the merchants or 'nail-masters', who frequently used their power
unscrupulously to reduce wages. In the hosiery industry of
Leicestershire and Nottinghamshire, where the 'stocking-frames'
on which the woollen stockings were knitted were expensive
pieces of machinery, the merchants secured an even greater hold
over the workers by their ownership of the machines on which
the 'frame-knitters' worked. In short, the domestic system was
far from being the ideal form of industrial organization as it has
sometimes been painted. Long hours, excessive employment of
children's labour, and low standards of living were all too often
the inevitable results of the system.

Side by side with this domestic industry, there began to
appear for the first time isolated examples of really large-scale
industry. These remained exceptional until the late eighteenth
century, but owe their importance to the example and experience they provided to industrialists of later ages. The biggest
units of industry before the eighteenth century were the naval
dockyards of the Thames estuary and the south coast. Here, at
Deptford, Woolwich, Chatham, Sheerness, Portsmouth and
Plymouth, the Crown employed hundreds of shipwrights,
carpenters, smiths and sailmakers, making and repairing ships.
The earliest examples of large 'factories' appeared in the woollen
industry. Thomas Spring, clothier of Lavenham in Suffolk, was
reputed to employ many hundreds of cloth-workers on his own
premises in the early sixteenth century, whilst John Stumpe
acquired the abbey of Malmesbury in Wiltshire after the
Dissolution of the Monasteries of the 1530's in which he set up
looms for hundreds of his weavers. Perhaps the most remarkable
example of early large-scale industry was in the factories of Sir
Ambrose Crowley outside Newcastle, where hundreds of smiths
mass-produced nails and other ironware. Here, from the late
seventeenth century, Sir Ambrose provided workshops, forges,
warehouses and houses for his workmen. By offering his workers
an elaborate scheme of social insurance which included education for their children, a free medical service for the families of
all his workmen, and the services of his own chaplain, Crowley
anticipated the better-known scheme of Robert Owen of a
century later, and proved that large-scale industry could both
pay its way and be humane.

CHAPTER 6

RURAL CHANGES

1. ADVANCES IN AGRICULTURE

By the end of the fifteenth century many features of
English farming which we tend to regard as characteristic
of the medieval system had ceased to exist or, if they still
survived, did so in a much modified form. Serfdom, for example,
had virtually disappeared. Labour services, a form of rent
payment-in-kind for land, had similarly disappeared by the
process of commutation described in Chapter 1. The manorial
demesne, too, formerly the pivot of the medieval farming
community, was now seldom farmed directly by the lord of the
manor or indirectly under the direction of his steward. Instead,
demesnes had mostly found their way by means of leases into the
hands of large independent farmers.

In spite of the apparent inflexibility of the medieval open field
system, there had been a steady growth in the later Middle
Ages in the amount of land held *in severalty*, that is, in separate
enclosed fields by individual farmers. This *enclosure* had been
achieved in three ways — by the clearance or drainage of new
land by individuals, in which case the land was never shared
out in strips; by the *consolidation* of existing strips by exchange or
purchase into compact blocks under single ownership or
tenancy; and by the sub-division of common or waste land.

The English farming village differed, therefore, in the late
fifteenth century from its predecessor in the earlier Middle
Ages. The difference was of organization rather than of
appearance, however, because in many areas the traditional
open fields still prevailed. Enclosures had so far only affected
some villages, and in some of these, only some parts. The typical
English farmer was still a tenant of his lord of the manor, cultivating his strips in the open fields and making full use of his
valued rights of common pasture.

Though the open fields still predominated in the central area, by 1500 they had ceased to exist in the outer ring of southern counties — Suffolk, Essex, Kent, Surrey, Sussex, Devon and Cornwall. Commons and wasteland still covered large areas, particularly in the north of England, providing rough grazing for large herds of sheep and cattle. But in most areas by 1500 the pressure of a growing population had caused persistent *assarting* (intakes of land for cultivation from the waste) and the increase of flocks and herds; land hunger was becoming more acute. So long as common or waste land exceeded normal demands for pasture, neighbouring villages could inter-common without difficulty. The stage came sooner or later in most areas when the reduction of the waste, coupled with the increase in the number of beasts, necessitated a division of the common grazing land between villages, or even between individual tenants. In this way Henfield Common in Lancashire was divided between the townships of Clayton-le-Moors, Altham and Accrington between 1576 and 1594. The tenants of Bradford Moor in Yorkshire met together in 1589 in order to make such a division of the moor between themselves. Further pressure on the commons led to a limit, known as a *stint*, being placed on the number of beasts any man might graze on the common. In Elizabeth I's reign the ploughing up of part of the waste at Burton Leonard in the West Riding of Yorkshire necessitated even a reduction in the stints.

This type of enclosure of common or waste land was a frequent occurrence in the sixteenth and seventeenth centuries, and was normally the result of amicable agreement between the villages or farmers involved, and was often confirmed by decrees of the Court of Chancery. There were, however, other types of enclosures taking place in response to new economic forces. Enclosures of both arable and common land to make more profitable use of land by specialization were made frequently in the sixteenth and seventeenth centuries. This was particularly the case in the broad belt of counties surrounding London. Kent, for example, concentrated on fruit growing, Essex on the production of vegetables and hops (a comparatively new crop in the sixteenth century), Lincolnshire on barley. When population was rising, as it was in the sixteenth century, agricultural productivity had to rise in step, and enclosure often made possible the better use of land.

Another important new trend in the sixteenth and seventeent
centuries was the growing appreciation of the value of *leys* o
sown grasslands. Grass was grown in a ley for a few years at a
stretch on land normally used for arable. This had the advan
tages of supporting greater flocks or herds (for meat, milk o
wool) and of resting and improving overworked ploughland
Leys were thus introduced as a variant in crop rotations, and
enclosures were often made in the sixteenth and seventeent
centuries to take advantage of leys.

All these types of agricultural change were productive o
nothing but good — they improved agricultural efficiency
raised the yield of food from the land, and made possible th
feeding of a population which may have doubled between 1450
and 1650. There remains, however, a further type of enclosur
which was a feature of the period after 1450 and which, becaus
it led to social disturbances, has attracted a great deal o
attention from both contemporary writers and modern his

*Sheep now graze on the site of the lost village of Wormleighton,
Oxfordshire. The depressions are the village fishponds. William
Cope, Cofferer to Henry VII, bought the manor in 1495, bought out
all the free-holders in 1498 and pulled down twelve houses and
three cottages, turning 240 acres from arable to grassland. Twelve
ploughs were displaced and sixty villagers lost their livelihood.*

torians. These enclosures were of both arable and commons for sheep and cattle rearing. Rising meat prices, combined with the great expansion of the woollen manufacturing industry in the late fifteenth century and the first half of the sixteenth century, made grazing an attractive form of specialization for farmers. Meat and wool production attracted particularly landowners who were anxious to increase their income from rents in the face of rising prices.

Not every kind of land is suitable for grazing, and enclosure for this purpose appears to have been confined largely to the midland counties of Leicestershire, Warwickshire, Northamptonshire and Bedfordshire. But within this area enclosure was widespread. In Leicestershire, for example, one in every three of its 370 villages was affected by enclosure between 1485 and 1607. Enclosures for pasture were mainly concentrated in the period 1475–1550. Probably by the end of this period wool production had risen to the new levels demanded by the expanded cloth industry, and the temporary stagnation of the cloth industry after 1550 discouraged further increases. Pasture farming made very small demands on labour compared with arable farming, and enclosure for grazing was often associated with a reduction of employment, or rural depopulation. 'All is taken up for pastures', complained a sixteenth-century writer with some exaggeration, 'either for shepe or for grasinge of cattell. So that I have knowen of late a dozen plowes within lesse compasse than 6 myles aboute me laide downe within theise 7 yeares; and wheare 40 persons had their livinges nowe one man and his shepherd hathe all.' Landlords who carried out this kind of depopulating enclosure ruthlessly, as did John Quarles who turned out the tenants of Cotesbach in Leicestershire to make way for pasture in 1603, stirred up immense hostility. Many English villages are known to have disappeared between the late Middle Ages and the seventeenth century: there were many and varied causes of the depopulation of these 'lost villages'; enclosure for pasture was only one.

During the first half of the sixteenth century the government was frequently under pressure to take steps to prevent the depopulation which enclosures for pasture sometimes produced in the Midlands. As early as 1489, an act of Parliament 'in restraint of sheep farming' had prohibited the destruction of farmhouses and the conversion of arable land to pasture Wolsey, as Henry VIII's Chancellor in 1517, appointed a Commission to enquire into the enclosure of arable land for pasture, but took little subsequent action. Acts of 1533 and 1536 ordered recently enclosed lands to be laid open once again, and tried to restrict the number of former holdings that could be occupied as well as the number of sheep to be kept by one man Another Commission appointed by Protector Somerset in 1548 during the reign of Edward VI provided further evidence of the persistence of the trend towards enclosures, particularly in the Midlands. Somerset believed that enclosures were partly responsible for much of the social unrest of his time and therefore opposed the movement. When, in 1549, the Earl of Warwick replaced Somerset as Protector, government opposition to enclosures ceased, for Warwick sympathized openly with the larger landowners. Though there were further attempts by Parliament to reverse the trend from arable to pasture, some years of good harvests towards the end of the century so lowered the price of corn that it was felt that there was still more than sufficient arable land under cultivation, and the existing laws against the conversion of arable land to pasture were repealed (1593). But a few years of corn shortage with high prices in the late 1590's reversed this policy and a further effort was made in 1598 to restore land to arable cultivation.

The laws against conversion of arable to pasture were mostly restricted to a limited number of counties in which the enclosures were mainly for pasture. They were seldom effectively enforced and are unlikely to have seriously checked the progress of the movement. The acts did little more than express the attitude of the government to the changes that were taking place for enforcement of the laws depended upon Justices of the Peace in each county and too often the Justices were sympathetic to the enclosers, if they were not themselves offenders.

The outcry by contemporaries, and the attempts by the government to arrest the trend towards more pasture farming have led to the belief that enclosures were a particular phenomenon of the sixteenth century. This is clearly a mistaken view, since enclosures were the constant accompaniment to agricultural development from the twelfth to the nineteenth century: more land, particularly common land, was enclosed

in the seventeenth century than in the sixteenth when the
outcry against enclosures was far louder.

2. THE RELIEF OF POVERTY

When the pace of economic development accelerates, some
kind of social disturbance is unavoidable. The agricultural and
industrial changes of the sixteenth century were accompanied
by a serious and prolonged inflation, a combination which
tended to produce periodic waves of unemployment and
poverty. Some causes of destitution in the sixteenth century were
self-apparent; the Midlands enclosures for pasture described in
the preceding section obliged thousands of rural workers to
leave their homes to find new occupations. One historian has
estimated that in twenty-four counties between thirty and fifty
thousand people suffered in this way. Another more recent
historian, by tracing the many hundreds of villages known to
have disappeared between about 1450 and 1600, believes that
the number of people displaced by enclosures for pasture must
have been even greater. But for every person displaced from the
countryside by sheep farming, two were employed in the woollen
industry which expanded in step with and as a result of the
enclosures. Indeed, rural unemployment arising from the spread
of pasture farming was mainly a local problem; but the periodic
depressions to which industry, particularly industry concerned
largely with export markets, was prone, affected much wider
regions. There was a particularly sharp decline in the output of
cloth in the late 1550's, followed by further depressions in the
early 1560's and early 1570's. Alderman Cockayne's disastrous
scheme of 1613 (see Chapter 5, section 2) was followed by a
serious depression in the early 1620's, and each of these set-backs
must have increased unemployment amongst industrial workers.

Over the country as a whole, however, the price rise must
have contributed more than any other factor to the increase of
poverty. Though wages rose, they did not rise as fast or to the
same extent as did the prices of the goods on which the wage-
earners spent their money. The quantity of goods which a
building labourer's weekly wage would buy fell by over 50%
between 1500 and 1600. In short, one effect of the sixteenth-
century inflation was a re-distribution of income, by which the

lower-paid workers became poorer (at least temporarily) while some groups, notably merchants and manufacturers, benefited. While this tendency towards inequality assisted the accumulation of capital, it increased the problems of poverty.

Equally important was the rise of population, whose growth from the late fifteenth century contrasted markedly with the stagnation of the preceding century and a half. It is believed that 40% was added to the country's population in the sixteenth century alone. Resources of land and capital could not provide additional employment fast enough. Industrial advances and some reversion to arable forms of farming provided the main solution to the employment problem in the long run, but the early stages of these momentous developments imposed strain and hardship on a society more accustomed to stability and conservatism than to rapid change. It is no coincidence that in the late sixteenth and early seventeenth centuries support for the establishment of colonies was given by many who believed that only extensive emigration would solve the social ills of the country.

There was, therefore, a great deal of poverty in the sixteenth century, but this was not new. One result of the Reformation had been to turn the relief of poverty from a purely Church affair into a matter of state concern. Poverty became no longer acceptable and the outcry against it in the sixteenth century has long deceived historians into believing that it was a problem of unusual severity in that century. As one modern historian puts it, in the Middle Ages 'many men died of hunger, but on the whole they died quietly'.

The agitation against poverty and its causes — the price rise, the excess of population, the irregularity of industrial employment and the spread of pasture farming — coincided, unfortunately, with the decay of some of the medieval institutions which had grappled with the problem in the past. In particular the gilds no longer played such a prominent part in the people's lives. Some older industries, like woollen manufacture, tended to move out of the towns into the countryside out of reach of the gilds, while the new industries, whose rise was such an important feature of the sixteenth century (see Chapter 5, section 2), never adopted the gild organization. Thus a growing proportion of the industrial population of the country was without the support which gild members traditionally provided for the poor of their own crafts at the very time when they were at the mercy of recurring periods of slackness and possibly unemployment in their occupations. Though some of these gaps were filled by extensive private charity, there are good grounds for believing that the price rise was also whittling away the value of these alms.

Small wonder then that the sixteenth century was a time of unrest, social disturbances and rioting. Contemporaries wrote of 'clothiers or other occupations, beinge forced to be withoute worke, are the most part of theise rude people that make theise uprores abroade, to the greate disquiet not only of the Kynges highenes, and also of his people', and the government looked on the increase of 'idle vagabonds' as one of the most pressing of its problems.

At first, the government's reaction was to suppress the 'vagabonds' brutally. In Henry VIII's reign, vagabonds were ordered to be whipped. Later, in Mary's reign, in 1557, persistent offenders were ordered to be branded with a letter 'V' on their shoulders. Another approach to the problem was to allow deserving cases to beg, but because of the great increase of beggars their numbers were restricted by licensing. Many of the poor flocked to London, believing, rightly, that where the greatest wealth lay, there was most to be gained by begging. Eventually London was forced to take steps to reduce the number of beggars, and licences for begging were limited to one thousand.

But the evils of poverty concerned more than just the large cities, and it was fast becoming apparent that some form of regional organization for the relief of poverty was necessary which would cover all parts of the country, rural as well as urban. Only the church parishes answered this need, and in 1572 an act of Parliament ordered Justices of the Peace in each county to appoint *Overseers of the Poor* in every parish, who were to be charged with the administration of poor relief in their parishes. They were to be empowered to collect a *poor rate* and distribute the money thus collected as they found need. Some parishes had already established *Houses of Correction* where the 'idle' poor were to be inured to the discipline of regular hard work. Others set up *workhouses*, where raw materials, bought out of the poor rate, provided useful work for the unemployed. Most adopted the practice of apprenticing orphans to craftsmen, so that they should grow up capable of earning a useful living.

By the end of Elizabeth's reign, a new system of poor relief had been created, replacing and even improving on the old charity of monastery, gild and private gift. An act of 1597, confirmed and amended by one of 1601, drew together all the piecemeal attempts of the previous half-century, requiring each of the ten thousand odd parishes in England to provide adequately for its own unemployed, sick, aged and orphans.

Though the Elizabethan *Poor Law*, as brought together in the Act of 1601, endured for two and one-third centuries, it had many imperfections and shortcomings so that frequent modification was necessary. The greatest difficulty lay in deciding exactly who was to be entitled to poor relief in each parish. If the overseers of one parish distributed over-generous relief to the poor, they ran the risk of attracting the poor from neighbouring parishes. They soon began, therefore, to make their own regulations in order to avoid taxing themselves unnecessarily highly. Ultimately, in 1662, a new act provided a solution to this problem, applicable to all parishes. Each person was to be *settled* in a parish, and could only have one parish of *settlement*. Settlement, entitling a person to poor relief in that parish, was normally acquired by being born there, but could also be acquired by serving an apprenticeship there, or occupying a house there assessed for poor rate at more than £10 per year. Naturally, overseers were concerned to keep the number of settlements in their own parish to a minimum in order to reduce their possible outlay on poor relief. This sometimes led to appalling inhumanity, as when women about to have illegitimate babies were hustled out of the parish in order that the child should not acquire settlement in the parish.

The *Act of Settlement* of 1662 had its shortcomings, too, for many people found themselves from time to time in need of poor relief when they were far from their parish of settlement. In an expanding economy, mobility of labour was essential, yet the loss of settlement imposed grave risks on anyone leaving his parish of settlement. Overseers came to demand certificates from the parish of settlement of anyone coming into their own parish to take up work, acknowledging responsibility in the event of the person becoming 'chargeable' for relief. These certificates were legalized by an act of 1697. In the event of unemployment, the person could then be removed to his parish of settlement — often an expensive business in itself. Not until 1795 was the settlement law amended so that a poor person could not be removed to the parish of his settlement until he had actually become destitute.

By the eighteenth century, the Poor Law with its accompanying law of settlement had become part of the background of the life of the English labouring classes. Probably half or more of the population, at one time or another, had occasion to have recourse to the 'parish'. The system was elaborate and unwieldy, a source of discord both inside the parish and between parishes. Yet when trade fluctuated between boom and depression, and years of good harvest were followed by periods of poor crops, poverty was always present, for few workers earned sufficient to set aside for bad times. The Poor Law re-distributed some of the wealth of the rich towards the needy poor in a tolerably efficient, if at times inhumane, manner.

CHAPTER 7

TUDOR AND STUART
ECONOMIC POLICY

The emergence in the late fifteenth and sixteenth centuries of strong nation-states, the decline of civil wars in Europe, the growing political strength of the merchant class, and the increasing ability of governments to enforce their policies all tended to encourage governments of the sixteenth and seventeenth centuries to direct their efforts to the increase of the wealth and power of the nation. A policy of this nature involved making fuller use of the country's own resources of labour and raw materials and led to determined measures to conserve the military and naval strength of the country. It involved the regulation of foreign trade and encouraged the establishment and exploitation of a colonial empire. These aims were far-reaching and sometimes contradictory; there is no real evidence that they were consciously pursued as part of a coherent economic and political plan. For the most part each aim was pursued individually for its own sake, in the belief that it would conduce to the general good of the country.

1. The State and Industry

The state's policy towards industry in the sixteenth century took two directions: it attempted to attract new industries to the country by the grant of special privileges and monopoly powers to foreigners and others willing to take the initiative in new processes; and in the older industries it endeavoured to preserve on the one hand the existing relationships between masters and servants threatened by the growing scale of industry, and, on the other, the control over industry by gild and borough.

There are many examples of the grant of special privileges to foreign skilled workers usually made conditional upon the new skill being taught to English workmen. Daniel Hochstetter, the representative of the Augsburg merchants, who came to England from southern Germany in 1564 to introduce the smelting of copper and the manufacture of brass to this country, was given, through the royal charter to the companies of the Mines Royal and the Mineral and Battery Works, the monopoly of these industries. In the second half of the sixteenth century there were attempts to introduce to this country the art of making the finer varieties of glass. In 1567, a *patent* (royal grant) of monopoly was given to two Antwerp glass-makers, Anthony Beckn and Jean Carre, to make one such type of glass in this country. Another patent was granted in 1574 to an Italian, Verselini, to make drinking glasses, but very little came of either of these attempts to establish the new industry. Later, towards the end of the seventeenth century, German sword-makers were established in County Durham by another chartered company, the Hollow Sword-Blade Company.

Even without the direct encouragement of privileges granted by the Crown, there was a constant immigration of foreign workers into England in the sixteenth and seventeenth centuries, bringing with them new skills and new trades. By giving facilities to these immigrants, and by refusing to listen to those who would have opposed this influx of skilled labour, the government did much to promote the growth of industry. Most of the immigrants were refugees from religious intolerance. There were Flemish and Dutch protestants fleeing from the fury of the Spanish efforts at reconquest of the Low Countries; French Huguenots warned by the Massacre of St. Bartholomew's Eve of 1572 of the fate that awaited them if they remained in France; and more Frenchmen, who, after Louis XIV's revocation of the tolerant Edict of Nantes in 1685, fled from Catholic persecution in their thousands.

From these continental persecutions England gained skilled French ironmasters in the early years of the sixteenth century who taught English workers the arts of casting goods from molten iron. Flemish weavers in the late sixteenth century brought the 'New Draperies' to the East Anglian clothmaking towns and villages, where they found their new homes. Silk-weaving was brought to the Spitalfields district of London by Huguenots in the late seventeenth century. Dutchmen established the manufacture of heavy cordage cables for shipbuilding.

and French Huguenots became the principal makers of glass in this country in the sixteenth century.

Another way in which the government attempted to assist the development of new industries in the country was through the grant of *patents of monopoly*. These were sole rights to use certain processes, or to manufacture certain goods. The aim of the patents was to foster the growth of new industries. The patents were first used, as has been seen, as incentives to foreign skilled workers to establish their methods in this country, and some of them proved both successful and valuable. In the 1560's, out of twenty-three patents fifteen were granted to foreigners. Among the most important grants of this kind in the sixteenth century were those for the manufacture of salt, soap, saltpetre (used in the making of gunpowder), and glass. But there was little consistency in the use of the grants of manufacturing monopolies, and applications for patents for at least two outstanding inventions of the late sixteenth century — Lee's stocking-frame (a knitting machine), and Harrington's water-closet — were rejected.

Moreover, as the Crown's practice of granting monopolies led to abuse of the system by grants which raised the price of the commodity to the consumer, opposition to the patents of monopoly grew. In 1601, after a bitter debate in the House of Commons, Queen Elizabeth admitted that some patents had resulted in 'the great loss and grievance of her loving subjects'. Many patents were withdrawn and permission given for others to be submitted to a test of legality in the law courts. In a test case, judgment was given against the holder of a patent for the sole importing and making of playing cards, on the grounds that such patents were contrary to the liberty of the subject and offended against common law. In spite of these developments, James I (1603–25) continued the practice of granting patents of monopoly, arousing new hostility. Ultimately, in 1624, Parliament passed an act — the *Statute of Monopolies* — which made illegal all forms of monopoly grants other than those made to genuine inventors or to companies.

Naturally the government lavished most attention on England's traditional source of wealth, its woollen manufacture. In the sixteenth century there was an important extension of this industry and there was no obvious need for government protection. The government, however, was not so much concerned to stimulate as to prevent the growth in the scale of industry from disturbing the existing balance between employer and worker. The government opposed equally the excessive concentration of power in the hands of a small group of wealthy capitalists and the degradation of the workers into an impoverished proletariat. The extension of the woollen industry in rural areas was disliked because the cloth-workers could no longer be controlled by gild and borough regulations. Further, expanding industry produced movements of labour, and, in an age already sufficiently racked by social disturbance, the government was anxious to reinforce the laws that bound servants to masters for long periods. Various acts of Parliament, particularly in the 1550's and 1560's, attempted to implement these various aims. Difficulties of enforcement rendered most of them ineffective and for the most part the industry developed along its own lines regardless of, and frequently contrary to, the policy of the government.

By the later seventeenth century, however, the situation had altered considerably. The East India Company was importing large quantities of Indian calico — a dyed or printed cotton cloth lighter and more attractive than woollen cloth. Calico became fashionable wear for the wealthier classes, and for the first time in the long history of the industry woollen manufacturers faced competition from a new type of textile. The woollen industry had, of course, immense influence in the country and in Parliament, and in 1667 this was used to procure an act which required the dead to be buried in shrouds of woollen cloth, 'forcing the dead to consume what the living were inadequate to purchase', as one modern historian has written. This was rather a forlorn hope for increasing the sales of woollen cloth, and as imports of Indian calico continued to grow, an act of 1700 prohibited the import of *printed* calico. This act, however, permitted the continued import of *plain* calico and gave a stimulus to the printing in this country of imported plain calico. In the face of the opposition of the wool manufacturers to this continued competition from calico, Parliament passed a further act of 1721 which prohibited entirely the *use* of printed or dyed calico in this country. However, a concession had to be made in 1736 (by the *Manchester Act*) to permit the manufacture of cloth made with a mixture of linen and cotton, and the 1721 act soon ceased to be effective. Protection of the woollen industry was seldom more than half-hearted and cannot have produced more than trifling benefit to the industry.

Another important aspect of government policy in the field of industry was concerned with arresting certain trends which arose inevitably out of economic progress, but which the government believed to be undesirable. These were the decay of municipal control over industry, the drift of population from the country to the town, and the gradual abandonment of the age-old practice of apprenticeship. The government's attack on these trends was best illustrated by the great *Statute of Artificers* (1563) which adopted few new approaches to these problems, but embodied and adapted many older laws relating to labour. The statute re-asserted the traditional obligation for the sons of all but the wealthy to undergo a period of apprenticeship of not less than seven years. Craftsmen and labourers in a great many occupations were to be engaged for a year at a time and were to be penalized if they left that employment during the con- tracted period. Anyone not already engaged in a useful trade, and not a moderately wealthy man (for the rich were not expected to work), was to be compelled to take up agricultural employment. Hours of work for all labourers were to be from five in the morning until seven or eight at night (with two and a half hours for meals) in summer, and the hours of daylight in winter. Finally, Justices of the Peace in every county were to meet once a year to determine rates of pay for all classes of labourers, making due allowance for variations in the cost of living; any employer giving, or labourer accepting, more than these wage assessments, was to be liable to fines or imprison- ment. Though the wage assessment clauses of the statute were not repealed until the early nineteenth century, and though in many areas Justices went through the ritual year by year of publishing lists of assessed wages, there is little evidence that these assessments had any real bearing on wages actually paid after the sixteenth century.

There was much in the Statute of Artificers which reflected the general attitude of the governing classes to the working class. An idle, restless reserve of unemployed labour was to be avoided at all costs, and the statute aimed to ease the problem of the relief of poverty. But there was in the statute also a broader assumption which underlay much Tudor economic policy — that the fullest employment of all resources (and labour was a country's most valuable resource) was the surest way to enrich a country. We may doubt today whether the provisions of the statute were likely to fulfil these aims, but it is still true that greater *productivity* (output per worker per year) is the key to rising standards of living.

2. THE BALANCE OF TRADE

When all these precautions had been taken to make the most of the nation's resources as the best means of increasing the economic and military power of the country, there still remained one weak point in the defence of the nation's wealth. If there was too great a reliance on imports, and exports failed to earn sufficient to meet the cost of these imports, the balance would necessarily have to be met in bullion (gold or silver). Whilst economists of the day recognized that a stock of gold did not itself make a country wealthy, they knew that a country could not afford to be without a substantial reserve on which to fall back in the event, say, of a war. For this reason a great deal of attention was paid to ensuring that the *balance of trade* (the difference between the values of exports and imports) was *favourable*, that is, would bring bullion into the country rather than drain it out. Trades which showed an excess of imports over exports came under heavy criticism. The French trade in the sixteenth century showed an unfavourable balance, largely because of the heavy imports of woad, salt, canvas and wines. 'No country robbeth England so much as France', complained Robert Cecil, later Lord Burghley, in 1559.

In the seventeenth century the East India Company was persistently attacked because it offended against this fundamental principle of trade. England's staple export — woollen cloth — was unfitted for the hot climates of the company's markets, and the enormous imports of spices, silk, calico and tea had to be paid for in bullion. In defence the company pointed out that much of its imports from the East were re-exported to Europe, and that these re-exports more than offset the outflow of bullion. This was probably true, but the political opposition to the company continued to use this argument, which might be expected to find popular approval with the uninformed. In the early eighteenth century attention was switched from the East India Company to a trade which was beginning to show a heavy unfavo'rable balance — that with Sweden and the Baltic countries (*Eastland*). These areas were England's sole source of several raw materials of the utmost importance in time of war — iron, hemp, pitch, and timber for masts and decking. It was hoped that the American colonies would come to the rescue by providing all these commodities, but the hope was never more than partly realized. Technical developments in the English iron industry did not rid the country of its dependence upon imports from Sweden until the end of the eighteenth century.

Another approach to the problem of trade balances was a series of direct attempts to encourage the production in this country of commodities normally imported. One such article was woad — a blue dyestuff in heavy demand. The attempts to introduce copper and glass manufacture have been mentioned earlier in another context. Government interference in the salt trade arose from a desire to reduce imports from France. The import of luxuries was universally condemned for its adverse effect on the trade balance. 'I marvel no man taketh heed', commented a writer of the 1540's, 'what number first of trifles cometh hither from beyond the seas, that we might either clean spare, or else make them within our own realm, for the which we pay inestimable treasure every year, or else exchange substantial wares and necessary for them, for the which we might receive great treasure.' An act of 1562 expressly forbade the import of a long list of trinkets in the hope of encouraging their manufacture in this country.

3. THE OLD COLONIAL SYSTEM

The first British Empire, consisting of colonies on the mainland of North America and on several West Indian islands, was founded consciously with a view to supplementing the resources of the homeland. The example of Spanish and Portuguese colonial development inspired an Elizabethan writer, a generation before the first English colonies were established, to assert that 'the trade, traffic and planting in these countries is likely to prove very profitable to the whole realm in general'. Some attempts were made in the 1580's to imitate the Spanish in the settlement of the newly discovered lands in the New World, but the first permanently successful colony was set up in Virginia in 1607 under the leadership of the resourceful Captain John Smith. Within twenty years other expeditions had established colonies in 'New England', the coastal area to the north of the

Captain John Smith, the founder of the colony of Virginia

Hudson River. During the seventeenth century, a steady stream of emigrants — some fleeing from religious persecution, but more seeking to take advantage of new opportunities — reinforced the diminutive communities scattered along the eastern coastline from Maine to Carolina. By the end of the century ten separate colonies were firmly established, peopled by 300,000 English-speaking colonists vigorously pursuing a wide range of economic activities ranging from tobacco-growing, through iron-making and shipbuilding, to overseas trade and fishing.

It was intended by those at home that the colonies should from the start serve as 'an inexhaustible mine of treasure'. However, hopes that the colonies would provide foodstuffs and raw materials hitherto imported from foreign countries were not wholly realized. Though the American colonies did provide a mighty flow of goods to the mother country, most of this consisted of commodities which had hitherto scarcely entered into foreign trade — mainly tobacco, sugar and dyewoods. Nevertheless, from the very first, these commodities at least were to be produced for the benefit of the mother country. From 1660, the principal products of the American and West Indian colonies — tobacco, sugar, rice and indigo — known as the *enumerated commodities*, were forbidden to be exported by the colonists to any destination other than Britain. Because several of these commodities were in high demand in other European markets, English (and, after the Union of 1707, Scottish) merchants made a substantial profit out of the re-export trade. Thus the colonists found their trade confined almost exclusively to a single market — the mother country.

In 1733, a further effort was made by the *Molasses Act* to regulate direct trade between the colonies and foreign countries. This act, designed to protect the export market of the Jamaican sugar planters, laid a heavy duty on molasses (a by-product of sugar used for making rum) entering the colonies from the French sugar-growing West Indian colonies.

To supply the urgent needs of the mother country certain industries were to be encouraged. This category comprised principally naval stores — masts, hemp, flax, pitch and turpentine — by which it was hoped to reduce the dependence on supplies from Sweden and the Baltic. To encourage the production of this range of commodities, from 1704 onwards *bounties* (subsidies) were granted on these goods when imported into England from the colonies.

A secondary purpose of the colonies was to create additional markets for the manufacturers of the mother country. To this end the import of certain manufactures from countries other than England and the manufacture of certain goods in the colonies were prohibited by the home government. An act of 1699 forbade the export from the colonies of any wool, woollen yarn or woollen cloth. The problem of the iron industry was more complex. There was an obvious need for imports of iron in England to supplement the inadequate home production, yet the manufacturers of ironware in England opposed any permission being given to the American colonists to produce their own finished ironware. The result was an act of 1750 which allowed American pig iron to enter London free of duty (and after 1757 all British ports), but forbade the erection of slitting and rolling mills by which the colonists would be able to manufacture their own finished ironware. In practice, however, it proved impossible to enforce these provisions of the act, and at the time of the revolt of the colonies in 1775, the output of the colonial iron industry probably equalled that of the home industry.

Finally, trade with the colonies was intended to remain the preserve of English merchants and English sailors. Colonial trade, in fact, was to be the means whereby the maritime strength of the nation would be increased. 'The Kings of Spain and Portugal', observed an Elizabethan writer, 'who, since the first discovery of the Indies, have not only mightily enlarged their dominions, greatly enriched themselves and their subjects, but have also, by just accounts, trebled the number of their ships, masters and mariners, a matter of no small moment and importance.' In this respect the colonial trade was only one aspect of a larger field of economic policy which merits a section to itself.

4. THE NAVIGATION SYSTEM

The *Navigation System* is the name given by historians to a series of acts of Parliament whose consistent aim was to protect the English shipping industry. There were several reasons why this was felt to be desirable. It was essential for an island nation to have not only an ample supply of trained mariners, but a fleet of well-built ships to serve in the defence of the country should need arise. 'The greatest jewel of this realm', commented a writer of 1583, 'and the chiefest strength and force of the same . . . is the multitude of ships, masters and mariners ready to assist the most stately and royal navy of her Majesty.' In the sixteenth century there was little structural difference between merchant and naval vessels, and many of the former, for example, were pressed into service when the Armada threatened England in 1588. In later centuries the Royal Navy, never adequately manned by volunteers, relied heavily on the press-ganging of merchant seamen. Equally important, in the eyes of contemporary statesmen, was the need to save the foreign currencies paid out to other countries — mainly Holland — for the use of their shipping. Finally — and what better justification could contemporaries have? — other countries were doing the same; and when France and Spain, for example, discouraged English shipping on their trade routes, the only effective answer was retaliation.

Though the Navigation System achieved its greatest effectiveness in the seventeenth century, its principles had been accepted since the fourteenth century, and some attempts made in succeeding centuries to put them into practice. By several acts of the early sixteenth century, the employment of foreign ships in trade with this country was forbidden. Queen Elizabeth, however, at the beginning of her reign, in 1559, wisely repealed these acts for fear of retaliation. Also in the sixteenth century other methods were used to encourage English shipping. An act of 1564, confirming earlier attempts, made every Wednesday a compulsory *fish day* — a day, that is, when it was an offence to eat meat: this was to increase the demand for fish, and so encourage the fishing industry.

Few of these early attempts to encourage English shipping were effective. It was not until the mid-seventeenth century that efficient measures were devised. The *Act of Navigation* of 1651 required all goods from Asia, Africa and America to be imported into this country in the ships of this country and its colonies only. Any goods from Europe were to be brought to this country in English ships or those of the country sending the goods. By eliminating the carriage of imports by independent ships, it was hoped to reserve the greater part of the shipping employed in overseas trade to English ships. This act was not very thoroughly enforced, and it became unpopular with merchants who found that freight rates rose. However, the moderate success of the 1651 act encouraged Charles II's government after the Restoration in 1660 to pass an improved Navigation Act. This Act of 1660 ordered that an English ship must have an English master and be manned by a crew at least three-quarters of whom were English. Another important addition to the earlier statute was the requirement that certain *enumerated commodities* — sugar, tobacco, cotton, indigo and other dyewoods (the principal products of the West Indian and American colonies) — might only be exported to England, Ireland and Wales, or to another English colony. In 1662, it was further enacted that for a ship to be classed as English, it must be built in England or in the colonies.

There was a steady increase in the tonnage of English shipping in the later seventeenth and eighteenth centuries, but it would be unwise to assume that this increase was necessarily the result of the Navigation Acts. Other European countries were increasing their merchant navies at the same time, but it does seem likely that, had it not been for the Navigation Acts, much of the increased demand for shipping arising out of the developing colonial trade in the seventeenth and eighteenth centuries would have passed to other maritime nations — particularly the Dutch — who possessed certain advantages over England in relation to supplies of shipbuilding materials. Nor is it unreasonable to see in this fostering of English merchant shipping the true foundation of England's naval supremacy which was so strikingly asserted in the wars against France from the end of the seventeenth century to Trafalgar in 1805.

This maritime strength was not achieved without cost. The expense of building ships in England, remote from supplies of many of the essential materials, was high and rose higher. This meant that freights, too, became high. Though there was a big increase in the amount of English shipping in the transatlantic trade, this seems to have been bought at the cost of some loss in England's share of shipping in European routes. But by far the greatest burden was a succession of wars. The Navigation

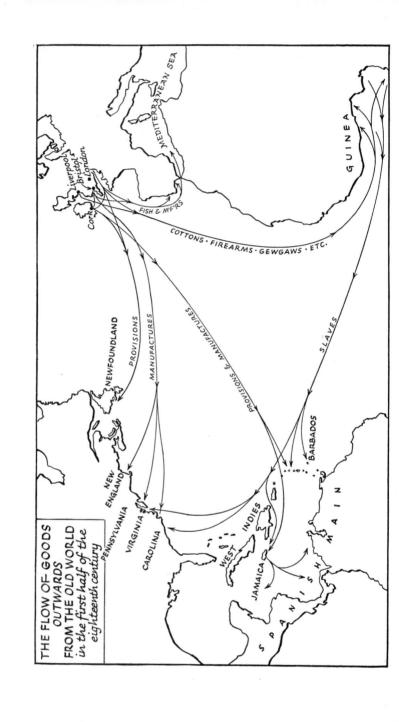

THE FLOW OF GOODS
OUTWARDS
FROM THE OLD WORLD
in the first half of the
eighteenth century

MEDITERRANEAN SEA

GUINEA

Liverpool
Bristol
London
Cork

FISH & MF'RS

COTTONS · FIREARMS · GEWGAWS · ETC.

NEWFOUNDLAND

PROVISIONS

MANUFACTURES

PROVISIONS & MANUFACTURES

SLAVES

NEW
ENGLAND

PENNSYLVANIA

VIRGINIA

CAROLINA

WEST INDIES

JAMAICA

BARBADOS

SPANISH MAIN

Acts were aimed principally against the Dutch. By skilful ship design and by careful specialization in certain types of ships for specific purposes, the Dutch had acquired in the seventeenth century a large share of the carrying trade of Europe. In some directions, particularly in the Baltic, they were supreme in the early seventeenth century, and it was mainly resentment at seeing so large a proportion of our imports come in Dutch ships that produced the acts of 1651 and 1660. Not surprisingly the Dutch bitterly resented these acts and their resentment is at least a measure of the success of the acts. This maritime jealousy was the principal cause of three wars between England and Holland in the mid-seventeenth century. Soon after the act of 1651, the first Dutch War (1652–4) broke out. Both countries possessed strong fleets and both great admirals. The struggle between the Dutch Van Tromp and the English Blake was indecisive, and one of Cromwell's first actions as Protector was to make peace with the Dutch in 1654. But confirmation of the Navigation Act in 1660 led to a renewal of hostilities in the second war of 1665–7. On this occasion, a Dutch fleet under de Ruyter sailed up the Medway and destroyed an English fleet at anchor at Chatham. This disgrace left a lasting impression on Englishmen's minds and was a real influence in the expansion of the navy in later reigns. A third war against the Dutch in 1672 was brought to a quick end by a change in political alliances, and the close association with Holland through a common king, William III, in 1688 brought Anglo-Dutch rivalry to an end. Though English naval strength had been effectively challenged by a smaller nation, the 'Navigation principle' won in the end; the Dutch never regained the dominance in world shipping that had been theirs in the first half of the seventeenth century.

A more serious outcome of the whole policy of the Navigation Acts and colonial regulation was the growing resentment of the colonists on the mainland of North America at the persistence of the home government in subordinating the interests of the colonies to those of the mother country. It is true that some concessions were made to the colonists — the English were forbidden, for example, to grow tobacco in competition with the plantations — but generally the aim of all regulations was to serve the needs of the homeland first. There were, of course, other and more important causes of the growing hostility to the home government in the colonies in the third quarter of the eighteenth century. Probably the persistence of the government in taxing the colonists without allowing them any representation in the Parliament authorizing the taxation was the most important single cause, but economic factors played an important subsidiary role. For over a century the market for colonial produce was artificially confined, whilst a great deal of perfectly 'natural' trade between the colonies and the French and Spanish West Indian islands was suppressed to the loss of the colonial planters and merchants. Not the least result, therefore, of British colonial economic policy in the seventeenth and eighteenth centuries was the loss of an Empire by the War of American Independence (1775–83).

PART TWO

1700–1830

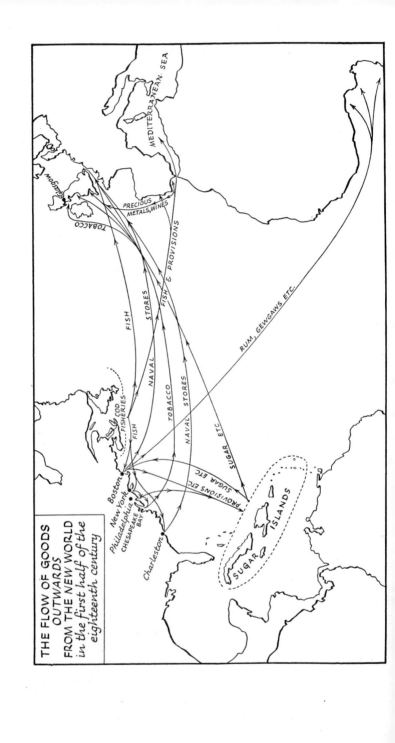

THE FLOW OF GOODS
OUTWARDS
FROM THE NEW WORLD
in the first half of the
eighteenth century

MEDITERRANEAN SEA

PRECIOUS
METALS, WINES

TOBACCO

Glasgow

FISH

STORES

FISH & PROVISIONS

RUM, GEWGAWS ETC.

COD
FISHERIES

FISH

NAVAL

TOBACCO

NAVAL STORES

Boston

New York

Philadelphia

CHESAPEAKE
BAY

Charleston

SUGAR ETC.

SUGAR ETC.

PROVISIONS ETC.

SUGAR ISLANDS

CHAPTER 8

POPULATION

For long periods in history changes in wealth and ways of life have often been slow, but in the second half of the eighteenth century there was a real speeding-up of the process of change. Not only were new methods increasing the yield of land and labour in agriculture; in industry, too, many factors combined to multiply rapidly the output of manufactured goods. This acceleration was accompanied by a similar increase in the rate at which the population of Britain was growing. In the 250 years before 1750, the population of Britain may have doubled itself. It required only seventy years to double itself again.

The coincidence of the acceleration of agricultural and industrial output in the second half of the eighteenth century with that of the growth of Britain's population is so striking that we are tempted to ask whether the needs of a much increased population caused the fruitful changes in agriculture and industry, or whether the greater output of improved farming and industry made possible the larger population. It is by no means easy to answer this question, but some of the points raised in this chapter may help to answer it.

1. How Population Grows

Briefly, there are two ways in which the population of a country may increase, apart from immigration. The proportion of the population that dies each year (the *death rate*) may be reduced; or the ratio between births and the total population in any year (the *birth rate*) may rise. A combination of a reduced death rate and a higher birth rate would lead to an even faster rate of growth.

There are many ways in which the death rate may be reduced. Medical knowledge may advance, enabling doctors to cure

hitherto fatal illnesses. A purer water supply may reduce the risk
of typhoid and other water-borne diseases. Improved housing
and domestic sanitation may reduce the spread of certain
diseases. A more varied and ample diet may strengthen the
human body's natural resistance to infection. New inventions
may reduce the physical effort demanded of workers in some
industries, or eliminate some of the dangers of other occupations. These and many other possibilities, singly or in combination, help to lengthen human life. The longer people may
expect to live (their *expectation of life*), the lower the death rate.

Similarly, there are ways in which the birth rate may be
increased. For people accustomed to a standard of living
which affords them no more than the bare necessities of life
any increase in wealth may well lead to earlier marriages and
hence larger families. The raised standard of living that might
in this way make possible earlier marriages may be caused by
a period of unusually good harvests, improved methods of agriculture increasing the yield per acre, or the lowering of prices
of commodities on which people's income is spent. The Reverend
Thomas Malthus, a late eighteenth-century writer on the subject of population, who warned of the danger of population
growing faster than the available food supplies, recommended
later marriages as a way of preventing the growth of population
from outstripping the increase of food supplies.

2. POPULATION CHANGES IN THE EIGHTEENTH CENTURY

The first Population Census in Britain was taken in the year
1801. Thereafter censuses were taken every ten years. For
periods before 1801 we are obliged to rely on estimates made by
contemporaries or on intelligent guesses made by modern
experts. The best and most reliable of the estimates by contemporaries is that of Gregory King made in 1695, when he
reckoned the population of England and Wales at 5·5 million.
By 1801 the population of Britain was almost 11 million. By
1831 this had risen to 16·5 million. These figures suggest that
population was growing faster in the early nineteenth century.
Before 1695, estimates of population are likely to be much less
accurate than Gregory King's, but the population is unlikely

to have risen during the seventeenth century by much more than 1 million, or between 20% and 25%. The indications, therefore, are that the rate of population increase (percentage increase in population per year) rose steadily during the eighteenth and early nineteenth centuries.

In the middle years of the eighteenth century, population was densest in the southern counties of England. It has been estimated, for example, that in the early eighteenth century one third of the whole population was concentrated in the seven counties of Middlesex, Surrey, Kent, Gloucestershire, Somerset, Wiltshire and Devon. Within this area, London accounted for the major concentration. Its population, steadily reinforced by a drift from the provinces, may have numbered more than 750,000, or nearly 15% of that of the whole country, in the middle of the century. Bristol was the second town, followed by Norwich and Exeter. The population was concentrated in the South and the Midlands largely because agriculture was still by far the most important occupation, and the richest and most easily cultivated lands were in those areas. Where industry existed before the Industrial Revolution — in the north-east (coal), the West Riding of Yorkshire (wool), Birmingham and the Black Country (metal-working), and Shropshire and South Wales (iron and coal), there were smaller concentrations of population; but these were not sufficient to balance the relatively dense areas of the South.

3. THE BIRTH RATE

In the absence of any census returns for the eighteenth century, very little is known about changes in the birth rate. It is possible to explain the rapid growth of population entirely in terms of a decline in the death rate, and to assume that there was no change in the birth rate at this time. What evidence there is, however, does suggest that there was some rise in the birth rate in the eighteenth century.

The decline of the practice of long periods of apprenticeship tended to reduce the ages at which men married, but unless the women, too, married earlier, there is no reason to believe that this change would lead to a higher birth rate. There is some evidence that in the eighteenth century a higher proportion of

E

women married than in earlier times and that some women married at earlier ages than hitherto. But at that time the probability of the death of infants was much higher in larger families than in smaller ones. In London in the 1770's, it was found that in families with only two children, on the average one child survived the age of five. In families with six children, fewer than three survived; and in families with more than eleven children, only a quarter of the children survived. Thus, even if there were some increase in the birth rate resulting from earlier marriages, it would almost certainly have produced a nearly equivalent rise in the death rate.

There remains the possibility that certain groups of the population have traditionally, for various reasons, always had larger families than others. Industrial workers in this country seem to have fallen into this class. Therefore, if a larger proportion of the population of the country entered industry during the eighteenth century, the class with the tendency to larger families would also increase in numbers, thus leading to a rise in the total population. Unfortunately, too little is known about these changes and we can only guess at their importance.

4. The Death Rate

When both birth and death rates are low, an increase in population is most likely to result from an increase in the birth rate, because it would be difficult to reduce an already low death rate, but easy to increase a low birth rate. Conversely, when both rates are high, an increased population is most likely to arise from a reduction in the death rate. In the early eighteenth century, both rates were relatively high — the death rate extremely so. The death rate was high largely because of the great number of children dying under the age of five. This high rate of *infant mortality* kept the population more or less stable.

Some earlier writers have suggested that the very great increase in the number of hospitals, particularly maternity hospitals, in the eighteenth century contributed materially towards a reduction of the death rate. The facts, however, indicate that the reverse was more likely to be true. The lack of knowledge of even elementary hygiene turned the hospitals nto places where infection was spread rather than prevented. To go into an eighteenth century hospital was to increase your chances of dying from a disease other than the one from which you originally suffered. Until knowledge of the use of anaesthetics was acquired in the late nineteenth century, surgery was primitive and frequently lethal. It has been estimated that one out of every two operations for amputation of a limb in the mid-eighteenth century proved fatal.

Nor were the advances in medical science of much material help in reducing the death rate. Some new medicines, of which the principal was quinine, were introduced during the eighteenth century, but these were either used wrongly or in doses too small to have any effect. Medical opinion today is against the view that any improvement in eighteenth century death rates resulted from the use of new drugs. Perhaps the most important development in preventive medicine during this period was the introduction of inoculation. First tried in 1721, inoculation against smallpox was not used on a wide scale until the last quarter of the century; but it is doubtful whether the methods of inoculation then were very effective, for there does not seem to have been any noticeable reduction in the number of deaths from smallpox in the eighteenth century. Once again, it seems unlikely that this innovation made much impression on death-rate figures.

Not only was there little improvement in health during the eighteenth century; there were forces at work more likely to shorten life. Thanks to the work of the great cartoonist Hogarth (1697–1764), the social evil of gin-drinking has become well known. Early in the century cheap gin was widely sold in London. Encouraged by a very low excise duty (an *excise* is a tax on home-produced goods) the consumption of this potent spirit rose rapidly in London, acquiring the proportions of a serious social problem. In the first forty years of the century the output of spirits grew about sixfold, and the death rate in London rose noticeably. Not until 1751 was the gin evil brought to an end by an act of Parliament forbidding the retail sale of spirits by distillers and raising the excise duties.

As towns grew in size, overcrowding occurred, and the pressure of population on sanitation and water supplies must have led to some deterioration in these services with a consequent increase in the risk of infection. It is true that many towns took active steps to increase their water supplies. In London, for example, where the river Thames had previously provided both the source of water for domestic consumption and a convenient outlet for the disposal of sewage, the purer spring waters of Hertfordshire were brought by the 'New River' early in the seventeenth century. In the provinces, Bridgwater and Exeter in the south-west and Newcastle in the north-east provide examples of towns where new sources of water supply were provided through the enterprise of private companies. The *quantity* of water for domestic consumption was increased during the eighteenth century, but it is doubtful whether the increased supply kept pace with the growth of population in some towns. It is even more doubtful whether there was any corresponding improvement in the *quality* of the water, for knowledge of disease-spreading bacteria was non-existent and few precautions were taken to ensure purity. It took a serious nation-wide epidemic of cholera in the 1830's to awaken local authorities to the need for urgent action.

How, then, was the death rate reduced? Such improvements in health services and the science of medicine as took place cannot apparently have made a very marked difference. On the other hand there is some evidence that the incidence of plagues and epidemics was becoming less. There have been no plagues in Britain since 1666, and the disappearance of the black rat may help to account for this. Some substantial sections of the population may have experienced rises in standards of living (standard of living includes both the quantity and quality of food, clothing and housing a worker's wage will buy). Certain aspects of social change during the eighteenth and early nineteenth centuries indicate obvious improvement. There was, for example, a greatly increased consumption of wheat bread in place of bread made from the coarser grains (rye and oats) in the diet of many of the working classes in town and country. Changes in agriculture improved the quality of meat and dairy produce and permitted specialization of farming in the neighbourhood of the large towns, which materially improved the supply of milk. Not all the housing produced during the period of the Industrial Revolution was shoddy and insanitary. Fine stone cottages built by big industrialists like Samuel

Oldknow at Marple in Cheshire bear witness to high standards in some quarters. Some changes in industry, such as those that produced plentiful supplies of cheap cotton cloth or improved and cheaper soap, must also have been generally beneficial to health. It has been said that one of the main effects of the Industrial Revolution was that people washed a great deal more frequently than before as a result of the availability of cheaper soap. Cheaper and more plentiful coal reduced the incidence of rheumatic complaints arising out of damp houses and damp clothes.

These factors, small in themselves, may have added up to important changes in health during the century. More important, however, was the question of wages. Two kinds of changes could affect wages — a change in wage levels themselves, and a change in the prices of goods bought by wage-earners. For example, the fact that the worker of the early nineteenth century could buy very cheap cotton clothes instead of relatively expensive woollen clothes brought a big improvement in standards of clothing and hygiene as well as leaving the worker more money to spend on, say, food. So far as wages are concerned, there was some rise in the wages of skilled workers over the period from 1750 to 1830, but some unskilled labourers and workers, like the old hand-loom weavers, suffered from a progressive decline in earnings. Some groups of workers were therefore worse off at the end of the period; but the class of skilled labourers and mechanics was growing rapidly in numbers, so that, on the average, wages, and therefore standards of living, were probably a little higher in the early nineteenth century than they had been in the mid-eighteenth century. This must have led to greater expectation of life, and a reduced death rate.

5. The Distribution of the Population

As population grew during the eighteenth and early nineteenth centuries, the centre of gravity of population shifted northwards. In spite of this trend, the censuses from 1801 to 1831 record that none of the southern counties actually declined in population. The concentration of population to the North merely implies that population grew faster there than in

the South. Growth was quicker in the North because of th
steady rise of industry there. The South remained largely agri
cultural. Possibly the population in industrial areas reproduce
itself a little more quickly than that in agricultural areas; bu
the explanation lies mainly in the fact that *surplus* populatio
in agricultural areas tended to drift to the towns. In Chapte
11, section 5, it is shown that the agricultural changes c

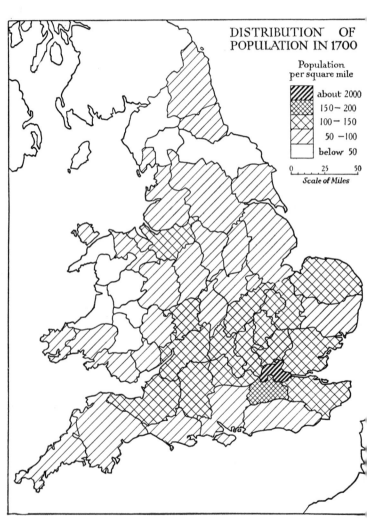

DISTRIBUTION OF
POPULATION IN 1700

Population
per square mile

about 2000
150 – 200
100 – 150
50 – 100
below 50

0   25   50
Scale of Miles

the eighteenth century led to little reduction of employment.

The single most important factor in the shift of the centres of population was the increased use of coal in industry. In England nearly all the coalfields are in the North and the Midlands. When industries turned to the use of coal as a source of power, and as they grew in size, so the concentration of population on the coalfields increased too. Until the middle of the eighteenth

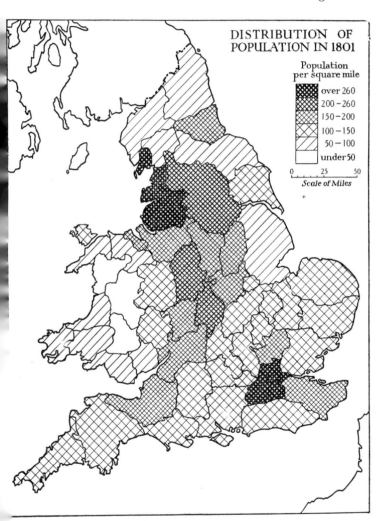

DISTRIBUTION OF
POPULATION IN 1801

Population
per square mile

over 260
200 – 260
150 – 200
100 – 150
50 – 100
under 50

0   25   50
Scale of Miles

century the iron industry had used charcoal as fuel for its furnaces and forges, and there had been a concentration of iron manufacture in the Weald of Sussex and Surrey and in the Furness district of north Lancashire. When coal was used for smelting, the industry expanded exclusively on the coalfields — in the Black Country, south Yorkshire, north Shropshire and south Wales. So long as textile machinery was operated by human power, as were the spinning-wheels and handlooms of the early eighteenth century, the industry remained in its traditional homes in the wool-growing areas or near the ports of export to European markets — in East Anglia, Gloucestershire, Wiltshire and the south-west. When water-power was used to drive the looms and spindles, both woollen and cotton industries tended to concentrate in the hilly Pennine areas of northern England and southern Scotland. Later, when steampower replaced water-power, the centres of industry shifted slightly to the coalfields of south-east Lancashire, south-west Yorkshire and Clydeside. These, and other similar movements of industry, led to the building up of concentrations of population in midland and northern areas.

Major concentrations of population sprang up in the later eighteenth century in groups of towns in south Wales, south Lancashire, west Yorkshire, the north-east coast, and the Midlands. In each case one major industry provided the nucleus around which the new concentration grew up. The development of south-east Lancashire may be taken as an example of a process that was repeated with only slight variations in the other areas. In the early eighteenth century the only important centre of population in this area was Manchester and in about 1770 its population was estimated at 30,000. The expansion of the cotton industry in and around the town after about 1775 led to a rapid growth not only in Manchester itself, but in many of the surrounding towns. Manchester's population rose to 95,000 in 1801, and to 238,000 in 1831. Stockport, another cotton town some six miles to the south, acquired more than twenty-five cotton mills between 1770 and 1790, and its population rose from about 5,000 in 1770 to 28,000 in 1841. Oldham, seven miles to the east of Manchester, had some 300 or 400 inhabitants in 1760; between 1776 and 1788, twenty-five cotton factories were built in the town, and by 1801 its population had risen to 20,000. Bolton, ten miles to the north-west, which was a small country town with 2–3,000 inhabitants in 1700, had a population of 17,000 one hundred years later. Similar trends were evident in Bury and Rochdale, other fast-growing towns in this cotton group.

In the same way, the growing metal industries of the Midlands were building up Birmingham as a centre, with its group of smaller but similarly expanding towns — Wolverhampton, Stourbridge, Walsall, Dudley and Wednesbury. In the West Riding of Yorkshire, Leeds was the centre and largest town, but nearby Bradford, Huddersfield, Halifax, Sowerby Bridge and many smaller places were also growing fast. In South Wales, however, although the ports of Swansea, Cardiff and Newport remained the principal centres, the development of the coal and iron industries further inland in the narrow valleys produced few large centres. Instead, population growth multiplied the number of industrial villages, a form of settlement also common in other parts of Britain where it created areas of high population density.

Where did the population of these new towns and urban areas come from? For the most part the actual movements of population were small. Many people moved, but they moved for short distances. A continuing surplus from the agricultural areas was being 'mopped up' by the towns. There was a steady drift from rural areas to towns, but mainly to the nearest towns. There is little evidence of mass movement from, say, south of the Thames to the industrial North. For the most part the new industrial areas drew their populations from the surrounding districts. Only a small proportion came from more than fifty miles away.

A second source, however, was of importance in some of the areas — immigration. By far the most important source of immigrants in the late eighteenth and early nineteenth centuries was Ireland. Passages across the Irish Sea could be bought for as little as 2s. 6d., the Irish population was growing even more rapidly than the English, and industry was almost non-existent in Ireland. The Irish immigrants mostly entered England through Liverpool, so it is not surprising to find many of them settling in Manchester. By 1836 one fifth of the population of Manchester was of Irish origin. The Irish also penetrated into the Lowlands of Scotland and further inland from Liverpool, but the main concentration remained in south Lancashire. There was a further stream of immigrants from the Highlands of Scotland, but few of these penetrated further than the Scottish Lowlands.

To offset these streams of immigrants, there was, throughout the eighteenth century, a steady flow of emigrants from Britain to the New World. The numbers increased during the nineteenth century, but were never great enough to counteract the natural growth of the population plus the Irish immigrants. After 1825 the emigration of skilled artisans was legally permitted for the first time.

6. Social Effects of the Growth of Population

In 1840 the population of Britain was twice what it had been seventy years before, and three times what it had been seventy years before that. There had been an appreciable increase in the output of foodstuffs during this period, but not sufficient to provide for this great rise in numbers. Moreover, for many sections of the population there was some improvement in standards of living. The first and most important effect of the population growth of the period 1750–1830 was to turn this country from a net exporter of grain into a net importer. That is to say, at the beginning of that period Britain exported more corn than it imported (importing only rarely in years of poor harvests), and at the end of the period it imported far more than it exported. To pay for this ever-increasing quantity of imported foodstuffs, Britain had to devote an increasing proportion of her manufactures to the export market. By being the first country in the world to industrialize, Britain had little difficulty at first in finding overseas markets for her manufactures, but there were dangers in this specialization in foreign trade. In the 1830's, for example, over 80% of Britain's cotton manufactures was exported, and because foreign trade was notoriously subject to interruption from wars or restriction by tariffs, a large section of our manufacturing industry became liable to periodical losses of markets, with the resulting unemployment and hardship.

Secondly, most people lived longer. In particular, the death-rate of children under five was very much reduced. Finally, the concentration of the increased population into crowded towns raised many new problems of health, education, municipal government and the preservation of law and order. Before these could be solved on the lines with which we are familiar today, much disease, suffering and discontent occurred. A society that expands so rapidly cannot expect to avoid growing-pains, and Britain's experience of social suffering at a time of industrial revolution has been shared by other countries in varying degrees at later times.

CHAPTER 9

TRANSPORT

Some of the most important changes in Britain during the period 1700–1830 took place in the sphere of industry and involved a very rapid increase in the number of mines, mills and factories. This, of course, meant that larger quantities of raw materials had to be transported to the manufacturers, and that greater quantities of finished goods had to be distributed to the consumers both at home and overseas. There was a substantial increase of population in the second half of the eighteenth century, and clearly a population of 14 millions in 1820 required at least twice the amount of transport services available in 1750 for a population of about 7 millions. Thus, the demand for additional transport for agricultural marketing coincided with a striking increase in the demand for the carriage of the raw materials and products of industry.

When the value of goods transported was high in relation to weight, as in the case of watches, silk or hosiery, transport costs would probably add little to the final cost of the goods. When value was low in relation to weight, as in the case of coal, iron or timber, the cost of transport would be an important consideration. If the cost of transport added too much to the final cost of the article, then people would simply not buy it. In the middle of the eighteenth century, it was seldom worth while to carry coal more than ten or fifteen miles overland, as its cost when delivered was out of all proportion to the mere cost of mining. Thus, no matter how much the mills, mines and factories increased their production, the selling price, particularly of heavy and bulky articles, depended to a great extent on the costs of transport.

1. Industrial Transport in the Early Eighteenth Century

How far were the existing means of transport in the early eighteenth century capable of carrying the industrial loads required of them? So far as industrial transport was concerned, there were three main methods — by road using packhorse or horse-drawn cart, by river where the depth of water permitted, and by coastal navigation. A few moments' consideration will show that all these three methods had severe limitations. A great many packhorses or carts were required, for example, to feed even the smallest blast-furnaces of the eighteenth century with iron ore and charcoal all the year round. The want of sufficient depth of water, though important, was far from being the only hindrance to river navigation in eighteenth-century Britain. In fact, in the case of both river and coastal navigation, only those districts immediately in the neighbourhood of a river or seaport could be served. Many important areas, particularly in the Midlands, had no access to sea or navigable river. Even where a fortunately-sited coalfield, like that near Newcastle-upon-Tyne, was able to make easy use of river and coast routes, the potential consumers of such an article as coal were often widely dispersed and remote from convenient water transport.

A great deal depended, therefore, on the roads. It is well known that the Romans, during their occupation of this country in the first four centuries A.D., equipped the country with a fine system of well-constructed main roads. It is, moreover, scarcely an exaggeration to say that, between the departure of the Romans in the early fifth century, and the middle of the eighteenth century, no attempt was made even to imitate the very thorough Roman methods of road-building, let alone improve them. Celia Fiennes, an adventurous woman traveller in the late seventeenth century, for example, described how she went along a main road in Gloucestershire 'over one common of some miles length on a narrow causeway that a coach can scarce pass, all pitched with slatts and stones. Our coach was once wedged in the wheele in the stones that severall men were forced to lift us out.' Apart from a few cobbled streets in towns, roads were without hard surfaces of the kind we know today.

Even loose stones were seldom used in road construction except to fill up deep ruts worn by carts and carriages forced to keep in the same narrow track. Small wonder that ironworks contrived to do as much as possible of their transporting of raw materials in the four or five summer months, building up during that time a stock sufficient to last the winter.

In view of the smallness of loads that could be conveyed easily by road and the expense of this form of transport even for short distances, river and coastal navigation were used wherever possible for industrial transport. When the growth of population and overseas trade led to an increase in the demand for transport services, it was to the development of river navigation that engineers first turned their attention.

2. RIVER NAVIGATION

Britain's natural waterways had served as trade routes from the Middle Ages. Some of the most important trading and industrial centres were situated on navigable rivers — London, Bristol, Gloucester, Chester, York and Newcastle. Few rivers, however, were sufficiently deep and unobstructed to permit navigation for very great distances. The most used rivers in the seventeenth century for commercial traffic were the Thames, navigable as far as Oxford, the Severn as far as Shrewsbury, and the Trent as far as Nottingham. In the main, however, these great rivers served agricultural areas, and the eighteenth century saw the intensification of the movement to improve the navigability of the rivers giving access to industrial regions.

Hindrances to navigation were many and were created both by nature and by man. Firstly, the depth of the water might be insufficient in places owing to silting up, to rapids, or simply to an inadequacy of the flow. Secondly, the tortuous loops and 'meanders' of some lowland rivers sometimes increased the travelling distance between two points up to four or fivefold. Thirdly, the construction of weirs across rivers in connection with water-driven fulling and flour mills created absolute barriers to navigation. Fourthly, the existence of fords had sometimes involved the artificial raising of the bed of the river in order to make the ford as shallow as possible. Fifthly, low-built medieval bridges, whilst not actually preventing navigation,

Water transport in the late seventeenth century

sometimes obstructed the passing of large boats. Sixthly, the susceptibility of some lowland rivers to flooding meant that any alterations in the interests of improved navigation might increase the liability to flood.

How were these problems solved by the eighteenth-century river engineers? Some of them could be dealt with quite easily; others were insoluble and have never been overcome. Towns, for example, were not easily persuaded to pull down their fine medieval bridges, nor were mill-owners with long-established legal rights to their weirs in a hurry to sacrifice their means of livelihood. As a first step towards increasing the depth of water, attempts were made in some instances to increase the rate of flow of the water. This action, by making use of the natural movement of the water to scour the bed of the river, helped to

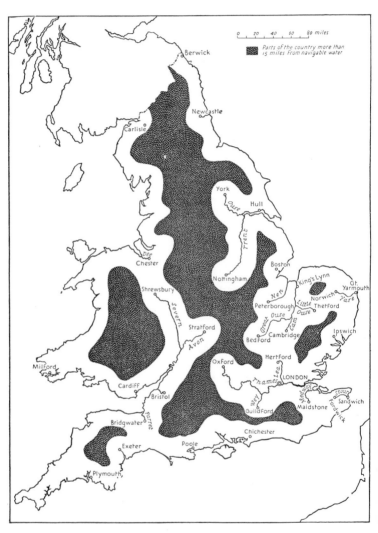

Navigable rivers of England 1600–60, showing the areas more than fifteen miles from navigable water

increase the depth of water without the great expense of dredging. This result could best be achieved by shortening the distance to the river's mouth, and thus increasing the angle of fall. This was achieved through the elimination of long meanders by short 'cuts' across the neck of the loops. In this

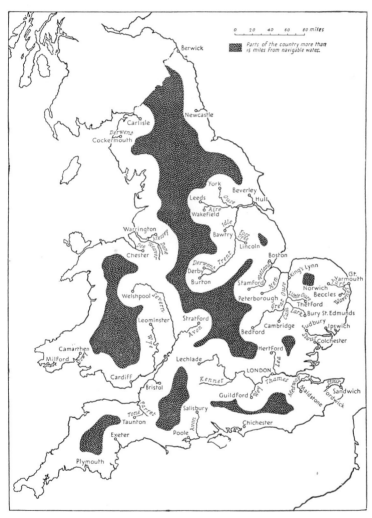

Navigable rivers of England and Wales 1724–7, showing the areas more than fifteen miles from navigable water

way, inconvenient sharp bends with their accompanying shallows were also avoided. But more commonly the depth of water was increased artificially by holding up the water behind weirs. These weirs, together with the mill weirs already mentioned, were then by-passed by short loop cuts, and the difference in level negotiated by means of a *pound lock*. The pound lock therefore became the key to successful river improvement. The principle of its operation will be familiar to all who live near a canal. The lock was an Italian invention of the fifteenth century, and was first used in England in the sixteenth century. Although we are familiar today with locks on canals, until the middle of the eighteenth century they were exclusively used in this country to improve the navigation of rivers.

In the eighteenth century a great many schemes for the improvement of the navigation of rivers were carried out, resulting in the addition of many hundreds of miles of navigable waterways in Britain. An important scheme of this kind was that to improve the river Weaver in Cheshire. In 1721 the proprietors of salt works in the neighbourhood of Nantwich and Middlewich secured an act of Parliament giving them authority to deepen and clear the little river Weaver which flowed northwards into the navigable lower stretch of the river Mersey. This brought the coal of south Lancashire more cheaply to the salt works and reduced the marketing costs of the manufactured salt. Another important scheme of this kind completed between the years 1726 and 1733 made the river Don, a tributary of the Yorkshire Ouse, navigable to within three miles of Sheffield, thus cheapening the transport of bar iron, the raw material of the Sheffield steel and cutlery industry.

The improvement of river navigation had important results for industry. By the mid-eighteenth century it had opened up many new areas to heavy industry. This permitted the development of the coalfields of Derbyshire and south Lancashire by the extension of the navigable portions of the rivers Trent, Derwent, Mersey and their tributaries, and of the woollen cloth manufacturing districts of Gloucestershire and the West Riding of Yorkshire by the upper Thames and the Aire.

3. CANALS

There were obvious limits to the adaptation of rivers in Britain for industrial transport. Many growing industrial districts lay beyond any hope of access to improved river navigation. These included much of the mining and textile region of Lancashire, the large mining and metal-working district around Birmingham and Wolverhampton, and the pottery region of Staffordshire.

Canals had been constructed and used for industrial transport on the Continent from the sixteenth century, and indeed many of the schemes of river improvement in this country involved little less than the construction of canals of varying lengths. But the construction of canals quite independently of existing water-courses involved several difficulties which held up their development in this country until the growing urgency of the demand for additional means of transport led to their development from the middle years of the eighteenth century onwards. Foremost among these difficulties was the expense of canal construction, which was so great that people were not easily convinced that canals could earn sufficient profit to repay the costs of building. There were also several technical difficulties facing the would-be canal builder. A canal required replenishing with water at its highest levels, whilst in a country-side liberally intersected by valleys and ranges of hills, problems of negotiating inclines looked like being acute.

In the circumstances, what was needed was the construction of just one or two successful canals which would demonstrate to engineers and manufacturers all over the country that canals would solve their transport problems *and* could be made to pay. Two such canals were built in the 1750's. Both were in south Lancashire and both were very short, but they showed unmistakeably the immense value of this new form of transport. The first to be built was the Sankey Brook Navigation, completed in 1757. This canal replaced the Sankey Brook, too small for navigation, and connected the south Lancashire coalfield around St. Helens with the navigable river Mersey near Warrington. It secured a cheap outlet for Lancashire coal, and completed the process of taking the coal to the salt of north

Brindley's aqueduct for the Bridgewater Canal over the River Irwell

Cheshire begun thirty-six years before with the Weaver Navigation.

The second of these pioneering canals achieved more fame, and established the reputation of two of the greatest men in canal engineering — James Brindley and the Duke of Bridgewater. The latter, owning coalmines at Worsley, some seven miles from Manchester, found that transport added so much to the cost of the coal, that it proved too dear to find many purchasers even in nearby Manchester. In 1759, securing the services of James Brindley, a Cheshire millwright, he began the construction of a canal linking his Worsley mines to Manchester. The work involved carrying the canal over the river Irwell by means of an aqueduct, an astonishing feat of engineering in the mid-eighteenth century. The canal was completed in 1764, and was the means of reducing the price of coal in Manchester to less than half its former figure.

The success of this canal encouraged the Duke of Bridgewater to extend his canal-building activities, and in 1762 he obtained Parliament's permission to link his Worsley canal to the river Mersey at Runcorn, a distance of about thirty-five miles. This greater canal, which became known as the Bridgewater Canal, was not finished until 1776, by which time other canals had begun to be constructed. The most important of these was the Grand Trunk Canal, completed in 1778, linking the Mersey and the Bridgewater Canal with the river Trent via the Potteries of Staffordshire.

There followed a great boom in canal-building lasting until the early years of the nineteenth century. During this boom the country came to be covered by a network of canals, linking all important industrial areas with the main navigable rivers. Regions like Birmingham and the Black Country, which had hitherto been badly handicapped by absence of water transport, rapidly acquired a complicated web of new waterways. The great river systems were linked by new canals such as the Thames-Severn Canal completed in 1799, the Forth-Clyde Canal in Scotland completed in 1790, and the Ellesmere Canal linking the Dee with the Severn completed in 1793. Industrial towns were connected to their markets or sources of raw materials, as Birmingham to London by the Grand Junction Canal of 1793, Leeds to Liverpool in 1777, and the iron-making centre of Merthyr Tydfil in South Wales to Cardiff in 1812.

It is clear then that the difficulties mentioned earlier were somehow overcome. It was said that money presented the first hurdle. The earlier canals were financed with difficulty. The Sankey Brook Navigation was financed out of capital subscribed by Liverpool merchants and the owners of Cheshire salt works. The Duke of Bridgewater raised the entire cost of his two canals from his own private resources, straining these to the uttermost in the process, and having recourse to borrowing on the security of his estates before completing the work. Josiah Wedgwood and other Staffordshire potters subscribed to the Grand Trunk Canal. No sooner was it demonstrated by these early ventures that canal-building could pay good dividends than money flowed in from all sources. Many of the early canals were extremely profitable. The Bridgewater Canal was reputed to be earning regularly nearly £100,000 a year in the early years of the nineteenth century. But while many paid handsome dividends to their fortunate shareholders, in other instances money had been less wisely invested. In the early 1790's, for example, so great had been the enthusiasm to build canals that many were planned for areas in which the volume of traffic never could justify the expense of canal-building. Some of these had been built in agricultural areas in the east Midlands and southern England, and failed to repay the cost of construction.

The other difficulties were technical, and most of them were concerned with the negotiation of inclines. Locks were used extensively for this purpose. To cut down expense, locks were made no bigger than was necessary to accommodate a single barge. This led to a serious problem, because, as each canal was constructed by a different group of businessmen, there was no standard width or length of barge. A lock built to accommodate a barge six feet wide would be impassable to wider boats. In this way the wide (fourteen feet) boats of the Bridgewater Canal could not negotiate the narrow locks and bridges of most other canals. However, six feet gradually became adopted as the standard width for barges, though there remained difficulties concerning lengths. Where hills were steep and long, as in the Pennines, great stairways of locks were built. The Rochdale Canal, for example, contained 92 locks in a distance of 33 miles. Where conditions permitted, tunnels were sometimes

Canal and lock gates at Stoke Hammond, Buckinghamshire, in the early nineteenth century

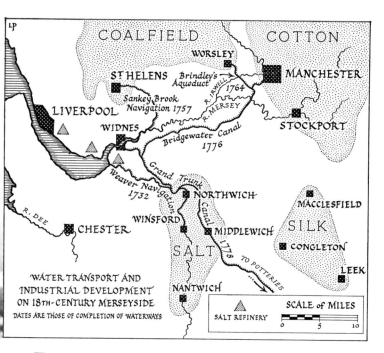

The map is labelled:

LP

COALFIELD • COTTON

WORSLEY

ST HELENS • Brindley's Aqueduct

MANCHESTER

Sankey Brook Navigation 1757 • R. IRWELL • 1764 • R. MERSEY

LIVERPOOL

WIDNES • Bridgewater Canal 1776 • STOCKPORT

Weaver Navigation 1732 • Grand Trunk • NORTHWICH

R. DEE • CHESTER • WINSFORD • Canal 1778 • MIDDLEWICH • MACCLESFIELD

SALT • SILK • CONGLETON

LEEK

TO POTTERIES

WATER TRANSPORT AND
INDUSTRIAL DEVELOPMENT
ON 18TH-CENTURY MERSEYSIDE
DATES ARE THOSE OF COMPLETION OF WATERWAYS

NANTWICH

SALT REFINERY

SCALE of MILES
0 • 5 • 10

The rock salt deposits of north Cheshire began to be worked intensively from the late seventeenth century, using coal to evaporate the brine. The nearest coalfield was in south Lancashire, and Liverpool merchants engaged in the export of refined salt built the Mersey salt refineries in the 1690's. As a first step towards reducing the cost of transport of rock salt and coal, the Liverpool merchants secured an act in 1721 for improving the navigation of the river Weaver to Winsford. Later, in the 1750's, they built the Sankey Brook Navigation to make cheap coal available for salt-making. As a result of the development of these new waterways, the output of salt from north Cheshire rose from 14,000 tons in 1732 to 28,000 tons in 1752, to pass the 100,000 tons mark by the end of the century. The original Bridgewater Canal of 1764 brought coal cheaply to the textile manufacturing centre of Manchester, and its extension in 1776 made possible the immense expansion of the cotton industry by the cheap water carriage of American raw cotton from Liverpool and the finished cotton goods from Manchester to Liverpool for export. The Grand Trunk Canal of 1778 gave the Potteries and the silk towns of the Cheshire-Staffordshire border access to the port of Liverpool.

used to save the construction of ascending and descending stairways. The most famous of these was the two-miles-long Sapperton tunnel in Gloucestershire on the Thames-Severn Canal, built in 1799 at a cost of £245,000. Lastly, the inclined plane was occasionally used on steep inclines in Shropshire, by means of which the barge was carried up or down the incline on a wheeled carriage running on rails.

The canals succeeded in unifying the country in this period in a way that the roads and rivers never achieved. By their means the products of each and every industrial region were made available to consumers in all parts of the country, whilst the newly acquired access of many important industrial areas to seaports greatly assisted the growth of export trade. Finally, one other aspect of canals should be noted. The construction of the canal network of this country, confined as it was to a relatively short period of time, employed large numbers of labourers. These were the 'navigators', or 'navvies'. In the days when excavation had to be done entirely by the spade, many thousands were employed in the construction of a single canal. They were the beginnings of a growing army of unskilled labourers, a type of workman hitherto uncommon in Britain. Many of them were immigrants from Ireland. On the other hand, canals also bred another important class of worker, the skilled engineer, a group which was to grow enormously in importance in the nineteenth century.

4. ROADS

The heavy investment in canals and improvements to river navigation discussed in the preceding sections was the result of the failure of the roads to cater for the growing volume of traffic in the eighteenth century. British roads were bad for two reasons — there was a lack of technical knowledge of road-building, and, perhaps more important, there was no system of administration capable of raising sufficient money even to keep the existing roads in a decent state of repair, let alone to build new roads.

For centuries the maintenance of roads and bridges had been the responsibility of the parish in which they lay. This caused little difficulty in an out-of-the-way country parish where the

Three types of land transport in the late seventeenth century
top: A stage waggon; centre: Packhorses; bottom: Coach and dray

roads were used mainly by the local inhabitants, but matters were very different in a poor agricultural parish which had the misfortune to bestride a great main road. In this case the road-users were mainly those who lived outside the parish concerned, and it was natural for those who bore the expense of road maintenance in the parish to resent the heavy burden of repair for the benefit of others. In the circumstances this situation invariably meant that the duty of maintaining the road in good condition was neglected, and even the busiest of main roads remained without any form of hard surface. As a result, in winter they were deep quagmires, and in summer when the ruts hardened, severe jolting kept down the pace of carriages and carts to a snail's pace.

This problem of administration was tackled by what were known as *Turnpike Trusts*, which took their name from the turnpikes or toll-gates at which tolls were collected of all road-users. A turnpike road was normally planned and financed by a group of people interested (often on account of their local industrial activities) in improving a certain road. They secured permission by act of Parliament to collect tolls from all users of the road in question, on condition that they maintained the road in a good state of repair. They embodied the principle that 'every person ought to contribute to the repair of roads in proportion to the use they make of, or the convenience they derive from them'. As in the case of canals, as soon as it became evident that investment of money in a turnpike road could be very profitable, there was no shortage of money coming forward, and much of this was put to very good use during the eighteenth century. Already by the 1720's Defoe was writing enthusiastically about the benefits of the earlier turnpike roads. 'It must be acknowledged', he wrote, 'that they are very great things, and very great things are done by them, and 'tis well worth recording, for the honour of the present age, that this work has begun, and is in an extraordinary manner carried on, and perhaps may, in a great measure, be completed within our memory.'

The first turnpike trust was established in 1706 in Buckinghamshire, though since 1663 Justices of the Peace in several counties had been levying tolls for road repair. Throughout the early decades of the century there was a steady growth of the number of turnpike trusts, but the rapid increase in their numbers only began after 1748. Between then and 1770 the number of turnpike trusts rose from 150 to 530. By the late 1830's, when the coming of the railways brought the creation of new turnpikes to a halt, over 1,100 trusts had been created, covering 22,000 miles of roads, including most of the main roads of the country. There remained 105,000 miles of roads in the country still under the care of individual parishes. In 1773 Parliament had passed a General Turnpike Act which regulated the actions of turnpike trustees everywhere. This Act, with some modification in 1822, remained the basis for the administration of all turnpike roads. Unfortunately it gave legal authority to many of the undesirable characteristics of turnpike administration, and at the same time failed to remedy the more obvious shortcomings, thus perpetuating both good and bad features of the system.

Though the turnpikes effected a great deal of improvement to the road system of the country, they were far from providing the perfect answer to the demand for better roads. There was, firstly, no obligation on the trustees to spend any fixed proportion of their revenue from tolls on the maintenance of their stretch of road. In practice this sometimes meant that little or nothing was spent on repair work, so that the travelling public received little value for its payment of tolls. Secondly, because a trust was rarely given authority over more than a comparatively short stretch of road, travellers on long journeys found themselves obliged to pay a considerable number of tolls in the course of their journeys. Thirdly, the system did not sufficiently recognize the needs of the purely local traveller, whose daily journey to work might take him past a toll-bar. This problem led, firstly, to considerable evasion of tolls, and secondly to local hostility to the turnpikes which occasionally took the form of rioting and the destruction of toll-bars. The turnpike trusts failed to meet the needs of the times because they were a piecemeal and purely local answer to the problem. Where roads crossed many parishes and even counties on the way from one large town to another, only a truly national system of road administration could have answered completely.

The turnpike trusts, for all their shortcomings, spent a great deal more money on road maintenance than had hitherto been available. By 1838, for example, turnpike trustees were spending, on the average, £51 a year on each mile of road under their care, whilst parishes were only devoting £11 to the same purpose. The additional money made available encouraged the rise of road engineers, and it is therefore no coincidence that the turnpike trusts developed hand-in-hand with the science of road engineering. The period is famous for the activities of three great pioneers in road construction — John Metcalf ('Blind Jack of Knaresborough'), Thomas Telford, and John Loudon McAdam.

John Metcalf, who was blind from the age of six, was remarkable for his diverse talents. Beginning life as a horse-dealer, in 1754 he started a regular coach service between York and Knaresborough. This led him to take an interest in road-building, and in 1765 he secured a contract to construct a three-mile stretch of road on a new turnpike between Harrogate

A stage-coach and turnpike in the late eighteenth century

and Boroughbridge. His success in this, as well as at bridge-building, led him to undertake further work of this kind, and by the time he gave up road-building in 1792 he had supervised the construction of about 180 miles of turnpike roads in Lancashire and Yorkshire.

Thomas Telford, born in 1757 in Scotland, trained in his youth as a stonemason, and before he was thirty had been appointed surveyor of public works for Shropshire. In this capacity he gained valuable experience as supervisor during the construction of the Ellesmere Canal. The building of two immense aqueducts carrying the canal over the valleys of the Ceiriog and the Dee immediately established Telford's reputation as an outstanding engineer. He turned later to road and bridge-building. He greatly improved the methods of creating a firm road surface, and was responsible for the planning of many important roads and bridges. Perhaps the most famous of these was the Shrewsbury-Holyhead road, which involved the construction in 1825 of his most famous bridge, the Menai Suspension Bridge.

John McAdam, also a Scot, was born in 1756, but spent part

of his early life in America, where he acquired a fortune during the War of Independence. Returning to England, he experimented in the construction of roads, using broken stones for surfacing. On being appointed surveyor-general of roads in Bristol in 1815, he put his theories into practice. The merits of the new 'macadamized' surface were immediately recognized, and the nation's debt to him was recognized by Parliament in a grant of £10,000.

The improvement of roads thus made possible by the turnpike trusts and the technical contributions of the road engineers led to a great acceleration of coach traffic. The stage-coach, travelling at speeds of up to ten miles an hour, and covering 100 to 120 miles in a day, enjoyed a brief spell of popularity. The stage-coach was lighter and more rapid than earlier carriages had been. It carried six passengers inside, with room for more on the roof. Drawn by teams of up to six horses that were changed in relays along the route, the stage-coaches did much to reduce the time spent in travelling. Travel, though still an expensive luxury, became less of a physical hardship. But the railways, coming hard on the heels of the stage-coaches, gradually displaced this form of road traffic.

The transport changes discussed in this chapter covered a period of well over a century. The improvement of river navigation was a continuous process of development which was merely accelerated in the eighteenth century. The age of the turnpikes coincided closely with that of the canals, and both suffered eclipse with the coming of the railways in the 1830's. The combined effect of intensive development of all three methods of transport during the eighteenth and early nineteenth centuries was twofold — to reduce substantially the cost of carriage of industrial products, and to permit an enormous increase in the quantities of goods carried. How these changes interacted with the industrial, agricultural and social development of the nation will be studied in later chapters.

CHAPTER 10

INDUSTRY

1. THE CONDITIONS OF INDUSTRIAL GROWTH

Of all the changes that took place in Britain during the eighteenth century, those that occurred in industry were probably the most striking. The Britain of 1700 was predominantly agricultural, but the 1831 census revealed that only 25% of all the families in Britain were engaged in agriculture. In that year, too, one quarter of the population of Britain was living in towns of 20,000 inhabitants or more, and probably half of all the people in the country lived in towns of all sizes. In most cases, industry was the magnet that drew people from the rural areas.

The most obvious way through which demand for the products of industry could grow was through an increase of population. Without any change in standards of living, the population of 14 millions of 1820 would consume twice as many goods as would the population of 7 millions of 1750. Any rise in the standard of living would lead to a further increase in demand. But the home market was not the sole outlet for British manufactures; some industries, particularly the woollen industry, had always exported a considerable proportion of their output. In the later eighteenth century there was a remarkable growth of overseas trade from Britain. Some of the newer industries, like cotton and pottery, exported a high proportion (as much as 80%) of their total output; some of the older industries, like iron and woollen cloth, increased the exported proportion of their output. New markets overseas added considerably to the demand for British manufactures in the late eighteenth and early nineteenth centuries.

Of the factors influencing supply, those that tended to reduce costs were most important. An invention, for example, that substituted a simple mechanical device for human labour reduced the time and labour expended in the production of a commodity, thus lowering its cost. When two shirts can be supplied for the same amount of money as one, more shirts will be bought. Many of the inventions of the eighteenth and early nineteenth centuries achieved this result. For example, it was noted in 1800 that whereas with the old methods of woollen manufacture it required 101 workers to turn a pack of wool into woollen yarn, by the newer methods recently developed, only 22 were needed. By making possible the manufacture of two or more commodities for the price of one they did not necessarily reduce the number of men and women employed in an industry, as many people feared would happen. In some cases the rise in demand consequent upon the reduction in cost more than compensated for the displacement of human labour by the new machine. In the first half of the eighteenth century and earlier, some industries such as iron were unable to meet even the home demand for their products, and it was necessary to import additional quantities. This was because existing techniques of manufacture did not admit of any very great increase in output. Where inventions made possible the use of alternative or new raw materials, the supply of which was greater or cheaper than existing materials, then a further lowering of cost, or an expansion of output, was made possible.

Industrial expansion requires capital. The Industrial Revolution was only made possible by an increased flow of capital as well as by the development of essential banking and credit facilities. In all ages industry has financed its own expansion in part from its former profits, and the eighteenth century was no exception. The century after 1660 was one of active, if slow, expansion in many industries, and the spurt in several industries in the late eighteenth and early nineteenth centuries was the result of this earlier prosperity.

Another equally important source of capital was overseas trade. Merchants' profits were turned over to industry. When the outbreak of the War of American Independence in 1775 cut off the extremely profitable tobacco trade of the Glasgow merchants, many turned to industry. David Dale, a Glasgow merchant of this period who traded mainly in linen yarn, used the profits of this trade to found the New Lanark cotton mill, made famous in later years by Robert Owen. The profits of the Bristol transatlantic trade were used extensively to finance the industries of the Severn basin.

The eighteenth century saw the real beginnings of the finance of industry by banks. In particular, the many hundreds of country banks (see Chapter 4, section 4) which appeared during the eighteenth century played a vital part in raising capital for industry. Many industrialists turned to banking and, as bankers, used their industrial experience to serve the needs of growing industry. Banks served to bring together the savings of all kinds of people and to make part of these, at least, available as loans to industry. A further factor which contributed to encourage the supply of capital was the steady fall over a long period in the rate of interest at which capital could be borrowed.

Towards the end of the eighteenth century, immense demands were made on the supply of capital — from industry, from agriculture (for enclosures and other improvements), from transport (for canals and turnpikes) and from building (to house the rapidly growing population). The marvel that made the Industrial Revolution possible was that the supply of capital responded at the same time to all these calls.

Industry, particularly heavy industry, could not develop without adequate transport facilities. Though coastal and river navigation was used extensively by industry in early eighteenth-century Britain, these methods alone could never have met the needs of modern large-scale industry. Industrial expansion before 1830 depended to a large extent on the canals built after 1750. For this reason canal construction in the late eighteenth century was a pre-requisite of industrial growth. Wagon-ways and improved roads and harbours also helped. These improvements so far reduced the cost of transport of heavy or bulky goods that local markets were turned into national markets.

2. Iron and Steel

The manufacture of iron in the early eighteenth century was a long and expensive business involving several separate processes. Iron ore was smelted in the blast furnace using charcoal as fuel. Some iron goods could be cast directly from the blast furnace (*cast iron*), but most of the iron from the blast furnace was run off into sand moulds as *pig iron* for further treatment. Pig iron contained some impurities, and its brittleness made it valueless for most purposes. The impurities were therefore removed in the *forge*, where repeated hammering and re-heating removed the impurities and produced *bar iron*, pliable and tough, from which the whole range of ironware could be made. In the days of wooden ships, houses and machines, the demand for nails was very great, and possibly one third of the iron manufactured in Britain was made into nails. This involved rolling the bars of iron by power-driven rollers into *plates*, slitting the plates into thin *rods* at the *slitting-mill*, and cutting and shaping the rods into nails by hand. Other kinds of ironware were made by *smiths* directly from bar iron, while the production of steel from bar iron required such lengthy and expensive processes that very little of it was made at all. Most of these processes required the use of water-power. The water-wheels worked the bellows of the blast furnaces, lifted the great forge hammers by means of cams, or turned the rollers and cutting blades of the rolling- and slitting-mills.

In the first half of the eighteenth century the industry was fairly well dispersed over the country. The great activity of the sixteenth century in the Weald of Sussex and Surrey had abated during the seventeenth century, and this area, though not completely decayed, was no longer important in the iron industry, which flourished in South Wales, in the Forest of Dean in Gloucestershire, in Shropshire, in the Midlands from Staffordshire to the Stour, in south Yorkshire and Derbyshire, in the Furness district of north Lancashire, and in the north-east near Newcastle.

In the early eighteenth century the English industry barely supplied half the country's requirements. To make good the deficiency, bar iron was imported at first from Sweden and later in the century also from Russia. In the early eighteenth century English manufacturers produced about 20,000 tons of bar iron, and a further 20,000 tons was imported mainly from Sweden. The reasons for the inadequacy of the English supply were three-fold. Furnaces and forges had to be sited near to deposits of ore and supplies of wood for charcoal. These were seldom to be found adjacent to the larger rivers, so that the industry was normally forced to rely upon the smaller streams for water-power and these often failed to provide sufficient power during the summer months. Secondly, both iron ore, with its high proportion of waste (more than half of English iron ore is non-

F

metallic waste), and finished iron are bulky and heavy. In Chapter 9 it has already been shown how inadequate the country's transport system was until quite late in the eighteenth century. Before the coming of canals and hard-surfaced roads the iron industry was frequently unable to transport either its raw materials or finished products for a substantial part of each year when the winter conditions made the roads virtually unusable for heavy traffic. Finally, and most important, charcoal was expensive, and because a great deal of charcoal was used to make iron, this raised the price of English iron so much that countries with plentiful supplies of easily-obtained charcoal, like Sweden and Russia, were able to make iron much more cheaply and sell it in this country at the same or even a lower price despite shipping freights and heavy import duties. Charcoal was dear in England because most of the land is very fertile and could be farmed more profitably for crops or animals than for slow-growing timber.

Thus, in the early eighteenth century, there were three pressing needs in the English iron industry — an alternative source of power to water, providing power for twelve months of the year; an improved transport system which allowed the carriage of iron all the year round; and a substitute fuel for charcoal. The first had to wait until Watt's steam engine could be adapted towards the end of the century. The midlands iron-master, John Wilkinson, was the first to apply steam power to the blast furnace in 1776. The second need was largely met by the improvements referred to in Chapter 9, while the third problem was only solved after many efforts and a series of important inventions.

After more than a hundred years of experiments, during which several patents for unsuccessful processes were taken out by Dud Dudley and others, the first commercially successful production of iron using coked coal as the fuel in the blast furnace instead of charcoal was achieved shortly after 1709 by Abraham Darby I, a Quaker ironmaster of Coalbrookdale in Shropshire. Darby was fortunate in the fact that both his local coal and ore were of the right chemical constitution; ironmasters in other areas who attempted to imitate him were not immediately successful. In any case the iron produced in Darby's coke furnaces was only suitable for casting. Not until 1749, after further experiments by his son, Abraham Darby II, was it possible to make pig iron with coke suitable for refining into bar iron at the forge.

After 1760 there began a steady expansion of the industry. The new blast furnaces were nearly all coke-fired, and the industry naturally expanded most in areas where coal was easily available — South Wales, Shropshire, the Midlands, south Yorkshire and the Scottish Lowlands. Areas where the industry had flourished during the charcoal era but which were without coal declined rapidly — the Weald, the Forest of Dean and the Furness district.

The solution of the fuel problem, combined with the improvements in transport in the second half of the century, left a major bottle-neck in the industry. The forging of pig iron into bar was a slow and laborious process, and there could be little expansion in the industry until some way was found to speed it up. The important discovery was made by Henry Cort, who in 1783 and 1784 patented processes for rolling and puddling. In Cort's puddling furnace the impurities were removed from the pig iron while it was still molten, and on cooling, the refined and purified iron was rolled into bars. These inventions made possible an enormous increase in the output of bar iron, and allowed the industry to respond to a rapidly growing demand for iron manufactures without having to rely on imports as formerly. Output of pig iron grew from under 30,000 tons in 1750 to 68,000 tons in 1788, and 250,000 tons in 1806. The industry, formerly producing iron mainly for nails and iron tools, by the early nineteenth century had to cater for a much increased demand for steam engines, boilers, iron boats, rails, bridges, and a wide range of machinery.

In the early eighteenth century, steel was made in two different ways, but both were slow and costly. A steel furnace took between two and three weeks to convert eight or ten tons of iron into steel, and it then required repeated forging to produce the metal in a commercially usable form. As a result, steel was very expensive compared with iron, and its quality left much to be desired. An important step forward was made in 1740 by Benjamin Huntsman, a Doncaster watchmaker. Huntsman was anxious to find a steel of the highest quality suitable for watch and clock springs. In the *crucible* process of steelmaking invented by him, the steel was produced in clay crucibles in molten form. The process produced steel of a quality that has never since been exceeded, but it did nothing to reduce its high price. Thus its use remained limited until well into the nineteenth century. Although the output did expand, mainly as a result of the big demand from the Sheffield cutlery industry, steel remained expensive and relatively unimportant until the middle years of the nineteenth century.

Casting steel ingots from Huntsman's crucibles in the eighteenth century

3. ENGINEERING

The most important developments in engineering during the eighteenth century were connected with the steam engine, or 'fire engine', as it was commonly called. The desire to harness the power of steam had led to experiments from Roman times onwards, but the first successful machine operated by steam power was the steam pump patented by Thomas Savery in

1698. Savery's engine made use of the atmospheric pressure created by the condensation of steam in a cylinder to draw water up a pipe for mine drainage. His engine was not very efficient and could only pump water from a limited depth. His

A Newcomen steam pump

principle was utilized by Thomas Newcomen in a much superior form of pump invented in 1709. In Newcomen's engine, steam from a boiler was condensed in a cylinder by an injection of cold water. The contraction of the condensed steam drew down a piston which, linked to a rocker arm, operated the rod of a pump or series of pumps. Newcomen's engine was capable of pumping water from a considerable depth, but was still inefficient, consuming a great deal of coal. However, it was mainly used to draw water from coal-mines, and the high consumption of coal was of small importance. Unfortunately for Newcomen, he was unable to take out a separate patent for his invention and was obliged to share in Savery's patent. Newcomen's engine made possible the working of deeper seams in coal mines, and many hundreds of engines were built and installed during the eighteenth century. The production of metal parts, particularly the casting of the huge iron cylinders (five or six feet in diameter), gave a valuable stimulus to the iron industry.

The Newcomen engine was extremely inefficient, however, as it was necessary to consume steam in re-heating the cylinder at each stroke of the piston. Moreover, with the very crude means available, it was not possible in the early eighteenth century to manufacture working parts with any precision, and much power was lost through ill-fitting valves and inaccurately-bored cylinders. In 1757 a model of a Newcomen engine used for demonstration purposes in the University of Glasgow was given to a young laboratory mechanic, James Watt, to repair. Watt easily appreciated the shortcomings of Newcomen's machine and devoted himself to improving it. At last, in 1765, after some years of experiment, he designed an engine with a coal consumption less than half that of Newcomen's. He

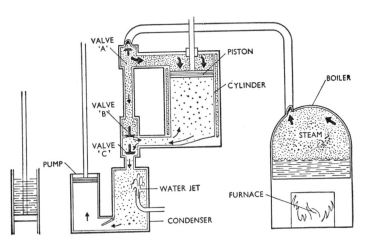

A diagram to show how Watt's steam engine worked

realized that the re-heating of the cylinder between each stroke of the piston was extremely wasteful, and devised a separate cylinder into which the steam from the main cylinder could be drawn to be condensed by cold water. Thus he avoided cooling the main cylinder, with a consequent saving of steam and fuel. Watt patented his invention in 1769.

Watt's invention of the *separate condensing cylinder* reduced the cost of operating steam pumps considerably and accordingly extended the field of their use. Watt's skill and his valuable patent could therefore be put to profitable use by a businessman with just the right combination of enterprise and resources. In Scotland, John Roebuck, owner of coal-mines and ironworks, took Watt into partnership, but Roebuck went bankrupt in 1773, leaving Watt to look for another partner to assist him in the exploitation of his invention. For some years he had been in touch with a Birmingham manufacturer of metalware, Matthew Boulton, and when Boulton heard of Roebuck's bankruptcy he immediately invited Watt to join him as a partner in his firm to manufacture the new steam engine at his factory at Soho near Birmingham. Thus, in 1774, there came into existence the most famous firm in the history of engineering, the firm which was to make steam engines on a scale large enough to revolutionize many of the principal industries of the country. Boulton and Watt were fortunate in securing an extension of Watt's patent for a further twenty-five years from 1775, so that until 1800 steam engines could only be erected and operated under licence from the firm of Boulton and Watt.

But in 1775 the engine could still only pump water from a mine. True, both Newcomen's and Watt's engines had been used to pump back water that had passed over a water-wheel, so permitting water-power to be used the whole year round; but the engine still had obvious limitations. The key to future development lay in the adaptation of the reciprocating motion of the rocker beam to the rotary motion of a shaft. Boulton realized the possibilities of rotary steam engines from an early date, but it was not until 1781 that Watt produced the invention that paved the way for the power-driven factory and the locomotive. He was unable to make use of a simple crank and flywheel motion, as another engineer, Pickard, held a patent for that. Watt therefore devised a substitute for the crank, the *sun and planet motion*, which was used until Pickard's patent expired in 1794.

The rotary motion raised another problem that had to be solved before the machine could be said to be effective. The use of the piston to turn a shaft instead of working a pump required a rigid link between piston and beam. The end of the beam described an arc, while the piston rod could only move vertically. Watt's brilliantly devised *parallel motion*, patented in 1784, solved this problem. Later he introduced other devices that improved the efficiency of his engine. In 1787, for example, he invented a *centrifugal governor* which automatically controlled the engine at a constant speed through a linkage to the steam inlet valve.

Owing to the high cost of licences for Watt engines, Newcomen engines continued to be widely used, particularly in the textile industry of Lancashire, until the expiry of Watt's patent in 1800. So long as the steam engine existed only in the reciprocating form of Savery's, Newcomen's or Watt's early machines, its use was limited to pumping for mine drainage or for pumping water back into a mill-pond after it had passed over a water-wheel. The invention of rotary motion enormously extended the range of uses to which steam power could be put, and in the last quarter of the eighteenth century it was used to drive all kinds of textile machinery, brewing and pottery machinery, malt, sugar and flour mills.

Watt's inventions paved the way for the growth of a new industry — engineering. In the thirty years following the expiry of his patent in 1800, there were many new developments to the steam engine as well as in other spheres of engineering, and to man the engineering works that grew up rapidly in the Midlands, Lancashire and the North-east there arose a new class of workers, the skilled mechanics and engineers. One of the best examples of this class, William Murdock, gained his earliest engineering experience in Cornwall where he assisted in the erection of Boulton and Watt's engines in the copper mines. He showed his resourcefulness in his invention of the slide valve of 1799, but his reputation was chiefly earned by his being the first to make use of coal gas for lighting. Boulton and Watt's factory at Soho was lit by gas as early as 1798.

The whole field of engineering is a very wide one, and great strides were being made at this time in machine-making, and road and canal engineering. John Smeaton, for example, is famous for his many improvements to steam engines during the 1750's and 1760's. John Wilkinson, the great Midlands iron-master, facilitated the development of the steam engine by his invention for the boring of iron cylinders. Towards the end of the century, engineers like Joseph Bramah and Henry Maudslay set up general engineering workshops in London. Workshops for the manufacture of textile machinery in Lancashire were established by Dobson and Barlow — an industry that was to become very important in the textile regions. William Galloway, a Scots millwright, started an engineering business in Manchester in 1790 which his son, John, later developed into an important locomotive engineering works. These men, and many others like them, were rapidly creating from very small beginnings the great British engineering industry.

4. COAL

Early in the eighteenth century coal was mined in north-eastern England in the valleys of the Tyne and the Wear, in

The pit-head of an eighteenth-century coal-mine, with a Newcomen steam pump

A colliery pit-head at Broseley, Shropshire, in the eighteenth century,

south Yorkshire, south Lancashire, Derbyshire, Nottingham-shire, the Midlands, the Forest of Dean, and in Somersetshire near Bristol. The first of these districts was overwhelmingly the most important. Coal, being both bulky and heavy, was not easily carried by land, and for the most part it was carried by water — by coastal or river navigation. Thus mines without easy access to water transport could expect to sell only to a very restricted local market. By far the largest centre for the domestic consumption of coal was London, and this market was most cheaply served by the north-east coalfield.

The mines in the north-east were situated on either bank of the rivers Tyne and Wear. As the earlier pits became exhausted, new ones were sunk further away from the rivers. To convey the coal to the *staiths* or loading quays on the rivers, wooden wagon-ways were developed. These consisted of horse-drawn wagons whose flanged wheels ran on flat wooden rails. Some of these wagon-ways had been built in the late sixteenth century and were therefore the first railways in Britain. By the eighteenth century a great many had been constructed, the longest ways carrying coal as far as ten or twelve miles down to the rivers. At the staiths, the coal was loaded from the wagon-ways into *keels*, the riverboats that carried about twenty tons of coal down river to the exporting ports of Newcastle, Shields and Sunderland. There the coal was transferred to the *colliers*, the coastal vessels sailing between London and the coal ports. Many hundreds of colliers plied the east-coast route during the eighteenth century, and this trade was rightly regarded as the greatest nursery of English seamen.

Pits tended to be small in size, seldom employing more than 40 or 50 miners and frequently less than 20. They rarely penetrated very deeply into the ground, for the miner's greatest problems of drainage and ventilation prohibited deep workings. When the expansion of river and canal navigation opened up new markets for coal, and new industries like coke-smelted iron and pottery added to the demand for coal, it became essential for the mining industry to master the problems of drainage and ventilation. During the eighteenth century some small im-provements in ventilation were made. Boys were employed down mines to operate trap-doors and fans to control the dangerous gases. Braziers were suspended in the shaft so that

A collier in the early nineteenth century

the rising convection currents could circulate fresh air. Shafts were divided vertically into two parts so that fresh air could go down one side while foul air was expelled up the other. In 1815 Davy invented the safety lamp for miners which contributed materially to reducing the accident rate. Nevertheless the danger of explosion from the ever-present gases remained high. The miner's life was exceptionally hazardous, and catastrophic explosions were regarded as the unfortunate but inevitable accompaniment to mining.

So long as mine-owners were prepared to risk men's lives in inadequately ventilated pits — and some were — the real obstacles to increased output were drainage and winding. Until the invention of the steam engine for pumping, the only satisfactory system of underground drainage was the *adit*, or sloping shaft, down which water could flow, given a convenient hillside on to which the adit could discharge the water. The situation of some mines in the steep-sided Tyne and Wear valleys made adit drainage possible in many instances, but this form of natural drainage was normally only possible in shallow pits. Early in the eighteenth century Newcomen's engine provided a new method of deep drainage. Though expensive in fuel, the steam engine could pump water from greater depths than before, and the widespread adoption of the Newcomen engine on Tyneside during the first three-quarters of the eighteenth century (there were believed to have been one hundred erected around Newcastle alone) bears witness to its effectiveness in this respect. Because the main advantage of Watt's engine over Newcomen's — its saving in fuel — was of relatively little importance to mine-owners, the Watt engine was slow to replace the older Newcomen engine for pumping. It was not until the beginning of the nineteenth century that the steam engine began to be used extensively for winding.

Improvements in ventilation, drainage and transport made possible a great expansion of coal production in answer to growing demands from many sources. The mere growth of population accounted for some of this increased demand and the new and improved methods of transport brought coal to many districts hitherto without it. More important, however, was the growing demand for coal from industry. Darby's invention had created an important new market for coal. The development of the steam engine, as well as the steady growth of some smaller industries like pottery, glass-making and copper-making, all added to the growing demand for coal. Coal output in Britain had probably been barely 5 million tons in 1750, and this was doubled by 1800. In 1830, 22 million tons were being produced. These figures are small compared with outputs of over 200 million tons in the twentieth century, but the quadrupling of production in eighty years marked a very great advance in the industry.

5. COTTON

Since the early middle ages the principal industry in England had been the manufacture of woollen cloth. By the middle of the eighteenth century the slow march of economic development had diversified the industrial structure of the country, but in spite of rising competitors like the iron, shipbuilding and mining industries, the country's first industry was still wool: cotton manufacture offered little threat to the supremacy of wool.

Two factors in the early eighteenth century hindered the expansion of the textile industry. Raw cotton, grown only in the eastern Mediterranean and India, was expensive and was not cultivated on a sufficiently large scale to permit any great expansion of a cotton industry. For the most part, the cotton consumed in England in the seventeenth and early eighteenth centuries was not used on its own but mixed with wool or linen. Secondly, both spinning and weaving were slow and arduous processes requiring a great deal of human labour. The spinning wheel, by which the raw fibres were spun into yarn, had scarcely developed at all in several centuries, so that the output of yarn per spinner was little greater in 1750 than it had been in, say, 1350.

The eighteenth century saw the removal of both these barriers to progress. Firstly, the United States, having won their independence from Britain in 1783, developed the cultivation of cotton in the southern states with the aid of slave labour. Secondly, a series of inventions from 1733 onwards revolutionized the manufacture of cloth. These inventions were applicable equally to all branches of textile manufacture — cotton, wool, linen and silk alike — but in all cases were adopted first in the cotton industry and only later in the other branches.

*Apprentices at their silk looms in Spitalfields
in the mid-eighteenth century*

In the early eighteenth century spinning was so slow and laborious an occupation that it required the labour of about ten spinners to provide sufficient yarn to occupy a single weaver. Clearly the way to expand the output of cloth lay through the mechanization of spinning. But in 1733 a Lancashire cloth-worker, John Kay, invented a device for accelerating the weaving process. By means of a simple system of flexible linkages, he found a way of passing the shuttle automatically from side to side of the cloth. His *flying shuttle* speeded up weaving and enabled the weaver to dispense with the boy who had formerly assisted in the manufacture of all but the narrowest cloths. Kay's valuable invention, though only very slowly adopted, accentuated the disparity between the labour of spinning and weaving. Thereafter attention was focused more than ever on the development of spinning technique.

As early as 1738, Lewis Paul had contrived a simple mechanism that was ultimately to lead to the solution of the spinner's problem. Two sets of rollers, the second revolving faster than the first, were used to draw out the carded cotton or wool to the required thickness or 'count' before the twist was imparted. But Paul's method of *roller spinning* encountered practical difficulties, and little commercial use was made of his invention until almost the end of the century. Meanwhile, between 1764 and 1767, James Hargreaves, a Lancashire carpenter, produced an 'engine' or 'jenny' in which some half-dozen ordinary spindles were combined, so that a single spinner could produce six threads in the same time as he had formerly made one. Later adaptation multiplied the number of threads produced simultaneously by the spinning jenny, until as many as eighty threads could be spun at once. Here at last was the answer to the bottle-neck in production. Hargreaves' machine was adopted rapidly and it is estimated that 20,000 were in use by 1788. When, in 1768, Richard Arkwright, another Lanca-shire man, patented his *water frame*, a water-powered machine incorporating Paul's rollers that produced for the first time a cotton thread strong enough for use in the warp (the longi-tudinal threads in a piece of cloth), the disparity between spinning and weaving was removed. These inventions, by speeding up the process of spinning, only stressed the urgency of mechanizing the carding process by which the cotton fibres were prepared for spinning. Various inventions in the 1760's paved the way for a practical machine, but it was Arkwright in 1775 who finally produced, patented and employed on a large scale a rotary carding machine. It was this machine more than any other which made possible the mass-production of cotton yarn. In the 1780's yet another invention widened the scope as well as facilitated the spinning of yarn. Samuel Crompton's *mule*, perfected in 1785, not only spun many scores of thread at once, but also produced a soft, firm yarn, suitable for either warp or weft (cross threads).

In less than twenty years, after the late 1760's, the spinning branch of the textile industry had been completely transformed. Formerly spinning had been mainly the preserve of women and had been done almost entirely in the home. Little capital was required, for the only machinery was a simple wooden spinning wheel, while hand and foot supplied all the power needed. After 1770, spinning machines, operated by water (and later by steam) power, required to be grouped on a single site to make the most economical use of the power of a water-wheel or Watt engine. Spinning, in other words, passed from domestic industry to factory industry. In Lancashire, Derbyshire and Clydeside, spinning mills multiplied. In Derbyshire, Jedediah Strutt built one of the first at Cromford in 1771, followed a few years later by mills at Belper and Milford built by Arkwright. The latter also assisted Samuel Oldknow to build his huge mill at Marple in Cheshire. It was in Manchester, then as now the centre of the cotton industry, that Robert Owen, famous later for his work for trade unionism, first gained his experience in cotton spinning, and, in partnership with John Drinkwater, built new mills. From Lancashire he moved to the Clyde valley in Scotland. There he entered into a partnership with David Dale, a Glasgow merchant, and used Dale's famous cotton mill at New Lanark for the experiments in industrial organization referred to in Chapter 13, section 2.

The rapid development of factory spinning threatened to outstrip the capacity of the weavers. Although Kay's flying shuttle began to be adopted after 1760, the pace of the hand-loom weaver was slow, little faster, indeed, than it had been for five hundred years. The application of water or steam power to the loom was a logical step, but the complicated motions of the loom were not easily harnessed to a single shaft. Success came from an unexpected quarter — the Church. In 1784, the Reverend Edmund Cartwright designed an effective power-loom. It was not rapidly adopted. The causes of this delay were twofold. Firstly, Cartwright's machine was far from perfect, and some years of development were necessary before it could be used commercially on a wide scale. Secondly, weaving had always been a man's trade, and the men were less willing to desert the comparative freedom of the home for the discipline of the factory. So the loom went into the factory much more slowly than did the spinning-wheel. In 1813, it was estimated that there were still only 2,400 power-looms in the country. Thereafter the transfer of the loom from the home to the factory quickened, and twenty years later about 100,000 power-looms were in operation.

Most of the references in the preceding paragraphs have been to the cotton industry. In all branches the woollen industry was slow to follow the trends in the cotton industry. Whereas the cotton-weaving industry had gone over to the power-loom almost completely by the 1830's, there still remained a considerable proportion of hand-loom weavers in the woollen industry in the 1830's and 1840's. They have, indeed, never been completely eliminated, though their survival has only been in the specialized rural industries of Wales and Scotland. A more important effect of the transfer from the domestic to factory system in the woollen industry in this period was the consolidation of the industry in the West Riding of Yorkshire. Older areas of manufacture like Gloucestershire, Wiltshire, Devon and East Anglia lost ground in the early nineteenth century to Yorkshire where coal was available in ample quantities to supply the steam engines. In particular the worsted branch of the industry, originating in East Anglia and taking its name from the Norfolk village of Worstead, left that area completely, becoming concentrated in the Bradford district.

6. POTTERY

The industries discussed earlier in this chapter have all been major industries, and it is only right that they should receive pride of place. It would be wrong, however, to assume that the

Wedgwood's works at Etruria, Staffordshire

industrial changes of the late eighteenth century affected only a handful of major industries. Many smaller ones gained as a result of the availability of new sources of power, or raw materials, or new markets, and of the experience gained elsewhere in larger forms of industrial organization.

A pottery industry had, of course, existed in England from earliest times, but its products tended to be coarse, and the unit of industrial organization seldom exceeded half a dozen men. The rise in standards of living during the eighteenth century opened markets for finer pottery, whilst the growing habits of tea and coffee drinking added to the demand for fine china. The expansion of the English pottery industry in the eighteenth century came almost solely as the result of the efforts of one man — Josiah Wedgwood (1730–95). A cultured man with a flare for science, Wedgwood created the first real pottery factory in England in 1769 outside Burslem, at a place he called Etruria after the Italian source of pottery styles he admired and imitated. Unlike the iron or textile industries, there were no major technical innovations and only a few minor ones in pottery-making during Wedgwood's lifetime. His main contribution to the progress of the industry was to practise so far as was possible the principle of the division of labour. The varied skills of the old-fashioned potter — of mixing the clay, of shaping the work on the wheel, of firing and of glazing — were now divided between a multitude of specialist workers. Wedgwood, moreover, turned out a superior product: whereas, before his day, only coarse *pottery* could be made at a price accessible to the majority of consumers, he developed the economical manufacture of fine *china*, and found world-wide markets for it by energetic and enterprising techniques of salesmanship.

Wedgwood's success drew to Staffordshire many rivals and imitators. Among them was Josiah Spode, whose ware acquired a reputation second only to Wedgwood's. The creation of a substantial body of skilled workers and the advantages of local coal supplies and good transport services (thanks mainly to Wedgwood's work in the planning and financing of canals) led to a high degree of specialization in this district of Staffordshire. Though pottery was made there before 1769, the 'Potteries' were truly founded by Josiah Wedgwood.

CHAPTER 11

AGRICULTURE

1. FARMING IN THE MID-EIGHTEENTH CENTURY

Until the start of the eighteenth century probably as much as half of the arable land of the country was still farmed in open fields. Some open-field land had been enclosed during the Middle Ages by agreement between strip owners or by the purchase and consolidation of strips by individual owners, or since the fifteenth century by the varied enclosures described in Chapter 6, section 1. Some of the land under arable cultivation in Britain in the eighteenth century was the fruit of earlier reclamation from woodland, marsh or sea, and this land was normally enclosed from the start. In addition to the arable land there were great tracts of rough pasture land, particularly in Wales, Scotland and many areas of northern England. A country dependent upon wood for house construction and shipbuilding and for industrial fuel must necessarily also have devoted much land to the growing of timber. Much good land was, in fact, given over to the systematic growing of timber, copses being planted and cut at between twelve and twenty years' growth for charcoal. There were also a great many tracts of waste land amongst the arable areas.

Very little of this land was owned by the people who farmed it. During the century before 1700 there was a marked trend towards the concentration of the ownership of land. In the more settled times after the Civil War land was one of the safest investments, and many of those who made fortunes in trade, industry and politics bought landed estates. Probably little more than ten per cent of the land remained in the possession of owner-occupiers (freeholders farming their own land). Many of these holdings ranged from 30 to 300 acres, though there were some freeholders with smaller holdings — sometimes too small to be economically practicable, forcing the freeholder to supplement the produce of his holding by wage labour. The number of medium-sized freeholders (*yeomen*) had been much reduced in the century before 1700.

In the middle of the eighteenth century there was a wide range of tenant farmers, most of whom held their land by leasehold (an agreement between landlord and tenant to rent land for a fixed number of years for a fixed money rent). There were some large tenant farmers leasing farms of several hundred acres, but the average tenancy was of some 25–100 acres. At the lower end of the scale were landless labourers and cottagers with tenant holdings too small to provide a living in themselves. Some of these, in the open-field areas, retained rights of grazing in the common land; others, without any legal rights, were, by common consent of the other farmers, permitted to put a few cattle on the common.

Both open-field and enclosed areas concentrated on grain growing. Wheat, barley and oats, providing food and drink for man and fodder for animals, were the staple crops. There was as yet little field cultivation of vegetables, though the potato, turnip and mangel had already been introduced. The open-field system of farming was a mixed one, and catered normally for cows, horses for farm work, pigs, sheep and all varieties of poultry. Outside the open-field districts there were some areas of specialized farming. The higher districts of Leicestershire, the Cotswolds, Pennines and Wales concentrated on sheep farming, mainly for the wool; around London there was some specialization in market gardening, milk production and the fattening of cattle reared in Scotland and Wales and driven in great herds along the drove routes to the metropolis.

2. OPEN-FIELD FARMING IN THE EIGHTEENTH CENTURY

Open-field farming had limitations — limitations that ultimately became so pronounced that the system was discarded entirely. Today, only the village of Laxton in Nottinghamshire retains the system, at the request of the Ministry of Agriculture, as a living museum of the country's agrarian past.

The most serious objection to the system was its inflexibility. It stood in the way of innovations to agricultural techniques.

The times of sowing, of harvesting and of ploughing, even the choice of the crops themselves depended on majority decisions of the manorial courts, and new crops were hard to introduce. The system, originating almost a thousand years before, was devised to ensure livelihoods for all members of the communities. In protecting the weak, it inevitably hampered the strong and enterprising. Secondly, the dispersal of strips over the open-fields to give an equal share of good and bad land to all involved each farmer in an immense waste of time in going from one part of his farm to another. This limited the area of land a man could farm, reduced the product of his labour, and tied him to a lower standard of living. Thirdly, the absence of any physical division between strips (the boundaries were marked by posts, double furrows, or simply minutely remembered by the older farmers of the village) meant that the farmer who cared for his strip suffered from his neighbour who did not, for weeds spread rapidly regardless of man-made boundaries. Fourthly, the fact that all the cattle shared the grazing on the common meant that it was impossible to experiment or benefit from other people's experiments with the breeding of improved cattle. Selective breeding was only possible if herds were kept separate. Furthermore, the intermixing of cattle on the common guaranteed the maximum infection from disease; only by isolation can the ravages of cattle disease be checked. Fifthly, the use of three- or four-course crop rotation left one field in three or four fallow (idle) each year. This was a wasteful method of farming. Finally, the normal crop rotations in the open-field made little provision for winter feed for cattle. Hay from the meadow was generally so inadequate that a proportion of cattle had always to be killed off at the beginning of each winter and salted down for human consumption. The beasts kept over the winter were inevitably so short of food by the time the spring grass began to grow again on the common that they were undersized and gave poor yields of milk or wool.

The limitations of open-field farming described in the previous paragraph are generalizations which were not necessarily true of every individual open-field village. The system, though inflexible, was not wholly resistant to change, and in many villages by the early eighteenth century modifications to the traditional pattern had crept in. Whole furlongs, for example, were withdrawn from the customary rotation and laid down to grass. Exchange of strips by individuals had produced compact holdings in the open fields, which were also withdrawn from the common system.

Open-field farming had much to commend it when population was small and growing slowly. But when population began to grow more rapidly the demand for ever-increasing supplies of foodstuffs put a pressure on agriculture which made it imperative that more productive methods be adopted. This pressure was transmitted to the farmer through the price mechanism. Rising prices encouraged investment in enclosures and made arable farming in particular commercially attractive on land which could not hitherto have been cultivated profitably. Wheat, which had averaged 30s. a quarter in the 1730's and 1740's, sold for over 50s. on the average in the 1780's. The price of malt rose in the same way from 3s. 6d. a bushel in the 1720's to 5s. in the 1790's. The long war between 1793 and 1815 intensified this trend. Few countries in the world had much surplus agricultural produce to export, nor were Britain's exports of manufactures on a sufficiently large scale to make possible a greatly increased import of foodstuffs. For most of the eighteenth century Britain was to be dependent upon her own resources for foodstuffs, and in securing the greater harvests the old system was largely swept away.

3. New Farming Techniques

The impulse to enclose the open-field land of Britain in the second half of the eighteenth century and later came from the existence of new crops and new rotations, all of which had been tried and proved to be successful, making it possible to dispense with the fallow year. The problems of increasing agricultural productivity by providing more winter feed for the cattle and eliminating the wasteful fallow year could both be solved by the introduction of root crops. These served the dual purpose of resting the soil from the exhausting grain crops, and of feeding cattle in winter.

Peas and beans, grown as a field crop, were known in the Middle Ages and were quite commonly used in the sixteenth century, particularly in Lincolnshire, as winter feed for cattle to supplement limited supplies of hay. Turnips had been grown on the Continent early in the seventeenth century and are known to have been planted by enterprising farmers in this country from the middle of the seventeenth century. Sir Richard Weston (1591–1672), a Royalist who had taken refuge in Holland during the Cromwellian Protectorate, returned to England at the Restoration of 1660 and developed on his own estates a four-course rotation using turnips and clover and eliminating the fallow year. Andrew Yarranton, an enterprising landowner in the Midlands, introduced the use of clover to his county of Worcestershire in the 1670's. Potatoes, a native crop of the Andean Highlands of South America, were brought to this country as an exotic luxury in the early seventeenth century, and were being grown on a small scale in Lancashire in the late seventeenth century. In Norfolk, Robert Walpole senior (1650–1700), father of the great statesman of the same name, cultivated the turnip and clover extensively on his estate at Houghton from the 1670's onwards. He and other Norfolk farmers developed the *Norfolk four-course rotation* of turnips, barley, clover and wheat, later popularized by Lord Townshend (1674–1738), which successfully eliminated the wasteful fallow year.

Valuable experimental work was accomplished by Robert Bakewell (1725–95) who farmed an estate at Dishley in Leicestershire and specialized in the breeding of sheep and cattle. By the careful selection of the finest existing types of cattle as a basis for his experiments, he paved the way for modern breeding. In breeding both sheep and cows, Bakewell aimed specifically at producing high quality wool, milk or meat. As a result of the efforts of Bakewell and his imitators there began a steady and impressive improvement in the quality of cattle sold on Smithfield market in London.

There were many progressive farmers in the seventeenth and eighteenth centuries who were anxious to raise their incomes by the practical application of the most profitable methods of farming. They were, however, the exceptions, and it needed more widespread experience and propaganda work before the advantages of the new crops and rotations could be widely recognized. Progress on a national scale must inevitably have been slow. Much useful instruction was achieved by estate-owners like the Cokes of Norfolk who sought to teach by example their tenants and neighbours. The Coke family had farmed their estates at Holkham on the sandy coastal area of Norfolk since the early seventeenth century. The best known of the family was Thomas Coke (1750–1842), but in many ways he was simply carrying on with the good work of his father and grandfather. Like other progressive landlords of the eighteenth century, the Cokes sought to increase the rentals of their estates by exercising close control over the farming methods of their tenants. Under the terms of their leases, the Cokes' tenants were obliged to adopt crop rotations adapted carefully to the needs of the particular soils of their farms. The quantity of seeds to be used in sowing grass and clover were stipulated, while hoeing of turnips and the manuring of land were further conditions. Tenants were strictly forbidden to grow grain crops on the same soil in successive years. The annual sheep-shearing provided occasions for the spreading of sound and well-tried ideas by the Cokes amongst their tenant farmers; prizes were given for the best efforts in the various departments of farming, so that these meetings acquired something of the nature of private agricultural shows. The Cokes always returned a steady proportion of their rents to the land in the form of investment in improvements. As a result, the income from their estate rose steadily from about £6,000 in 1718 to £9,000 in 1748, £12,000 in 1776, and £25,000 in 1816.

The Cokes were not alone in their systematic development of farming techniques over extensive estates, but they were still the exception rather than the rule. Their importance lay in demonstrating the advantages of new methods from the point of view of both yields of foodstuffs per acre of land and of profitability to farmers and landowners. Even late in the eighteenth century the need was still for more publicity for the improved farming methods. Towards the end of the century this need began to be met by the diverse activities of Arthur Young, an unsuccessful farmer turned writer. Young travelled extensively in England and on the Continent from 1767 onwards, and was extremely observant and diligent in noting improvements wherever he saw them. He undertook the advocacy of improved farming. From 1784 onwards he edited a journal, *The Annals of Agriculture*, to which even the king,

George III, himself an enthusiastic farmer on his home farm at Windsor, contributed. With the help of a Scotsman, Sir John Sinclair, Young secured the creation of a government commission, the *Board of Agriculture*, of which he became the first secretary. With Sinclair he planned a series of surveys of every county in England and Scotland, writing many of them himself. A keen advocate of enclosures, he was nevertheless acutely aware of the social implications of sudden upheaval in established institutions.

Throughout the seventeenth and eighteenth centuries agricultural reformers observed, experimented, exhorted the less enterprising, and reaped their harvest of rents and profits. For a long time their success was limited, largely because the open-field system, still operating over more than half the arable land of Britain, made the adoption of the new methods, if not impossible, at least extremely slow and difficult. The enclosure movement, by sweeping away these hindrances to agricultural progress, made possible the increases of food production without which the rapidly growing population of the later eighteenth and early nineteenth centuries could not have been fed. It is to this movement, by which not only the physical appearance of great areas of the British landscape was materially altered, but a way of life that had satisfied village communities for many centuries was swept away, that we must now turn.

4. ENCLOSURES

Enclosure means the consolidation of scattered holdings of arable land and common rights into a single compact area of land, fenced or hedged so that each new holding, equal to the total area of the former scattered strips plus some of the common, is separated from its neighbours. It has already been suggested that the need for enclosures in eighteenth-century Britain was in order to improve arable farming by more intensive cultivation. This type of enclosure, however, was but one aspect of the movement. Most open-field villages included a certain amount of common pasture and waste or woodland, and the enclosure of these lands involved rather different problems from that of the arable fields. Once enclosed, the separate farms could employ their land in whatever way they chose. One of the great advantages of enclosure was that it permitted a degree of specialization previously impossible.

Enclosure of the open fields was no new thing in the eighteenth century. Where there was but a single landowner in an open-field village, providing the legal agreements with his tenants permitted, he could enforce enclosure. More frequently, however, the existence of some smaller freeholders or lease-holders made it difficult, if not impossible, for the major land-owner to use this method for enclosure. It was possible to secure voluntary agreement between all the landowners concerned. Enclosures of this kind were made from time to time from the late middle ages to the eighteenth century. But in the majority of cases it was necessary to coerce at least a small minority whose possible losses from enclosure determined their opposition to the change.

To overcome opposition of this kind it was necessary to secure a private act of Parliament; for this Parliament had to be petitioned by a majority of the landowners (by acreage) of the area it was desired to enclose. For a petition to be acceptable, those signing had to represent at least three-quarters of the land to be enclosed. Those opposing the enclosure were entitled to submit a counter-petition, though they rarely did so. There was seldom any difficulty in securing the passage of an act once sufficient local support for the enclosure had been obtained. The act appointed *commissioners* who were empowered to make an award, that is to re-distribute the land fairly in separate parcels. The commissioners, usually three, five or seven in number, were normally experienced local land agents or surveyors. Their first task was to have the land surveyed in order to ascertain exactly what land and common rights each claimant to a share of the enclosure possessed. (Common rights included the right to graze so many cattle on the common, the right to cut turf for burning, and the right to cut or gather firewood.) On the basis of the survey, the commissioners made their *award*, by which they allocated separate holdings of land to each claimant in proportion to their previous holding of arable land and common rights. (The commissioners' awards and maps, incidentally, provide a most valuable and interesting source of local history.) Provision was made for new roads, where necessary, to give access to detached farms.

Enclosure of the open fields at Almington, Warwickshire

above: The medieval furlongs are crossed by the hedges of the new
fields laid out at the enclosure of 1778.
below: The surveyor's sketch for new roads and hedges

Enclosure was expensive. The cost of securing the parliamentary permission fell on the landowners. This involved heavy legal fees as well as the expenses and fees of the commissioners and their surveyors. The cost of new roads had to be met, too. These costs of enclosures varied from place to place, from 5s. per acre to £5 per acre. The average was about 25s. per acre. But these costs were only the beginning. If a farmer, whether freeholder or tenant, wished to make the most of his newly-enclosed holding, there were many other calls for capital. There were fences to be erected or hedges to be set immediately; in all probability it would be necessary to build at least barns and sheds on the new enclosure, if not a farmhouse; and there would be expenditure on new stock, seeds and equipment.

There were a few enclosure acts in the first half of the eighteenth century, but enclosure by private act really got under way in the second half of the century. Between 1730 and 1740 there were 38 acts; between 1740 and 1750, 156 acts. In the next decade there were 480, and thereafter the numbers grew in each decade until the end of the century. In 1801, a *General Enclosure Act* simplified the procedure, standardizing certain clauses of the acts, thereby reducing the cost. Enclosures continued at a high rate in the early nineteenth century, diminishing only as the remaining open-fields and commons disappeared. An act of 1845 further facilitated enclosures by grouping them in a single act each year. By the end of the first quarter of the nineteenth century most of the open-field arable land was enclosed, and the majority of the enclosures of the nineteenth century were of common and waste land. The high prices of corn during the period when the French Wars (1793–1815) reduced the imports of grain had encouraged farmers and landowners to go ahead fast with their enclosures. Common and waste lands were frequently enclosed at different times from the arable land. For these lands the pressure to enclose was not so great and their enclosure continued until well after the middle of the nineteenth century.

5. The Results of Enclosures

The first effect of enclosure was an appreciable increase in the output of agricultural produce; and if the production of foodstuffs was increasing, then not only was the country as a whole profiting from enclosure but also the producer or landowner must have benefited. Because nearly all enclosures were initiated by landowners, there can be little doubt that landowners as a class benefited from the change in the shape of increased rents; rent is very closely related to the productivity of the land. Nor is it unreasonable to assume that the larger freehold and tenant farmers benefited from enclosure. With their more ample resources they were fully able to take advantage of the new possibilities. Moreover they, too, had often taken a leading part in initiating enclosures. But below the landowners and large farmers there was a very wide range of freehold and tenant farmers, and the effects of enclosures upon the fortunes of these classes have been much disputed.

Enclosures, for example, have been blamed for the decline of the yeomen (the owner-occupiers of medium-sized holdings). In the early nineteenth century there were fewer medium-sized holdings of arable farmland than there had been in the middle of the eighteenth century, and the ownership of land had become concentrated in fewer hands. It is doubtful, however, whether enclosure was responsible for this trend. In fact the number of small owner-occupiers had diminished noticeably during the century before 1750. Moreover the fact that some of the larger holdings had increased in size after 1750 should not be allowed to obscure the parallel increase in the number of very small holdings in the country. This may be explained by the steady growth of the arable acreage in the country, particularly during the French Wars of 1793–1815, and by the grant of small holdings during enclosures in place of former common rights.

If, then, landowners, larger farmers (whether freeholders or tenants), and medium freeholders (yeomen) mostly benefited from enclosure, or at least did not suffer, what justification is there for the view that enclosure produced a great deal of hardship? Though the expense of enclosure was roughly proportionate to the area of land allotted to each individual, smaller farmers, whether tenant or freehold, were less able to bear the cost, whilst those with the smallest holdings were sometimes obliged to sell part or all of their holding to pay for their share of the cost. Moreover the smaller farmers were less likely

be able to borrow money to meet their obligations. The
advantages of enclosure were less easily obtained from small
than from large farms, for the small farmers lacked the resources
to replace the implements and draught animals that had been
provided communally in the open-field communities. However,
some of those who sold their land for this reason continued to
farm in the same parish as tenants of one of the larger landowners. Most of the complaints against enclosures arose from
the enclosure of the commons. The ability to put one or two
cows, a few sheep, some geese or ducks on the common provided many of the poorer sections of the rural population with
the means of converting the earnings from an acre or two of
land, or a few days' work for a larger farmer each week, into a
modest livelihood. But the arable land, equivalent to the right
to graze beasts on the common, was not easily calculated and
was likely to be very small.

Moreover, many of the poorer classes had difficulty in proving their rights to the use of the common. Some clearly had no
legal rights at all. They were *squatters*, that is, people whose use
of the commons had simply been tolerated by others, but never
legally acknowledged. How were the commissioners to treat
these people when making their awards? Where rights existed
and could be proved, an allotment of enclosed land was made,
but all too frequently even the small proportion of the communal costs of enclosure was greater than this poorer class
could stand, and the inevitable result was for the small man to
sell out. Enclosure may, therefore, have turned the very small
tenant farmer into a landless labourer. Where no legal rights of
common could be proved, commissioners usually compensated
the squatter if he could claim more than twenty years' occupation. If less than twenty years, recognition and compensation
were not given. It is therefore almost certainly true that enclosure increased the number of landless labourers in the
countryside.

Whatever changes took place in the social structure of rural
England during the century of parliamentary enclosures (1750–
1850), it must be borne in mind that other factors were at work
at the same time which may, in fact, have been of equal or even
more importance. Firstly, population was growing rapidly.
Thus there was bound to be a certain redundancy of population

in agricultural districts whether enclosures took place or not. In most areas enclosure resulted in an increase in employment; because of the fast growth of population it was possible for this to occur and still leave a surplus of population to migrate to the growing towns. None of the counties of England showed a decline in population between 1801 and 1851. Where there was evidence of depopulation, this was most frequently the outcome of declining rural industries — ironmaking in the Weald, or cloth-making in the south-west and East Anglia. Secondly, after 1795 the Speenhamland system of poor relief (see Chapter 14, section 3) was adopted in many rural parishes, particularly in southern England. It was believed at the time that the system encouraged large families, and a modern writer has claimed that 'it led to an over-population of the agricultural villages'. In more ways than one the system of poor relief operating until 1834 debased rather than alleviated the condition of the agricultural worker, and some of the rural distress of the early nineteenth century must be attributed to this cause rather than to the enclosure movement. Thirdly, the country was at war with France almost continuously for twenty-two years (1793–1815). During the war prices rose sharply, and to add to the resulting hardship, taxation increased, and the prices of some commodities, particularly grain and bread, fluctuated severely.

There was certainly much distress amongst the poorer classes in the agricultural areas during the period 1790–1830, but it is clear that many influences were at work, of which enclosure was only one.

CHAPTER 12

WAR AND TRADE: 1793–1815

1. OVERSEAS TRADE: 1700–1815

Since the early Middle Ages Britain's export trade had een mainly concerned with wool. At first raw wool had been xported to the Continental cloth manufacturers. Later, in the fteenth and sixteenth centuries, as the manufacture of woollen loth in this country grew in importance, the export of cloth eplaced that of raw wool. Through a group of powerful rading companies, each based on monopoly trading rights in various parts of the world, this overseas trade in woollen cloth vas considerably expanded in the sixteenth and seventeenth enturies. The geographical discoveries of the sixteenth century and the resulting colonization of the seventeenth century xpanded the markets available to British exporters. The onditions that had produced the great trading companies in the ixteenth and seventeenth centuries, however, very largely eased to operate in the eighteenth century, and one by one the ompanies ceased to exercise control over the trade. By the middle of the eighteenth century, only one — the greatest of hem all, the East India Company — remained as an active orce in foreign trade. Elsewhere, overseas trade was largely in he hands of private merchants.

Britain's principal commodity of trade remained woollen cloth, and this accounted for possibly half of the value of all the exports. There was also a slowly rising export trade in coal, hough the high cost of transport restricted this trade to the nearer markets, Ireland and Holland between them taking the bulk of the total export. Small quantities of lead, tin, copper and ironware were exported, and there was a fluctuating trade n grain stimulated by the *corn bounty*, a government subsidy on exports to encourage corn production.

As in more recent times, the greater part of the imports at the beginning of the century was made up of foodstuffs and raw materials. From the New World came tobacco, rice, sugar, rum and timber. The lucrative East India trade brought spices, textiles and tea to this country. Raw-material imports came mainly from northern Europe — pitch, tar, hemp and timber for the navy from the Baltic countries, and bar iron from Sweden and Russia. The limited imports of manufactured goods comprised, surprisingly enough, mainly textiles — linens from Germany and Holland, silk and calico from the East India Company. (The *East Indies* in the eighteenth century meant the whole of the trading area of the East India Company — India, China and the East Indian islands.)

A very important aspect of overseas trade in the eighteenth century was the re-export trade. This related to goods imported into this country only to be exported immediately without undergoing any process of manufacture. Government regulation of the seventeenth century had aimed to increase the profits of English merchants by requiring that all enumerated commodities (see Chapter 7, section 3) shipped from the colonies must be imported first into England. In some trades — the East India Company's and that from the North American colonies — a high proportion of the goods shipped was destined ultimately for European markets outside Britain. Nevertheless, the *Navigation Laws* channelled these trades into English and (after the Union of 1707) Scottish ports. Sugar and tobacco from the New World and tea from the East formed the basis of the re-export trade. In 1724, for example, 75% of the four million lbs. of tobacco brought to Clyde ports was re-exported.

Amongst the markets for British exports in the early eighteenth century, the nearest ranked highest. Holland alone took one-third of all exports in the first ten years of the century, though many of Holland's imports were re-exported into her European hinterland up the Rhine and Meuse valleys. Germany, Portugal and Spain were the next most important markets. The exports to Portugal alone exceeded the total of exports to all the colonies in the New World. The remaining European countries were regular markets for British exporters, but apart from Ireland, Russia and the eastern Mediterranean countries, none of these was of any great importance. The East India Company's exports to the Far East represented only a fraction of their return cargoes in value, and a very small percentage of the total exports from this country.

The largest single source of imports was the East India Company. It was difficult to find a market in the East for Britain's major exports of woollen cloth and metals, and most of the Company's imports were paid for in bullion. Early in the eighteenth century imports from the New World were of slight importance, and the bulk of the trade came from European sources — Germany, Holland, Turkey and Sweden being the most important. In the first half of the eighteenth century about half of Britain's imports came from the Continent of Europe.

Early in the eighteenth century trade was expanding slowly. During the period between 1740 and 1783 there were many wars interrupting not merely European commerce, but also trade in America and India. The *Seven Years' War* (1756–63) led to the exclusion of France from India and added Canada to the British Empire. It is not surprising then, that, in spite of these interruptions to trade, British overseas trade continued to expand. In the first year of peace after the *American War of Independence* (1775–83) exports valued at £14 million were rather more than twice as great as they had been at the beginning of the century. After 1784, the expansion of trade was very rapid. From £14 million, exports grew to £19 million in 1790, and by the end of the century exceeded £40 million. The value of imports grew similarly.

These enormous changes in the value of exports and imports altered the balance between the different trading areas. The trade with Holland diminished in relative importance as the century wore on, while in the Mediterranean the French were successful in capturing much of the trade from Britain. The largest expansion in exports was to the mainland of North America, where, in spite of the fact that the colonies had just broken away from their allegiance to Britain, trade increased enormously. From an annual average of about £2 million between 1784 and 1788, exports to the United States rose to £7 million by 1798.

There were, similarly, many changes in the nature of the goods imported and exported as a result of the big expansion in trade in the last twenty years of the century. One effect of the growth of population and of industrialization was to make the country no longer self-supporting in food. Whereas in the first half of the century there had normally been a wheat surplus for export, by the end of the century imports exceeded exports by some seven million quarters. The vast increase of exports consisted almost entirely of manufactured goods — textiles, metalware and pottery. Of the textiles, woollen cloth showed a steady increase, and exports were valued at over £8 million in 1800. Starting from very small beginnings, cotton cloth exports grew rapidly, but did not overtake woollens until 1802. To supply the growing industries, and to feed the rapidly expanding population, imports of raw materials and foodstuffs were needed in ever-increasing quantities. At the beginning of the century such relatively small quantities of raw cotton as were required came mainly from the Levant and the West Indian Islands. By the end of the century its cultivation had spread to the American mainland which now supplied the bulk of British requirements. Changing tastes in drink led to an enormous growth in the amount of tea and coffee imported.

A well-known feature of British trade in the eighteenth century was the triangular trade route by means of which slaves from West Africa were taken to the plantations of the West Indies and American mainland. The prosperity of the west coast ports of Glasgow, Liverpool and Bristol was partly based on the profits of this trade. British manufactures, mainly cotton goods and small metal wares, were sent to West Africa, where they were bartered for slaves to be shipped to the plantations across the Atlantic. Most of the negroes were the victims of tribal warfare or of native slave-dealers in Africa. The sales of slaves helped to finance Britain's imports of West Indian sugar. The slave trade was one of high risks, and while some Bristol and Liverpool merchants made fortunes, others failed. It is not easy to distinguish the profits of slave-trading from those of the other less objectionable trades which were associated with it. Nevertheless, the triangular route was largely the means by which Bristol and Liverpool developed rapidly in the eighteenth century.

2. Britain and the French Revolution

In the last chapter it was shown that hardships and discontent in rural areas in the late eighteenth and early nineteenth centuries could not be explained solely in terms of the changes in farming methods. The wars against France, lasting for over twenty years, would have disturbed the normal functioning of the economy even had there been no other changes taking place at the same time; but as they coincided with a period when both industry and agriculture were being transformed it is not surprising that the effects of these wars on events in Britain were considerable.

The France that Britain fought after 1793 was not the France of earlier periods. The French Revolution, by deposing and guillotining the king, and by its crusading zeal for popular republicanism, stirred up ideas and aspirations in the hearts and minds of people in other countries. Britain was strongly affected by this wave of revolutionary enthusiasm, and it is not surprising that the seeds of revolution should have found fertile soil in the unstable conditions of that period.

The effects of the wars against revolutionary and Napoleonic France were twofold. They created conditions under which the normal functioning of the economy was impossible, lasting so long that some of the wartime changes became permanently engrafted into the economic structure of the country. Secondly, they stirred up a dissatisfaction with the existing forms of government which, after many years of acute social unrest and in spite of determined repression by successive governments, ultimately led to important changes in the relations between different social groups — between the government and the governed, between employer and employee, even between men and women.

In Britain, two distinct phases in the repercussions of the French Revolution may be noticed. The first, immediately after the outbreak of the Revolution in 1789, of enthusiasm and support; the second, particularly after the execution of the French king and queen, Louis XVI and Marie Antoinette, in 1793, of revulsion amongst the upper classes, and growing determination amongst the lower classes to go at least part of the way with the revolutionaries and extend the narrow limits of political power in Britain. For some years before the outbreak of the Revolution there had been a powerful movement working for the reform of Parliament in Britain. Neither in county nor borough did the working classes, or even the middle classes, have a vote in parliamentary elections, whilst the majority of members of parliament represented small boroughs in southern England, leaving the newer industrial towns without separate representation. The younger Pitt had tried to introduce a mild measure of reform in 1785, but his bill was rejected. The movement can scarcely be said to have achieved working-class popularity and support until the French Revolution demonstrated for all the impermanence of even the most apparently permanent of institutions, and until in 1792 Thomas Paine published his *Rights of Man*, a book in which he asserted that the hereditary government by King and Lords was 'an imposition on mankind', and that only completely representative government was just. His book was widely read and achieved immense influence amongst the working classes.

The *September Massacres* (1792), during which the revolutionary government in France massacred enormous numbers of political prisoners, and the execution of the French king in January, 1793, decisively turned opinion in British governing circles against the Revolution and against reform in Britain. Burke's *Reflections on the Revolution in France* of 1790, as reactionary as Paine's book was revolutionary, had an important influence within the governing classes. Amongst the working classes the desire for reform, powerfully stimulated by Paine, remained strong, and *Corresponding Societies* were formed in the 1790's to promote the interchange of ideas between French and British reformers. The crusading zeal of the revolutionary government in France after 1792, offering to liberate oppressed classes everywhere, effectively swung the British government against democratic reform, and after the outbreak of war in 1793 a systematic policy of repression was adopted.

The government's attack on the reformers was facilitated by the fact that the reformers' enthusiasm for the French revolutionaries made them unenthusiastic in their support of the war against France. Under the guise of wartime security, the government therefore prosecuted editors of reforming journals and indeed anyone who ventured publicly to criticize the existing system of government. In 1794 a charge of high treason was brought against Thomas Hardy, a London shoemaker, and founder of the London Corresponding Society. Fortunately Hardy and other equally respectable citizens were acquitted by the jury. But the government suppressed the Corresponding societies by its *Seditious Libels Act* of 1795, and more than once suspended *Habeas Corpus*, the traditional British safeguard against arbitrary imprisonment. Finally, in 1799 and 1800, Pitt's government endeavoured to suppress trade unionism by the *Anti-Combination Acts*.

3. ECONOMIC EFFECTS OF THE FRENCH WAR

The war affected the economy in two ways — through the direct effort of sustaining a long war on sea and land in many parts of the world, and indirectly through the dislocation of normal economic activities.

The war involved operations on a larger scale than had been known before. By its end in 1815 there were nearly half a million men under arms, about two-thirds of them in the army. During the course of the war Britain allied herself with a number of different countries, many of them unable to bear the expense of a long war by themselves. An important part of Britain's contribution to Europe's struggle against France was the financing of these allies by substantial loans. Between 1792 and 1816, Britain sent £57 million to the aid of her allies. To raise this huge sum and to pay for the maintenance of the army and the navy, taxation naturally rose to a high level. In 1799, Pitt introduced a new tax, the income tax. This was immediately removed when the temporary peace was signed at Amiens in 1802. Renewed when war broke out again in 1803, it was an extremely unpopular tax, and when it was abolished in 1816 Parliament voted for the destruction of all records of it. Though disliked, the tax proved a most valuable contribution to the Exchequer, yielding £142 million in the ten years before 1816. Other taxes, of which the customs and excise were the most important, were also raised. It has been estimated that by the end of the war taxation took away one sixth of the total of everybody's incomes.

Taxation alone could not pay for the war. In fact only 35% of the additional expenditure required to finance the war was met by taxation. The rest was borrowed. Hoping that the war would be a short one, Pitt's policy at the outbreak of war was not to increase taxation severely, but to rely mainly on borrowing. When the war became prolonged, it was clear that borrowing was a short-sighted policy, and that the war must be paid for out of current income. When war broke out in 1793, the *national debt* (the money owed by the government to individuals, mostly in this country, who had lent it money) stood at £240 million. The interest alone on this debt consumed annually nearly £10 million, or about half the government's total annual expenditure. Borrowing during the war raised the total of the national debt to £900 million, and required annual interest payments of £32 million, more than half as much again as the total government expenditure at the beginning of the war.

The demand for the materials of war fortunately came at a time when industrial output was expanding. The developments in the iron and textile industries were of material value to the war effort. It can also be argued that the demand for war materials constituted an important part of the greatly increased demand for manufactured goods noticed in Chapter 10, section 1. It is certainly true that in the metal-working industries of the Midlands the demand for war goods accelerated the introduction of steam power. Perhaps more important, the remittance of the subsidies to Britain's allies was only made possible by a big increase in exports. It was this ability to provide these increased exports that constituted industry's most valuable contribution to the war.

Unable to conquer Britain militarily (after Trafalgar in 1805, Napoleon gave up the attempt to invade England), France turned to economic blockade. By the Milan and Berlin Decrees of 1806 and 1807, France closed the ports of the greater part of Europe to British shipping and British goods. More than half Britain's trade was still with Europe in the early nineteenth century, and the loss of markets was as serious as the cutting-off of sources of raw materials and foodstuffs. To some extent the rapidly growing trade with America, both North and South compensated for the loss. Moreover, Napoleon's *Continental System* of blockade was never completely effective. In 1808 Britain sent an army into Portugal and Spain, partly with a view to keeping open that important doorway for trade with southern Europe. Smuggling was pursued on a large scale, the island of Heligoland near the mouth of the river Elbe in northern Germany being used as a base for this activity.

The most important effect of the blockade was to cut Britain off from her main sources of imported food supplies. Of these, by far the most important was corn, coming from many ports of northern Europe. From about 1760 onwards, Britain's imports of corn had begun to exceed her spasmodic exports, and by the outbreak of war imports had come to make a significant proportion of her total corn consumption. The loss of these imports seriously affected the nation's food supplies. Once again, the developments in agriculture — enclosures and improved techniques — materially increased the output of food at home. Nevertheless, the price of corn rose, and in years of deficient harvest at home, price levels were two or even three times as high as in pre-war years. The high prices encouraged farmers to concentrate more and more on grain production. The enclosure of much waste land was undertaken and every resource was utilized to increase the yield of corn per acre. It was estimated that the output of all crops was increased by 50% during the war years, most of this increase being due to higher yields. Agriculture prospered, high profits being made. Much of this profit was returned to the land in the form of investment in enclosure, new equipment, better stock and seeds, drainage and fertilizers. Inevitably, some of the advantage of higher prices was passed on to the landowners in the form of higher rents. Leases taken out in the later years of the war were for high rents. When prices fell dramatically at the end of the war under the combined effect of bumper harvests and renewed imports, the burden of these high rents reduced many farmers to bankruptcy.

4. CURRENCY AND INFLATION

Much of the hardship suffered by different sections of the population in the generation following the outbreak of war in 1793 is attributable to the rise in prices which was a feature of the war period. This rise in prices is to be explained by the lowering of the value of money. Broadly speaking, the value of money, indicated by the general level of prices, is determined by the amount of money available at any point in time to be exchanged for a given quantity of goods. Throughout nearly the whole of the eighteenth century the country used gold and silver coinage supplemented by notes for denominations larger than the golden guineas. The paper money was, however, merely a convenience in place of bulkier and heavy coins, and it was understood that the banks were prepared at all times to exchange their notes for the true coin of the realm — gold. Notes were issued in London by the Bank of England, which had been established for very nearly one hundred years when war broke out, and in the provinces by smaller private banks, known collectively as the *country banks*. It follows that a bank had always to be prepared to supply gold on demand to holders of its notes, so that banks issuing notes for a much greater value than their reserves of gold ran risks which occasionally proved disastrous.

Unfortunately, at the same time gold served a second purpose, that of an internationally acceptable currency. One country would accept gold from another in payment of a debt owed to it. Similarly, gold could be used to buy imports at a time when export markets were declining; or it could be used to subsidize an ally in time of war. The last two points explain why from 1793 onwards there began a drain of gold out of Britain which within a few years had seriously reduced the reserves held by the Bank of England. To add to this foreign drain, events nearer at home in 1796 and 1797 were far from reassuring. An attempted invasion of Ireland by the French in 1796, though a failure, revealed the danger to which the country was exposed, and encouraged the Irish to break out in rebellion against their English rulers. Bad conditions in the navy caused mutinies in the fleets at Spithead and the Nore in 1797. In these disturbing circumstances it is not surprising that holders of intrinsically valueless notes should have felt more inclination than usual to exchange them for gold. The combined effect of the internal and external drains of gold was to cause the government in 1797 to suspend the gold payments for notes, making it no longer possible for holders of notes to demand gold in exchange for them. Fortunately, more than a century's experience of notes had accustomed the public to their use, and there was no immediate fall in their value. But the banks were freed from the restraints under which they had previously issued notes.

Inevitably, under the pressure of high taxation and expanding business in many spheres of the economy, the note issue was increased and, just as inevitably, notes of a given face value began to exchange for a smaller and smaller quantity of goods. Looked at from another angle, prices were rising — an *inflation* had been started. Once initiated, an inflation will maintain, if not increase, its own momentum.

By 1810, the depreciation (lowering in value) of the currency had proceeded far enough for the government to feel some concern, and a committee was appointed to consider the situation. This *Bullion Committee* assumed that the inflation was the effect of an excessive issue of paper money, and recommended that the government restore *cash payments*, or the exchange of notes for gold on demand. The fault lay not so much with the Bank of England, whose policy over note issue had been consistently cautious, but mainly with the country banks. Some of the latter were dangerously liberal with their note issues; but the main trouble lay in the increase in the number of note-issuing country banks — their number was trebled during the war years. The government, however, supported by the Bank of England, was unable to accept the recommendations of the Bullion Committee, and so the suspension continued. Not until 1819, when the war had been over for four years, was a further committee appointed to reconsider the question of the currency. This committee, of which Robert Peel, the future prime minister, was the chairman, recommended once again the resumption of cash payments. This time the government complied, and from 1821 onwards, a gradual resumption restored the currency to its pre-war purchasing power.

Had the rise in prices during the war been steady, the effect on wage-earners would not have been too serious, although there is always a tendency for wage rises, even when obtainable, to lag behind rises in prices. But price movements were, in fact, very erratic, wheat prices fluctuating most violently of all. The demand for bread remains remarkably constant, fluctuating very little in relation to changes in price levels. As a result, quite a small deficiency in the harvest can lead to a big rise in price. Normally a deficient harvest at home could be compensated by imports, but during the war years imports were severely restricted, and in no year did imports amount to more than 5 % of consumption. It may be claimed that years of high prices were offset by years of low prices, so that over the whole period, on the average, nobody suffered. But bread cannot be stored in a cheap year and consumed in a dear year. In years when wheat was scarce and bread dear, the wage-earner went short of the principal item in his diet. The excessive fluctuations of commodity prices, and particularly of food prices, during the war years caused much hardship.

There were many ways, therefore, in which the prolonged war affected the economy, and brought suffering to one or another section of the population. Yet the war was only one factor influencing living and working conditions in this period. Agricultural and industrial changes discussed in other chapters played their parts, as did the operation of the poor laws. Often it is impossible to distinguish between the different elements that produced the changes so often deplored at this time. A tendency initiated by, for example, enclosures, might well have been accelerated or magnified by the peculiar circumstances of the war. It is important to consider all the elements operating in such a period of rapid change.

CHAPTER 13

IDEAS AND SOCIAL MOVEMENTS

1. *Laissez-faire*

From the sixteenth to the early eighteenth century, the government had pursued a very active economic policy. Believing that it was the government's duty to encourage certain industries, to preserve the influence of the craft gilds and to take steps to protect the nation's mercantile marine, many charters had been granted and acts of Parliament passed in the hope of achieving these aims. Not all these attempts to influence the process of economic development were successful, for in some spheres the government lacked the means of ensuring that its orders were carried out. Nor were the measures necessarily wise, so that all too frequently the results of the government's policy were unsatisfactory. In Chapter 7 some aspects of this policy and its results were discussed.

From the middle years of the eighteenth century, the number of economists and statesmen who criticized this type of economic policy increased. Foremost amongst these critics, and most outspoken in his criticism of the old policy, was the Scottish economist, Adam Smith. His great book, *An Inquiry into the Nature and Causes of the Wealth of Nations*, was published in 1776. His first concern was to attack the whole nature of the economic policy of governments for the preceding 250 years, and he then went on to explain why he thought it was wiser for governments not to attempt to influence the direction of economic development. For a government to force industry or trade into unnatural channels by prohibitions on imports, monopolies of manufacture, or similar devices, was, in Adam Smith's eyes, to deny the people of a country the cheapest and best source of production. 'To give the monopoly of the home market', he wrote in *The Wealth of Nations*, 'to the producer of domestic industry, in any particular art or manufacture, is in some measure to direct private people in what manner they ought to employ their capitals, and must, in almost all cases, be either a useless or a hurtful regulation.' A country would make the best use of its resources if every individual was allowed to choose those occupations and ways in which to invest his capital which seemed to him most likely to be advantageous. 'Generally speaking', wrote another economist of this period, Jeremy Bentham, 'there is no one who knows what is for your interest so well as yourself — no one who is disposed with so much ardour and constancy to pursue it.' In pursuing his own economic gain, the individual, Smith said, 'is in this, as in many other cases, led by an invisible hand to promote an end which was no part of his intention.' That end was to maximize the country's wealth.

Not all these ideas were original. Some of them had been expressed by other writers long before 1776, but Adam Smith combined them into an intelligible and persuasive scheme, and because he expressed them in some of the best English written in the eighteenth century they were widely read and accepted. Later economists, notably Thomas Malthus, David Ricardo and James Mill, developed and expanded some of Smith's ideas.

Thus there appeared, in the later eighteenth century, an approach to economic affairs which has been called *laissez-faire* (an expression first used earlier in the century by a French economist). By *laissez-faire*, these economic writers of the late eighteenth and early nineteenth century meant the absence of direct attempts by the government to control and regulate the nature and direction of economic development. Those who advocated *laissez-faire* recognized, however, that there were still many spheres in which it would be necessary for the government to take action, and they made it clear that an important field of government action lay in protecting the weaker members of society and in providing certain services such as poor relief, public health services and education which private enterprise of its own was unlikely to offer. The immediate aims of the *laissez-faire* economists were the abolition or reduction of import and export duties, of monopolies, of the Navigation Acts, and of the whole system of colonial regulation.

Amongst the statesmen, Adam Smith's chief ideas found a ready listener in the younger William Pitt, Prime Minister from 1783 to 1801 and from 1804 to 1806. Pitt was anxious to remove some of the restrictions on trade. In the ten years available to him for this purpose between the end of the War of American Independence in 1783 and the outbreak of the long war against revolutionary France in 1793, he took steps in two directions to put these ideas into practice. The first was to modify the Navigation system to give certain colonial ports freedom to trade directly with foreign countries instead of only being permitted to ship their main products to England. The first act creating such *Free Ports* in the colonies dated from before Pitt's time, in 1766, but the free port system saw its major extension under Pitt. Pitt's second, and more important, contribution to the freeing of trade was his simplification and reduction of the *tariff* — the list of import and export duties — accomplished between 1784 and 1787. He was primarily concerned to reduce smuggling by which the government was robbed of substantial revenues. To this end, in 1784, he reduced the heavy duty on tea to $12\frac{1}{2}\%$, thus removing almost entirely the incentive to smugglers. With the same end in view he reorganized and tightened the collection of duties on wines and tobacco.

In other spheres of government action, the policy advocated by Adam Smith and his disciples made less progress. Adam Smith had been quite clear that freedom of individuals to choose what occupation they thought fit for their own labour and capital involved the government in certain definite obligations — 'the duty of protecting the society from the violence and invasion of other independent societies; secondly, the duty of protecting, as far as possible, every member of society from the injustice or oppression of every other member of it; and thirdly, the duty of erecting and maintaining certain public works and certain public institutions, which it can never be for the interest of any individual, or small number of individuals, to erect and maintain.' What Smith had in mind was the need for governments to ensure that no group of people should be able to wield a power to the disadvantage of other groups; he had in mind the evils of monopoly in trade and industry, as well as the unscrupulous exploitation of labour by grasping employers. He foresaw, too, the need for governments to provide education, sanitation, water supplies and other public health services. But in these matters Smith and a few others were voices crying in the wilderness. Governments tolerated associations of manufacturers, which were, in effect, monopolies, using their power to raise prices artificially or to urge the government to raise protective tariffs; and on the other hand, they suppressed associations of workmen — trade unions — with all the power at their disposal. Scarcely a year passed in the eighteenth century without an act of parliament forbidding the formation of trade unions in specific trades. Early attempts by Sir Robert Peel senior, the father of the great prime minister, and Robert Owen, in 1802 and 1819, to secure factory acts restricting the hours of employment of children in factories met with so much opposition that the measures finally passed were hopelessly ineffective.

2. RADICALS AND PHILANTHROPISTS

After Adam Smith, probably the two most influential thinkers and writers were Jeremy Bentham (1748–1832) and Robert Owen (1771–1858).

Bentham, a man with a legal training, had the advantage of an ample private income. This provided him with the leisure in which to reflect on the social problems of his day, and to write about them. He surrounded himself with a broad circle of friends, some of whom lived for long periods on his hospitality, and he made a number of extensive tours in Europe. As a result, he was sure of a wide audience for his views not only in this country but also in Europe. Bentham demanded that all government action in whatever field should be submitted to the test of whether it would tend to produce 'the greatest happiness of the greatest number'. This principle was known as *Utilitarianism*, because every act of government was judged by its utility in increasing human happiness.

The increase of human happiness was most likely to be achieved, he believed, by the pursuit of four aims of social policy — of establishing universal social security (that is to say, removing the fear of want which, at some period of their lives, hung over most of the lower classes in his day), guaranteeing freedom from starvation, taking every step available to governments to increase the flow of goods and services, and reducing inequalities of wealth. To achieve these ends he advocated that governments should assume responsibility for a much wider range of social services than then existed — his list of proposed government departments shows a remarkable correspondence to the range existing in the mid-twentieth century. To ensure that the government acted in the interest of those it governed, rather than merely of one section, he recommended universal suffrage. His detailed plans for the administration of social services have led one modern economist to call him 'the father of the modern civil service'.

Through his disciple, Edwin Chadwick, Bentham exercised considerable influence on the social reforms of the 1830's and 1840's. His importance lay, however, not so much in his direct influence on this or that particular reform, as in his propagation of the view that it was the role of governments to pursue a deliberate policy of increasing human happiness.

Robert Owen was much more a man of action. Born in 1771 in Newtown in Montgomeryshire, he was apprenticed at the age of ten to a draper in Stamford in Lincolnshire. At the age of seventeen he went to Manchester, where he again worked in a draper's shop, but in 1791, in partnership with John Jones, and with the aid of £100 capital borrowed from his brother, the youthful Robert opened a small mule-spinning factory in Bridge Street, Manchester. A year later, still only twenty years of age, in reply to an advertisement, he applied for and obtained the post of manager of a large spinning-mill in Manchester owned by John Drinkwater, with a salary of £300 per year. But Owen only remained in Drinkwater's service for three years, after which he went into partnership with David Dale, a wealthy Glasgow merchant who, when the War of American Independence had cut off the valuable Scottish trade in Virginia tobacco, turned from overseas trade to cotton manufacture. Owen took over the management of Dale's large new cotton factory at New Lanark in upper Clydesdale in 1800. Here it was that he conducted his experiments in social and industrial organization by which his name became known all over the world.

Owen was alarmed at the extent of crime and lack of education among the working classes of his day, and attributed this to the bad living and working conditions of these people. He did not oppose the factory system of industry, though he acknowledged that this was often responsible for the bad conditions. Where Owen differed from many other employers of factory labour was in believing that it was possible to run a factory on humane lines and still make a profit. For he believed that the worker's surroundings — his working and living conditions, his hours of work, his enjoyment of leisure — shaped his character. Perhaps Owen placed too much faith in the ability of environment to mould human character, but in the unsavoury conditions of the working classes of this period, he could do nothing but good in applying his principles. Thus he set about making New Lanark into a model factory, where workers' homes were comfortable and hygienic, hours of work were short enough to allow some leisure, where no children under the age of ten were set to work, and where education was provided for all children from the age of two upwards. Many of his methods of education, such as his encouragement of play and movement, were far in advance of his time, and have only quite recently become commonly accepted as essential to the education of infants.

Owen's factory at New Lanark soon became an object of wonder and admiration, visitors coming from far and wide to inspect the unusual community of happy people working under humane conditions. Owen was anxious that his experiment should succeed, not merely for its own sake, but because he regarded it as a pilot scheme to point the way to later developments in industrial organization in all spheres of the country's industry. From the early years of the nineteenth century, therefore, finding that other mill-owners were not voluntarily imitating his methods, he turned his attention to the law as a means of compelling employers to improve working conditions. Joining forces with another great factory-owner, Sir Robert Peel senior, he initiated the *factory reform movement*. For many years the efforts of Peel and Owen achieved very poor results (factory legislation is dealt with in more detail in section 4 of this chapter and in Chapter 22, section 4), and long before success was finally won in the 1830's and '40's, Owen had turned to other ways of achieving his social aims.

There were two other avenues of social reform explored by Robert Owen. After the failure of his efforts to secure factory reform, he turned to the trade union movement after its legalization by the repeal of the Anti-Combination Laws in

1824. Realizing that the initiative for improving working conditions was no longer likely to come from the employers, he threw his tremendous energy and influence into promoting a nationwide organization of workers, which, by using the general strike, or *national holiday*, as he called it, would be able to secure compliance with its aims. Owen's Grand National Consolidated Trade Union of 1834 is referred to more fully in Chapter 20, section 4, where the reasons for its failure are discussed. Realizing, perhaps, that he had been trying to make the trade union movement run before it could walk, Owen finally turned his attention to yet another medium of social advancement — his *model communities*. During the 1820's he had experimented with the creation of *Villages of Unity and Co-operation* — communities of workers organized on communistic principles. In these villages, workers contributed skilled labour according to their varied abilities, and shared the produce of their common labour equitably between them. The purchase of land and the erection of houses and other buildings for these communities both in Britain and America was a costly business, but Owen willingly allowed these experiments to drain away his own vast fortune, built up in his earlier days in the cotton industry. Some of his model co-operative villages enjoyed a brief few years of existence; others were failures from the start. They could hardly succeed in an age when the scale of both industry and agriculture was growing, for the effect of trying to return to a medieval type of almost self-sufficient community revolving mainly around agriculture was almost certain to involve a reduction, rather than an improvement, in standards of living.

While Bentham and Owen were undoubtedly the greatest figures in the field of social theory in the first generation of the nineteenth century, there were several other important and influential reformers. The best-known and best-loved, of course, was William Wilberforce, who inspired and led the *Anti-Slavery Movement*. Wilberforce (1759–1833) devoted half a lifetime to the cause of freedom for the slaves in the British Empire, being assisted in this work by Thomas Clarkson and Zachary Macaulay, father of the great historian. Almost as well known was Elizabeth Fry (1780–1845), daughter of a Norfolk Quaker, who devoted her life to the improvement of conditions in English prisons.

William Cobbett (1763–1835) set out to influence a rather different type of audience. The working classes — and particularly the rural working classes — to whom he appealed possessed no direct influence on Parliament, and Cobbett, unlike Bentham or Owen, had accordingly little direct influence on the course of history. Nevertheless his popular writings played a vital role in stirring the under-privileged classes from their lethargy.

The prime of Cobbett's life was passed during the French Wars, and it was natural therefore that he should have concerned himself primarily with social evils arising out of war. Though he was a profuse writer of pamphlets, the principal medium of his propaganda was his weekly *Political Register*, first published in 1802 and continued until his death. To avoid the high newspaper tax which threatened to put his *Register* beyond the pockets of working-class readers, in 1816 Cobbett produced the *Register* in the form of a pamphlet, priced twopence. Though the *Register* soon became known as Cobbett's *Twopenny Trash*, it enjoyed a circulation far in excess of any other journal of the time. Cobbett did not understand the newer forms of industrial society emerging in his time; his ideal was the peasant cultivator making a comfortable, if frugal, living off his small-holding. He hated the corrupt parliamentary system of his day, and directed some of his most violent invective against the people he called 'tax-eaters' — those who drew income from interest on the national debt. For thirty years he waged war against the national debt, the unreformed Parliament, enclosures and high taxes.

3. Religion in England

The Reformation of the sixteenth century had replaced the medieval Catholic Church in England by the Church of England and in Scotland by the presbyterian Church of Scotland. In England the Revolution of 1688 was followed by the Act of Toleration of 1689, by which Englishmen were to have freedom to worship in the church of their choice (except in Unitarian or Roman Catholic churches), though the Church of England still remained the official, *established* church. By the middle of the eighteenth century the Church of England was probably at the lowest ebb of its history. This was a period in which very few new churches were built, while some old ones were allowed to fall into decay. Too many clergy neglected their duties or absented themselves from their parishes. But the traditions of the established Church were strong and for the greater proportion of the people of the country, life still centred on the parish church. For not only was belief in the fundamental doctrines of the Church of England unchallenged by all but a few, but the parish was the most important unit of administration for local government affairs. Law and order, poor relief, the upkeep of roads and bridges, the administration of charities and many other smaller aspects of community affairs were the business of the parish vestries. ('Vestry' was the name given to a committee which met in the church vestry.) The more substantial parishioners could all expect to serve in many parish offices during their lifetime, unless willing and able to pay the customary fine for exemption.

While the established Church failed to adjust itself to the changing conditions of eighteenth-century society, other Protestant Churches rose to meet the challenge. Because they disagreed with some of the doctrines of the official Church, they were known as *dissenting* or *non-conformist* bodies. Prominent amongst these in the eighteenth century, and enjoying an influence out of all proportion to its numerical strength, was the *Society of Friends* (the *Quakers*). Believing in the virtues of sobriety, honesty and hard work, and excluded by the law of the land from most official and professional careers, the Quakers established themselves as leading industrialists and scientists. In the iron industry, and in banking outside London, they were of supreme importance. The *dissenting academies* which they, the Unitarians and other non-conformists, established provided a practical education unique in this period, and turned out many distinguished scientists.

Dissatisfaction with the apathy of the Church of England also produced the *Methodist* Church. Finding that the Church of England did not meet the needs of the growing industrial areas, John Wesley, a minister of the Church, toured the country extensively, preaching and popularizing a creed understandable and acceptable to working men and women. His evangelistic work was supported by George Whitefield.

Although for a long time Wesley hoped to work within the framework of the Church of England, growing differences between him and the leadership of the Church forced his movement away, creating finally the *Wesleyan* or *Methodist* Church.

Thus, the early decades of the nineteenth century saw the fortunes of the Church of England in a very low state. Not only were the non-conformist churches thriving, but in the rapidly growing industrial towns the Church of England was losing contact with the mass of the people. This plight was recognized by a group of theologians in Oxford led by John Henry Newman and supported by Pusey and Keble. The leaders of the *Oxford Movement*, as these reformers were called, believed that the best way to put the Church of England on its feet again was to re-examine the beliefs of the Church and to establish anew the continuity of Christian worship in the English Church from the days of medieval Catholicism onwards. Their views were expressed in the *Tracts for the Times* — a series of pamphlets on theological matters. Some opponents of the *Tractarians*, as the leaders of the Oxford Movement thus became known, felt that there was a danger of the Church of England losing its distinctive middle way between Roman Catholicism on the one hand and the more extreme of the reformed Churches — the Non-conformists in England — on the other. That this danger was very real was revealed when, in 1845, Newman left the Church of England to become a Roman Catholic, and was followed by another leader of the movement, Manning. Both Newman and Manning subsequently became Cardinals of the Roman Catholic Church, but, by awakening the Anglican Church from its slumbers of the eighteenth century, they performed a service of the utmost value to that Church before they left it.

4. Early Social Legislation

The foregoing sections have shown that there were growing in the Britain of the early nineteenth century a number of small but powerful groups anxious to invoke the intervention of the government to remove some of the worst evils of society. But the barriers ahead of the reformers were many and strong. Few of the reformers had any direct influence in Parliament, which alone could pass laws compelling the removal of social evils, and neither of the main political parties in Parliament showed any great interest in reform. There were even people who felt that it was wrong for Parliament to interfere in any way with the liberty of the individual, and any social reform could be made out to restrict the liberty of some group of people. Nor was every member of the governing classes aware of the existence or immensity of some of the problems to be solved. Thus, it often became necessary for the would-be reformers to prepare the ground for reform by demanding a full-scale official enquiry into a given social problem, as a necessary preliminary to reform of the law. From the early years of the nineteenth century, a series of such enquiries, in the form of *Royal Commissions*, investigated such problems as the Poor Law, children's employment, the health of towns and the plight of the handloom weavers.

Wilberforce's efforts to secure the abolition of slavery have already been mentioned (in section 2 of this chapter). This movement, originated in the eighteenth century by the Quakers, worked hard for many years to convince the country that slavery was an evil institution which no civilized country should tolerate. But the opposition of the vested interests not only of the merchants in Liverpool and Bristol who were engaged in the slave-trade, but also of those who profited from the cheap cotton and sugar grown in the slave-plantations of North America and the West Indies, was both powerful and effective. However, in 1807, Wilberforce succeeded in persuading Parliament to prohibit the *slave trade* throughout the British Empire, though the institution of slavery itself still remained. Some years later, when the great powers of Europe met at Vienna in 1815 to make peace after the Napoleonic Wars, Castlereagh, Britain's Foreign Secretary, was able to persuade these powers to join in the suppression of the slave trade wherever it lay in their power to do so. It was to take many more years of effort before the anti-slavery movement could crown its efforts by securing the total abolition of slavery (1833) and Wilberforce died before this was achieved.

Nearer at home, Owen and Sir Robert Peel senior had opened the struggle for factory legislation early in the new century. Their main object was to persuade Parliament to make it illegal for women and children to be employed in factories for excessively long hours. Their opponents answered their attack with two arguments — that all labourers were free to make their own contracts with their employers, so that this was a matter for individuals rather than the state; and that in the conditions of the time, the employer's profit was only made with the last part of the worker's labour each day, for until then the goods produced only covered the cost of production. Neither of these arguments could stand very close scrutiny, but they served to bolster up an already powerful opposition. Sir Robert Peel persuaded Parliament in 1802 to pass his *Health and Morals of Apprentices Act*, which obliged employers of pauper apprentices to provide some education for the children, to whitewash the factories yearly, and, whilst limiting the working day of apprentices to twelve hours, aimed to abolish night work for them altogether. The act was to apply to cotton and woollen factories only (it was in these that at this time the worst abuses of child labour occurred) and was to be enforced by a system of inspection by local Justices of the Peace. Since the latter were all too often the offending employers themselves, it was the weakness of the provisions for enforcement that led to this act being totally ineffective from the start. The same defect marred the next attempt in which Robert Owen joined Sir Robert Peel. This *Factory Act* of 1819 prohibited the employment of children under the age of nine and renewed the limit of twelve hours on the working day. It fell very far short of what Owen and Peel had intended when they introduced their bill, having been drastically whittled down in its journey through Parliament.

Anti-slavery and factory legislation were forced on a reluctant Parliament by outside influences. Only in one field — albeit an important one — did the Tory government of the day initiate useful reform. This was the work of the younger Sir Robert Peel, who, as Home Secretary between 1822 and 1829, carried out an effective series of reforms of the penal system. He brought to an end the system of spying and repression which had so embittered the industrial working classes in the period of social unrest between 1815 and 1819; he abolished the death penalty for a long list of crimes; and in 1829 he established the Metropolitan Police Force. The idea of a paid full-time police force was not new: in the less happy circumstances of Ireland, the Royal Irish Constabulary had been created as far back as 1787; while both Middlesex and the City of London had established a kind of police office by the turn of the century. Thus the act of 1829 which brought into being the Metropolitan Police only extended an established system. Nevertheless, it paved the way for the replacement of the old 'Charlies' or night watchmen by proper police forces in most of the big cities within a few years.

5. The Rise of the Trade Unions

Perhaps the most important of the movements in their infancy in this period was the trade union movement. Trade unions, or *combinations* of workmen, as they were known in the eighteenth and early nineteenth centuries, first appeared during the eighteenth century, and originated in the journeymen gilds (see Chapter 5, section 3). When a numerous class of journeymen emerged in any occupation without the prospects of advancement to the status of master, it was natural that they should combine in the defence of their interests. These concerned primarily wages and hours of labour. As early as 1720, some 15,000 journeymen tailors in London were believed to have combined together against their masters, whilst a similar group had appeared amongst the journeymen tailors of Sheffield. Again, in 1778, there was formed in the Midlands the 'Stocking Makers' Association for the Mutual Protection in the Midland Counties of England'.

Until 1824, trade unions were made illegal in a number of different ways. The principal law used against the unions was that of conspiracy, for any workmen who met together to plan joint action against their masters were deemed to be guilty of entering into a conspiracy: many unionists were prosecuted under the laws of conspiracy throughout the eighteenth century and into the nineteenth. Even after the legalization of trade unions in 1824, the men who attempted to form a union of agricultural workers at Tolpuddle in Dorset in 1834 were prosecuted for taking 'illegal oaths' and sentenced to seven years' transportation to Australia. (See Chapter 20, section 4.)

To reinforce the conspiracy laws, acts of Parliament were passed during the eighteenth century declaring combinations of workmen in particular occupations to be illegal. Thus the combination of journeymen tailors of London mentioned above was prohibited by an act of 1721, while five years later a similar combination was forbidden in the woollen industry. At the very end of the century, driven by the fear of the governing classes in Britain that trade union action amongst the working classes might lead to an imitation of the upheavals of revolutionary France, Pitt's government passed acts which forbade combinations generally. The Anti-Combination Laws of 1799 and 1800 remained in force for a quarter of a century, but they must be regarded only as part of the general opposition to the growth of trade unionism by the governing classes.

These various legal methods that were used to suppress trade unionism were only partially successful. The most that can be said of them is that they hindered the development of trade unions, and perhaps forced the unions to develop along slightly different lines from those they might have chosen had they been free to do so. As it was, much trade union activity before the repeal of the Anti-Combination Laws in 1824 took place under cover of *Friendly Society* work. It was natural that groups of workmen who combined perhaps to raise their wages, should also contribute small sums weekly to provide a fund to help out needy members at times of sickness or unemployment. Some 'societies' were formed principally to administer such a 'box-fund', but many others used this quite legal form of organization as a cover for trade unions whose real aims were more definitely hostile to the employers.

In spite of these limitations on their activities, trade unions were a very active force in eighteenth century industrial relations. Strikes were not uncommon, as, for example, when the Durham miners struck in 1765, or when, in spite of the Anti-Combination Laws, the Cotton Spinners' General Union struck in 1810 in Preston and Stalybridge. Between 1775 and 1800, the journeymen tailors of London, who had been amongst the first to form trade unions, had succeeded by means of strikes in raising their wages from 18s. 9d. per week to 25s. Strike action required effective and well organized leadership which was not always present in the early unions. More frequently the protests against employers took the forms either of rioting and machine-breaking or the more orderly method of a petition to Parliament for the redress of grievances. The Spitalfields silk weavers' riots in London in 1764 and 1765 were sufficiently serious to induce Parliament to give way to their demands for the prohibition of imported silk, which was robbing the weavers of their employment. In 1777, the Hatters' journeymen petitioned Parliament to oppose a move by their employers to remove the restriction on the number of apprentices they could employ.

Active as these unions were — and occasionally effective — few of them had long histories in the eighteenth and early nineteenth centuries. Combinations mostly arose to meet specific problems or needs, and with the success or failure of the resulting action, the combination frequently broke up. Similarly the unions tended to be local rather than national: poor communications made it difficult to organize large-scale unions effectively. Thus the history of trade unionism before the mid-nineteenth century is one of small, local unions — often a succession of short-lived unions in a single occupation.

CHAPTER 14

THE CONDITION OF THE
WORKING CLASS

1. THE FACTORY SYSTEM

Many of the foregoing chapters have been concerned with outlining the nature of the changes which transformed Britain from a predominantly agricultural country into the leading industrial country in the world in the early nineteenth century. In this chapter the effect of these changes on the way of life of the working people must be considered. A most important effect of the industrial development of the country after 1700 was to change the occupation by which many people earned their livings. Not all these changes in occupations involved very drastic alterations to people's way of life, but one very significant trend was emerging during the late eighteenth and early nineteenth centuries — the unit of industrial organization was expanding rapidly. Formerly the unit had most frequently been the small workshop in which the master workman worked on his own account, or as the employee of, say, a clothier, nailmaster or hosier, who supplied him with his raw material and paid him 'by the piece' for the work he did on it. This 'domestic' system of organization was common to many industries, could be operated in conjunction with small agricultural holdings, and encouraged the employment of the whole family as an industrial unit. There were, of course, many exceptions to this general pattern of industrial organization, particularly in the metal, brewing and ship-building industries. It was the application of power — at first water power, and later steam power — to machinery formerly operated by human power that ultimately destroyed the domestic system, and raised the standard unit of employment from the family workshop to the factory with many hundreds of workers of both sexes and all ages.

This revolutionary change occurred first in the silk-throwing (spinning) industry in the second quarter of the eighteenth century, reached the cotton-spinning industry between about 1770 and 1800, then the cotton-weaving industry from about 1810 to 1840, and was imitated in the woollen industry from about 1830 onwards, to become gradually the rule in the growing engineering and clothing industries from the second quarter of the nineteenth century onwards.

When water or steam power was applied to machinery, particularly light textile machinery, it was found that a single water wheel or steam engine provided sufficient power to operate many machines at once, and the expense of installing this form of power was uneconomic if applied to the single machines which formed the basis of industrial organization under the domestic system. The first real textile factory was built at Derby in 1721 by the brothers Sir Thomas and John Lombe. It was a five-storey building employing three hundred workers. There were few imitators of this large-scale type of organization at first, but in the 1750's several similar silk mills were built in Stockport, Cheshire. An account of this town of the following decade described how 'the raw silk is thrown and prepared for the Spitalfields (London) weavers by six engines (machines) the buildings of which are of prodigious bulk, one of them containing above 45,000 movements which fill the spacious room up to the fifth storey, and all are put in motion by one wheel that goes by water.'

The really important extension of the factory system of organization came in Manchester and the surrounding towns after about 1770, and arose directly out of Arkwright's successful application of water power to cotton-spinning machinery. A large number of cotton-spinning factories were built in south Lancashire and the adjoining counties of Cheshire and Derbyshire in the 1770's and 1780's, and Watt's successful application of his steam engine to rotary motion, which permitted it to be used to drive machinery, accelerated the building of factories in the 1790's and after. The factories were grouped near important commercial centres like Manchester, or on rivers like the Mersey and the Derbyshire Derwent, which provided water and water-power, and the immediate outcome of the application of power to machinery was the rapid growth of the textile towns of these areas of the North of England. This meant that the

Cotton mills near Preston, Lancashire, early nineteenth century

population of these districts tended to depend entirely upon a single industry for employment.

For the worker there were both bad and good features about factory employment, though on balance the bad seem generally to have outweighed the good. Because the factories took advantage of the latest forms of power-driven machinery they were often able to offer more attractive wages than those earned by workers in the competing but dying domestic industries. Indeed, only by offering relatively good wages were the mill-owners able to attract to the textile towns the vast numbers of workers they needed. But the factory demanded forms of discipline from the workers to which they were not accustomed. Firstly, the factory employer required regular hours of work: though these may have been no longer than those worked by the domestic worker, the latter had always been free to choose when to work and when to take time off, and the change to the strict routine of the factory bell proved irksome. Once inside the factory the worker was tied to his machine. So long as the machine was in operation, he was kept constantly at work, and the machine was driven, of course, by water or steam power controlled not by the worker himself but by his employer — the worker became a slave to the machine. Work inside the factory was subject to the oversight of the supervisor or foreman, whose duty it was to see that there was no slackness amongst the workers and that the quality of work done was satisfactory. The mills were seldom well lit or adequately ventilated — early nineteenth century techniques of lighting and ventilation would not permit of this — so that the conditions of work were often far from satisfactory. The result of long hours of work tending machinery in a mill was often deformity, disease or proneness to rheumatic or internal complaints.

But perhaps the most serious indictment of the early factories was the excessive use they made of child labour. Poor working conditions and the employment of children were evils common to both factory and domestic systems, but it was the use made of pauper apprentices that made the early factories obnoxious. Pauper apprentices were orphans or the children of parents in receipt of poor relief and unable to provide for their children. Because of the heavy charge incurred in this way on the poor rate of a parish, overseers put these children out as 'apprentices' to any employer willing to provide board and lodging. There were many jobs in factories suitable for this kind of child labour, and some of the early cotton factories employed large numbers of these pauper apprentices, who both lived and worked on the same premises. The earliest factory legislation was concerned to reduce the evils of this aspect of the early factory system. (See Chapter 13, section 4.)

2. TOWN LIFE

A secondary but equally important effect of the application of power to industry, as well as of the increase in the scale of industry generally, was the rapid growth of the towns in which those fast-growing industries were concentrated. There was a substantial group of cotton towns in south-east Lancashire — Bolton, Bury, Oldham, Rochdale, Ashton-under-Lyne and Stockport, clustering round the nucleus of Manchester; another important group of woollen towns expanding fast in the first half of the nineteenth century in Yorkshire — Leeds, Bradford, Huddersfield, Halifax, Shipley and Otley; a metal-working and engineering group in the Midlands, mainly within the triangle formed by Birmingham, Wolverhampton and Stourbridge; another group of iron and coal towns in Wales — Merthyr Tydfil, Cardiff, Newport, Swansea and Port Talbot, with extensive urban development in the Rhondda, Taff and Tawe valleys; a trio of small silk-manufacturing towns in Cheshire — Congleton, Leek and Macclesfield; the 'six towns' of the potteries — the outcome of Josiah Wedgwood's eighteenth-century enter-prise — Stoke, Hanley, Burslem, Longton, Fenton and Tunstall; and a few of the older seaports of the country whose docks, ship-building and miscellaneous industries attracted rapidly increasing populations — London, Liverpool, Glasgow and Newcastle.

Two unsatisfactory features marked the new industrial towns of the late eighteenth and early nineteenth centuries — the overcrowding of the population into inadequate housing, and the lack of effective sanitary provisions to safeguard the health of the urban population. The overcrowding resulted from the failure of house-building to keep pace with the immense influx of people into the new towns. In towns like Manchester, Liver-pool and London, which attracted large numbers of Irish immigrants, overcrowding was most acute, for the Irish had been accustomed to low standards of living. Many towns contained large numbers of families occupying only a single room, and in some areas there were two or three families sharing a room. Three-quarters of the 5,000 families living in two parishes of Westminster in 1840 occupied single rooms. In some towns there were a great many cellar dwellings. Dr. Ferriar gave the following description of cellar dwellings in Manchester in 1796:

'Each consists of two rooms under ground, the front apartment of which is used as a kitchen, and though frequently noxious by its dampness and closeness, is greatly preferable to the back room: the latter has only one small window, which though on a level with the outer ground, is near the roof of the cellar; it is often patched with boards or paper, and in its best state is so much covered with mud as to admit very little either of air or light. In this cell, the beds of the whole family, sometimes consisting of seven or eight, are placed. The floor of this room is often unpaved: the beds are fixed on the damp earth. But the floor, even when paved, is always damp. In such places, where a candle is required even at noon-day, to examine a patient, I have seen the sick without bedsteads, lying on rags; they can seldom afford straw.'

Engels, a visiting German merchant, who described living conditions in the North of England in the early 1840's, found more inhabited cellars in Stockport, for example, than in any other town he had visited.

Not only were there far too many inhabitants to each house or room in the early nineteenth century, but the houses themselves were built far too closely together. This frequently involved 'back-to-back' houses — houses which shared the rear wall in common with the adjacent house in the next street. These houses had no back door, and, of course, no through ventilation. To achieve a high density of housing, houses were often built round courtyards, the only access to which was through narrow passages. Not unnaturally these courtyards were ill-ventilated and unhygienic.

The lack of paving, drains and proper sanitation, however, contributed much more than the overcrowding towards making the industrial towns of England nasty and unhealthy places in which to live. Probably the absence of adequate sewerage was the most serious nuisance, particularly in view of the grossly inadequate provision of lavatories. The water-closet, invented in the sixteenth century, began to be more widely employed after 1830, but was not general in working-class housing until the later nineteenth century; in some districts one lavatory between ten or twenty houses was not uncommon. Also, when streets were unpaved and unlit, garbage thrown from the houses was left to rot. Many districts had no regular arrangements for the collection of waste and garbage until later in the nineteenth century.

Engels' famous description of Manchester in the 1840's is too long to quote here in full, but the following extract reveals something of the squalor and filth of a working-class district of an industrial town of this period. It is an account of a small part of Manchester:

'The area is full of ruined or half-ruined buildings. Some of them are actually uninhabited and that means a great deal in this quarter of the town. In the houses one seldom sees a wooden or a stone floor, while the doors and windows are nearly always broken and badly fitting. And as for the dirt! Everywhere one sees heaps of refuse, garbage and filth. There are stagnant pools instead of gutters and the stench alone is so over-powering that no human being, even partially civilized, would find it bearable to live in such a district. The recently constructed extension of the Leeds railway which crosses the Irk at this point has swept away some of these courts and alleys, but it has thrown open to public gaze some of the others. So it comes about that there is to be found immediately under the railway bridge a court which is even filthier and more revolting than all the others. This is simply because it was formerly so hidden and secluded that it could only be reached with considerable difficulty, but is now exposed to the human eye. I thought I knew this district well, but even I would never have found it had not the railway viaduct made a breach in the slums at this point. One walks along a very rough path on the river bank, in between clothes-posts and washing lines to reach a chaotic group of little, one-storied, one-roomed cabins. Most of them have earth floors, and working, living and sleeping all take place in the one room. In such a hole, barely six feet long and five feet wide, I saw two beds — and what beds and bedding! — which filled the room, except for the fireplace and the doorstep. Several of

Colliers' houses on the road to Newcastle
in the late eighteenth century

these huts, as far as I could see, were completely empty, although the door was open and the inhabitants were leaning against the door posts. In front of the doors filth and garbage abounded. I could not see the pavement, but from time to time, I felt it was there because my feet scraped it. This whole collection of cattle sheds for human beings was surrounded on two sides by houses and a factory and on a third side by the river.'

These conditions were far from exceptional, and many tens of thousands of families must have lived under similar circumstances. It is only fair to add that not all working-areas were as bad as that in Manchester described by Engels. Engels himself spoke very highly, for example, of the neighbouring town of Ashton-under-Lyne, which, he said, 'has a much more agreeable appearance than most of the other manufacturing towns. The streets are broader and cleaner, while the new bright red cottages give every appearance of comfort.' About the same time, workers' houses in Coventry were described as 'good, comfortable dwellings; some of them very well furnished; many have nice clocks and beds, and drawers; are ornamented with prints; and some have comfortable parlours.'

A major result of the lack of elementary safeguards to health was the prevalence of disease in the towns. Epidemics, particularly of cholera and typhoid, which are caused by contaminated drinking water, spread with alarming rapidity amongst the urban population. The smoke- and germ-laden atmosphere bred a race of consumptives, and few working men and women in these circumstances survived the age of forty-five. Disease was rife and resistance to it almost nil; infant mortality in the towns remained high, and an early death was the common lot of town dwellers.

There was a wide range of conditions in English towns, but on the whole the over-crowded, insanitary, unventilated, filthy and unhealthy conditions which prevailed in Manchester probably affected a large proportion of the industrial working classes. Since the rapid growth of the industrial towns was involving an ever-increasing proportion of the population in squalor and discomfort, the immensity of the social evil was beginning to cause concern, particularly amongst doctors, and efforts, tentative and ineffective at first, were beginning to be made in the early nineteenth century to improve conditions. In the last quarter of the eighteenth century, doctors and scientists began to undertake careful investigations of urban conditions and to make recommendations as to how they might be improved. Though little practical good came of these early enquiries, they showed that at least one body of intelligent opinion recognized the existence of a serious social problem, and the publicity which their books gave to the question proved ultimately to be the means which forced Parliament to take steps to improve conditions.

The fundamental obstacle to the improvement of urban living conditions was the absence of any efficient local government. Few of the growing industrial towns were chartered boroughs, and in the absence of a corporation parish vestries and the local Justices of the Peace were ill-equipped to tackle tasks of such frightening immensity. In some towns, particularly in the suburbs of London, private acts of Parliament had created from the early eighteenth century local *Improvement Commissions*. The Commissioners appointed by these acts were charged specifically with the provision of lighting, paving, draining or sewering of a given area (often a particular parish or group of parishes). The Commissioners were empowered to levy a local rate to pay for their 'improvements'. In 1759, for example, Commissioners were appointed in one section of the parish of

Spitalfields (now in the 'East End' of London) 'for better lighting, cleansing and watching'. These were active and effective Commissioners who, in 1813, signed a contract with the Gas Light and Coke Company for lighting their streets with gas — making Spitalfields one of the first places to have its streets lit by gas. Portsmouth had been paved in this way in 1769, and the great sanitary reformer, Edwin Chadwick, believed that this had saved the inhabitants from recurring epidemics. By the early nineteenth century there were a great many Improvement Commissions at work, but equally there were many areas in which their achievements were negligible or for which no Commissioners had been appointed. The neighbouring industrial towns of Manchester and Stockport, for example, had been connected by one of the longest stretches of paved roads in the eighteenth century, but both towns were largely unpaved. The root of the trouble lay in the fact that the Improvement Commissioners were inadequate to the tasks ahead of them. Their authority covered too small areas. A town might be covered by several authorities, no two of which had the same responsibilities. None had powers to control new building, so that slums were being created faster than they could provide the barest minimum of essential services. In spite of valuable achievements in some towns, the Improvement Commissioners did little more than touch the fringes of the problem of making industrial towns at least as healthy to live in as villages and country towns.

The foundation of future reform was laid by the important *Municipal Corporations Act* of 1835. This Act provided for the creation of town councils to be elected on a wide franchise. Many of the new industrial towns, formerly without self-government apart from the hopelessly inadequate vestries or Improvement Commissions, took advantage of the Act of 1835 to secure *incorporation* (grant of powers of local self-government by an elected corporation). The new town councils were given powers to undertake all the work formerly done by the Commissions, and to levy local rates. At last authorities had been created that were both competent to take on the work of raising the standards of urban life, and were given access to the necessary legal powers to do so. But even under the more favourable conditions created by the Municipal Corporations Act, urban conditions only improved very slowly in the nineteenth century. (Improvements after 1835 are discussed in Chapter 22, sections 5–7.)

3. The Poor Law

So long as agriculture had remained the predominant occupation of British labourers, and so long as industry was frequently combined with agricultural small-holdings, variations in the level of trade seldom produced much unemployment. For the most part the parish *Overseers of the Poor* (see Chapter 6, section 2) in the seventeenth and early eighteenth century had used their Poor Rates to provide relief for the orphans, the sick and the aged. The *Old Poor Law*, as the Elizabethan parish system became known in the nineteenth century, was not designed to cope with the larger numbers of unemployed industrial workers which the fluctuations in trade threw out of work from time to time. In addition to these periodical waves of unemployment, the rapid rise of some industries and occupations at the expense of others tended to cause falling wages and unemployment in the declining occupations. Nor could the Old Poor Law deal adequately with the poverty caused periodically by exceptionally high prices for foodstuffs such as occurred during the wars against France between 1793 and 1815.

The Old Poor Law never succeeded in dealing satisfactorily with these new problems of large-scale unemployment mainly because the nature of the problem of poor relief was changing. Adaptation of the machinery for poor relief inevitably lagged behind the needs of the changing times. The main cause of the inadequacy of the Old Poor Law was its dependence on the parish as the unit of organization. The parish was too small a unit and could never raise sufficient money to cope adequately with the varied needs of the poor. An act of Parliament of 1782 known as *Gilbert's Act* had recognized this deficiency and allowed parishes to group together into *Unions* for the purposes of the Poor Law; but very few parishes availed themselves of this advantage, and for the most part the parish remained the unit of organization until 1834. Because it was uneconomical for each parish to run its own workhouse, some parishes availed themselves of privately-run workhouses, the owners of which accepted the poor from nearby parishes for a weekly fee. Needless to say, workhouses which were run by private individuals for the sake of the profit that could be made from them aimed to cut their costs to a minimum, and provided some of the worst and most inhumane examples of the eighteenth-century Poor Law at work.

The sharply rising prices of the French Wars after 1793 presented a new problem because wages, particularly in agriculture, tended not to rise so fast, and the standard of living of large sections of the working class was threatened. In an attempt to solve this problem, the Berkshire Justices of the Peace met together in the Pelican Inn in the village of Speenhamland on 6 May 1795. Their decision to use money from the poor rates to supplement the wages of labourers judged to be inadequate to support a reasonable standard of life proved to be a momentous one. They ruled that the Overseers of the Poor in Berkshire were to grant allowances to supplement wages which should vary with the number of adults and children in the worker's family. The amount given would take into account the changes in the cost of living as measured by the price of the 'gallon' loaf of bread. Their method of estimating what they considered to be the necessary minimum income is given here in their own words:

'When the Gallon Loaf of Second (quality) Flour, weighing 8 lb. 11 ozs. shall cost 1s.

'Then every poor and industrious man shall have for his own support 3s. weekly, either produced by his own or his family's labour, or an allowance from the poor rates, and for the support of his wife and every other of his family, 1s 6d.

'When the Gallon Loaf shall cost 1s. 4d

'Then every poor and industrious man shall have 4s. weekly for his own, and 1s. and 10d. for the support of every other of his family.

'And so in proportion, as the price of bread rise or falls (that is to say) 3d. to the man, and 1d. to every other of the family, on every 1d. which the loaf rise above 1s.'

This system of allowances, known as the *Speenhamland System*, was widely adopted, and within a few years was employed mainly in agricultural areas, in southern and midland England.

There is not a great deal of evidence of its use in the industrial areas of northern England. Some rural districts modified the system by the adoption of what was called the 'roundsman' system. By this, the workers who received allowances were allotted by the parish Overseers to each of the employers in turn. Where sufficient work was not available, the Overseers did their best to find unpaid work, possibly on the roads, and the allowances then constituted the whole of the labourer's earnings.

The Speenhamland system probably rescued many hundreds of families from starvation during years of scarcity and high prices; but the evils it created were perhaps worse than those it sought to cure. Employers realized that the worker's standards of living no longer depended entirely on the wages they paid them, with the result that all incentive to raise wages to keep up with rising prices was removed. The employer knew that what he did not pay in wages would have to be paid in the greatly increased poor rates. But not every employer was able to offset higher poor rates by lower wage bills. The employer of large numbers of labourers had the advantage over the small farmer, who was able to cultivate his holding with his own labour and that of his family, but was still obliged to pay the higher poor rates.

More serious, however, was the demoralizing effect of the system upon the labourer himself. For the lazy, the allowances removed the incentive to work, for there was now a certainty that a living wage would be provided whatever was actually earned; for the industrious the system denied the satisfaction of a decent wage honestly earned; for all who were forced on to 'the parish' for allowances to supplement inadequate earnings, there was the indignity of accepting charity and this affronted the pride of many hitherto independent workers.

In the eyes of the middle and upper classes, the most objectionable feature of the Speenhamland system was that it led to a sharp rise in the poor rates. In the years preceding 1795, about £2 million per year had been collected in poor rates throughout the country; by 1803 this total had doubled, and by 1812, when prices were almost at their highest, it had more than trebled. Another objection, raised principally by the economist, Thomas Malthus, was that by increasing the money allowances with the size of the family, the system encouraged the poor to have larger families; and, by guaranteeing an income to the rural worker, prevented the movement of surplus labour away from the countryside into the towns. According to this view, over-population of rural areas was a direct result of the system of poor relief.

Ultimately it was the disproportionately high cost of poor relief that led to a revision of the Poor Law. In 1832, a Royal Commission was appointed to investigate the state of poor relief and the *Poor Law Amendment Act* of 1834 was based closely upon its recommendations. The Commissioners were strongly influenced by the views of Edwin Chadwick, who, in turn, drew his ideas largely from Bentham. The act of 1834 was built on the basic assumptions that, apart from the special problems of the orphans, the sick and the aged, poverty resulted from idleness, and that expenditure on poor relief tended to encourage idleness. It followed that, if poor relief was given in such a way as to discourage those seeking it, the problem of the 'able-bodied poor' would simply vanish. The Commissioners showed little understanding of the nature of mass unemployment arising out of the fluctuations in the level of trade and industry.

The Poor Law Amendment Act was concerned with two aspects of the problem — of administration, and of principle. Recognizing the unsuitability of the parish as a unit of administration for poor relief, the act extended the principle of Gilbert's Act of 1782 by joining groups of parishes into Unions in all parts of the country. Poor relief in each union was to be administered by elected *Boards of Guardians*, while a central *Poor Law Commission*, consisting of three permanent commissioners, was to supervise the work of the boards from London. Edwin Chadwick was appointed as the Commission's first full-time secretary. The principle according to which the local boards were to administer the *New Poor Law* involved distinguishing between *outdoor* and *indoor* relief — relief given in money or in kind to the poor in their own houses, or relief given within the workhouse. The act ordered that the able-bodied should not be eligible for outdoor relief, and that in order to discourage 'idleness', the conditions in the workhouses should be 'less eligible' (less comfortable or attractive) than the circumstances of the lowest-paid labourer outside the workhouses.

Husbands and wives were to be separated inside the work
houses, for at least in the workhouses the poor were not to be
allowed to produce more children to be a public liability.

Administratively, the act was a success. Within six years
ninety-five parishes out of every hundred had been absorbed
into one of the new Unions. The 'workhouse test' of poverty
was applied in many districts, and met with what the Commissioners would have regarded as success. Large numbers of the
poor elected to refuse poor relief rather than enter the work
houses. But in some areas, particularly in the industrial North
the act aroused immense hostility. For the denial of outdoor
relief to the unemployed worker took no account of the in-
voluntary unemployment to which the industrial worker was
occasionally subject. This defect in the act was immediately
made clear, for the passing of the act was followed by one of the
most severe depressions of the nineteenth century — between
1837 and 1842 there was widespread unemployment and destitution in the North of England. Commissioners and Assistant
Commissioners who visited Boards of Guardians in the North of
England to enforce the 'workhouse test' were stoned, and a
strong movement organized by Richard Oastler expressed the
bitter opposition of the northern industrial workers to the New
Poor Law. In the face of this defiance, the Guardians had no
option but to overlook the 'workhouse test', and outdoor relief
continued to be given to the unemployed. In the agricultural
districts of the South, in which the Speenhamland system had
prevailed for almost forty years, the Act of 1834 effected a
genuine improvement. The abolition of outdoor relief to the
able-bodied caused some initial hardship, but wages were
gradually restored to their normal levels. Prices of food and
clothing were much lower in the 1830's than they had been
for example, during the French Wars, and arable farming was
slowly recovering from the effects of the post-war depression
The mid-1830's, moreover, were years of active railway construction which provided employment in rural areas.

The New Poor Law of 1834 remained fundamentally unchanged until after the First World War (1914–18), but during
the intervening period many changes took place which radically
altered the nature of the problem of poverty. These changes are
discussed in Chapter 22, section 3.

4. Britain in Depression: 1815–1819

The war against France lasted, with a short break in 1802–3, for twenty-two years. During this time profound changes were taking place in the structure and organization of both industry and agriculture. Napoleon's 'Continental System', the Orders-in-Council and the American Non-Importation Acts restricted England's overseas trade. The advent of peace in 1815 brought no immediate relief to the misfortunes which the war heaped on the working class. The effects of unemployment which periodically struck wide groups of workers were worsened by prices made artificially high by the taxation and inflation of the war years. In the years immediately following the end of the war, three-quarters of the revenue of the government was drawn from the taxes on wine, spirits, tea, coffee and tobacco. The immense wartime debt remained, and the interest on it added to the burden of taxation.

Though the general trend of industry in the early nineteenth century was towards steady expansion, the supply of labour for industry more than kept pace with this growth. Each successive failure of the potato crop in Ireland — an event which recurred frequently throughout the first half of the nineteenth century — brought fresh waves of Irish immigrants into the industrial North of England, while the growth of rural population, fostered by the working of the Poor Law, created a surplus of agricultural workers which tended to force wages down. After 1815, both the over-saturated agricultural and industrial labour markets were flooded by large numbers of soldiers and sailors demobilized at the end of the war from the swollen wartime army and navy. This coincided with the falling-off in government orders for textiles, metal-wares and ships. European countries which had contrived to manage for over twenty years largely without their former imports of British manufactures, had taken the first steps towards building their own industries, so that there was no immediate resumption of exports to these countries.

For these varied reasons, the five years following the final defeat of Napoleon at Waterloo were years of high living costs, unemployment and destitution for many sections of the working class. The area worst hit by the post-war depression was the cotton-manufacturing district around Manchester. Here, to add to the difficulties which affected all sections of the community, the growing adoption of the power-loom after about 1806 was steadily reducing the wages of the tens of thousands of hand-loom weavers. The weekly earnings of one class of weavers, for example, which had been 21s. in 1810, fell to 10s. 3d. by 1819; for another grade, from 12s. to 8s. 9d. in the same period. The wages of factory spinners also fell, but not to the same extent. During this period there was but little fall in the price of foodstuffs.

5. Working-class Agitation

Not surprisingly there was a great deal of unrest, the cause of which was principally economic. However, nobody, from the working-class agitators to the members of the government itself, had any constructive ideas for remedying the condition of unemployment, low wages and high prices. Some minor measures — an alteration in the basis of taxation which would shift some of the burden from the poorer to the wealthier classes, the removal of the import duty on raw cotton, and the repeal of the Corn Law — were urged upon the government by the working-class leaders, but these could only have alleviated slightly the evils arising from a temporary serious depression, whose causes were only imperfectly understood at the time, and whose cure lay beyond the techniques of early nineteenth-century economic policy. In the absence of an effective economic policy for remedying their unhappy position, the working class rested their hope in a programme of political reform. Given an active working-class share in parliament and government, they believed, the policy of the state would then automatically be directed in the interests of the greater part of the people in the country, instead of in the selfish interest of a small minority, and the economic problems which after 1815 were bringing such hardship to wide sections of the population, would cease to exist.

Thus the leadership of the working-class agitation after 1815 fell to the *Radicals* — a party with few active representatives in Parliament, and these all middle-class — who worked for manhood suffrage (votes for all men in parliamentary elections), annual parliaments (parliaments re-elected each year), and adequate and fair representation of the industrial areas. The last demand was particularly urgent, since none of the growing industrial towns of the Midlands and the North sent their own members to Parliament, which was therefore inevitably composed predominantly of the representatives of the smaller boroughs of the South of England (see Chapter 22, section 1).

This *Radical Reform* movement found expression during the period 1815–19 in a variety of ways. There was an extensive network of *Hampden Clubs* (named after the great seventeenth-century parliamentary leader), which held numerous public meetings in 1816 and 1817. Radical newspapers, like the *Manchester Political Register*, were founded. Another type of local organization was the *Union Society*, in which the working class endeavoured by means of weekly reading and discussion classes to educate themselves in preparation for the responsibilities of political leadership which they hoped shortly to assume. There were many strikes, particularly in the year 1818. Marches and processions were frequent. Of these the best known was the *March of the Blanketeers* in March 1817. Starting with a large meeting in Manchester, some three hundred men, carrying 'blankets, rugs, or large coats, rolled up and tied, knap-sack like, on their backs', set off to march to London to present a petition to the Prince Regent bearing the usual Radical political demands. A body of troops cut off the greater number of Blanketeers before they reached Stockport, the first town after leaving Manchester, and only one man eventually reached London.

More effective, however, in attracting large numbers and in frightening both the government and the local magistrates, were the mass meetings which were the most striking feature of working-class agitation in the post-war period. These were customarily addressed by the middle-class radical leaders, of whom the most persuasive orator was Henry Hunt. Hunt addressed a meeting of about 8,000 cotton workers in Manchester in January 1819, and similar meetings were held throughout the summer of 1819 in all the surrounding industrial towns. The culmination of the great series of reform meetings was planned for 16 August 1819 on St. Peter's Fields, Manchester. Contingents of workers poured in from the towns all around Manchester, and by mid-day an immense crowd of 60,000 was assembled ready to hear Henry Hunt. Rumours (untrue, in the event) that some of the crowd were preparing to come armed, had led the Manchester magistrates to assemble several troops of cavalry in the immediate neighbourhood of the meeting place, while many hundreds of infantrymen were kept in readiness in the surrounding streets. The magistrates could find no ground for declaring the meeting illegal, yet they were prepared to take action against Hunt and the other Radical leaders should they say anything in their speeches which might be interpreted as 'seditious'.

However, Hunt had scarcely begun to speak when the magistrates, thoroughly alarmed at the immensity of the gathering and the enthusiasm the people displayed towards the Radical leaders, decided to order the arrest of Hunt immediately. The Manchester Yeomanry, a part-time cavalry regiment of local middle-class supporters of the government, was ordered to make its way through the crowd to the platform to arrest the Radical leaders.

> 'At first, (wrote an eye-witness) their movement was not rapid, and there was some show of an attempt to follow their officer in regular succession, five or six abreast; but they soon increased their speed, and with a zeal and ardour which might naturally be expected from men acting with delegated power against a foe by whom they had long been insulted with taunts of cowardice, continued their course, seeming to vie individually with each other which should be first. As the cavalry approached the dense mass of people they used their utmost efforts to escape; but so closely were they pressed in opposite directions by the soldiers, the special constables, the position of the hustings, and their own immense numbers, that immediate escape was impossible. On their arrival at the hustings a scene of dreadful confusion ensued. The orators fell or were forced off the scaffold in quick succession; fortunately for them, the stage being rather elevated, they were in great degree beyond the reach of the many swords which gleamed around them.'

The crowd now began to break up. Panic and confusion reigned. Tempers rose, and the Yeomanry, unskilled in the tactics of crowd control, began to use their swords. In ten minutes the field was cleared, leaving behind eleven persons killed. Many

Peterloo, 1819

hundreds more were injured. The crowd, who had assembled
with none but peaceful intentions, streamed back to their
homes in the outlying towns, bearing a vastly increased resentment against the governing classes. The 'massacre', for such it
was held to be, was immediately dubbed 'Peterloo' in mocking
memory of the glorious achievement of the British army against
Napoleon four years before at Waterloo.

After Peterloo, the Radical movement fell away sharply. The
effect of the 'massacre' was to create a fatal division in the
movement between those whose despair led them to believe
that only violent action could bring victory in the face of the
government's determination to use the military to preserve the
existing order of society, and those, on the other hand, who
shunned violence and advocated patience and the continuance
of peaceful pressure. Furthermore the government took immediate drastic steps to suppress the reform movement.
Already, under the stress of widespread disturbance in 1817, it
had temporarily suspended *Habeas Corpus*, the traditional
English legal safeguard against arbitrary arrest. In the autumn
of 1819, the *Six Acts* were hustled through Parliament. These
gave the government additional powers to prevent drilling and
training in the use of arms, to prohibit all public meetings of

more than fifty people, and to suppress 'seditious' newspapers; they also extended the heavy tax on newspapers.

Perhaps the most important explanation of the decline of the Radical Reform movement after Peterloo lay in the general improvement in trade and industry from 1820. Reports from the industrial areas early in 1820 indicated a reduction in unemployment, the first increases in wages, and a resumption of the upward trend in output and export figures. This recovery continued until 1825, when once again trade fell off, and the year 1826 joined 1811, 1816 and 1819 as years of exceptional distress amongst the working class.

PART THREE

BRITAIN SINCE 1830

CHAPTER 15

THE FRAMEWORK OF
INDUSTRIAL BRITAIN

1. BRITAIN'S INDUSTRIAL LEAD

In the summer of 1851 Britain's *Great Exhibition* was held in the newly-built Crystal Palace, the 'blazing arch of lucid glass' designed and built in a matter of weeks by Joseph Paxton. The Exhibition, the Prince Consort's brain-child, displayed to all the world Britain's unquestioned mastery of the arts of manufacture. Here were textiles, pottery and manufactures of every kind of metal produced on a scale and at a price which left all Britain's competitors far behind. The Crystal Palace itself, a miracle of cast iron and glass, symbolized Britain's achievement in a new medium. (The Crystal Palace was not, in fact, the first glass and iron building; this was the Great Palm House at Kew built in 1844–8, but the Crystal Palace was much larger.) The Exhibition emphasized and symbolized the obvious fact of Britain's industrial leadership in the world.

The industrial changes described in Part II of this book were not immediately imitated by other countries. Some of the new techniques on which Britain's industrial achievements had been built were employed in other countries, but nowhere had there been expansion in the basic heavy industries on anything like the same scale as in Britain. Much of what advance there was on the Continent was the result of British emigrant skill and exported British machinery. In the countries which became Britain's most serious industrial competitors in the later part of the nineteenth century — Germany, the United States and Belgium — there was little sign in the first half of the century of the immense strides in industry which had been initiated in Britain in the last quarter of the eighteenth century.

This absence of serious competition gave Britain some valuable advantages. There was, in the first place, little fear of

The Great Exhibition, 1851

competition, in the home market at least, in cotton, iron, engineering, coal-mining and shipbuilding, though in some older industries, like silk and wool, Britain's lead was less clearly established. High tariffs in many foreign countries still made it difficult to compete with local, if less efficient and high-cost, industries. But in more distant markets — all parts of the Empire, in the United States and in South America — British exported manufactures enjoyed extensive, safe markets. Because of this favoured situation, the newer industries whose growth had occurred since the late eighteenth century were able to export a very high proportion of their total output. In the first quarter of the nineteenth century, for example, almost 90% of British cotton manufactures were exported. The profits from the vast overseas trade contributed to the unceasing flow of capital needed for further expansion: once economic progress has been initiated, it generates within itself the means of sustaining growth. It is much easier to sustain an established rate of growth than to stimulate new growth in a stagnant economy; by starting first on the road to industrialization, Britain was able to retain her lead for a long time — almost a century, in fact.

For a small country with a rapidly expanding population, this lead in industry, with its accompanying lion's share of the world export trade in manufactures, carried one overwhelming and vital advantage — it provided the means to feed its in-creasingly numerous people. At the end of the eighteenth century an economist, the Reverend Thomas R. Malthus, had voiced the fear in his *Essay on Population* (1798) that population tended to outgrow the means of subsistence. He could not see that it would be possible for a country like Britain to go on increasing her output of foodstuffs at the same rate as her population. Since population was indeed expanding at the rate of nearly 2% every year, and was to double itself within fifty years of the publication of Malthus's views, and since in the first few decades of the nineteenth century there was ample evidence of extensive poverty and periodic starvation, there seemed to be more than a little justification for Malthus's argument. But Malthus failed to take account of the process of industrialization which produced an ever-growing surplus of manufactures which could be exchanged in international trade for foodstuffs. Though the productivity of Britain's agricultural acres and of her farmers could only be increased slowly, the great advances in productivity of her industrial population provided the means, through international trade, whereby the growing population might be fed not merely at its existing standards, but, as time went on, at ever-rising standards. Without industrialization, in other words, Britain must have remained a poor, over-populated country. Industrialization has made it possible to accommodate on this small island a population denser than almost anywhere else in the world, yet at a standard of living which, until the twentieth century, exceeded that of any other country in the world.

But this fortunate outcome of industrialization was not achieved without cost. The initial growth of these industries could only be achieved by the regimentation of vast armies of cheap labour. Herded together in the slum towns of the nineteenth century, these victims of industrial progress had to wait until hard-won experience in handling the new problems of urban life slowly rescued them from their unhealthy squalor. In the long run industrialization was essential to Britain's survival; in the short run, who can blame the workers of Manchester, Birmingham or Bradford for doubting the advantages of industrial progress?

And if rapid industrialization carried with it social hazards, it was also not without some economic disadvantages. So long as Britain could retain its industrial lead, it could enjoy a disproportionate share of world trade, and British industry could be built on the expectation of substantial export markets. But when other nations, too, entered the competition for the world export trade, Britain must sacrifice some of her share; other nations would make particular efforts to oust Britain from overseas markets. Accordingly it was inevitable that British industry would have to adjust itself to loss of overseas markets, at least in the trades in the older established manufactures. Only drastic reorganization of the basic structure of British industry, to allow for the emergence of new industries with new commodities for export, would permit Britain to retain the substantial imports o food and raw materials essential to the maintenance of the standards of life of her people. This painful re-adjustment, which was forced on Britain from the last decades of the nineteenth century, was inherent in the industrial lead Britain had gained a century earlier. But while, in the long run, Britain's early industrialization created in this way a whole range of problems for the future, in the short run, during most of the nineteenth century at least, the prospects seem boundlessly bright. Those who marvelled at the Exhibition of 1851 had no cause to worry about the immediate future.

2. The Organization of Industry

The industrial changes of the late eighteenth and early nineteenth centuries had merely *begun* the process of transforming Britain from an agricultural into an industrial country; modern large-scale industry is the outcome mainly of the steady expansion of the older industries and the birth of new industries in the later nineteenth century. A recent attempt to measure this growth estimates a tenfold increase in industrial output between 1820 and 1913, a one-third increase between the two World Wars of the twentieth century, and a further doubling in the first fifteen years after the second World War. In the century before 1914 the population of this country was trebled, so that the output of industrial goods per head of population multiplied roughly three times during the same period. In the forty years since 1918, during which the population has grown by 20%, industrial output per head has more than doubled.

These striking advances in industrial output and productivity are not to be explained entirely in terms of technical advances, though the inventive genius of men like Bessemer and Parsons has clearly played a vital part. Capital needed to be made available for industry; developments in industrial organization were the essential prerequisites for an ever-increasing flow of investment into industry. The growth of the joint-stock banks, more fully described in section 3 of this chapter, helped to canalize capital into industry; by the creation of a stable paper money and by the provision of many other useful services, the banks have made possible the advance of large-scale industry. The speedy construction in the middle third of the nineteenth century of the railway network was another necessary condition of industrial development. Equally important, however, was the emergence in the middle decades of the nineteenth century of the limited liability company as a means of safeguarding the

Going to the

investor and therefore of encouraging the small investor to lend to industry. *Limited liability* limits the liability of an investor for the debts of the firm in which he has invested to the amount of the paid-up value of his shares. Every investor must take the risk of the loss of his investment, but before the coming of limited liability he was also liable to meet the debts of the firm from the rest of his property. In these circumstances, much capital that might have been poured into industry was invested in 'safe', non-productive directions. An act of 1844 began the registration of companies, making them legal corporations with the right to go to law as a company, but left liability unlimited. Limited liability was first made accessible to joint-stock companies by an act of 1856, a concession extended to banks two years later. Finally, in 1862, the whole body of law relating to companies and limited liability was revised and consolidated in a new act.

The coming of limited liability opened the door to immense new resources for industry. Vast numbers of small investors began to make their savings available to all branches of business enterprise. Later, the institutional investors — the insurance companies and pension funds — taking advantage of the new security in industrial investment, poured the small savings of

millions who would never have invested directly, into industry. Not all businessmen, however, were in a hurry to adopt limited liability; bankers, in particular, were reluctant to make any change which might imply that their ability to meet liabilities was in any way restricted, while in many branches of industry the family firm continued for several decades to meet all financial requirements. But the day when the needs of industry could be met by the resources of a single entrepreneur with perhaps a handful of partners was nevertheless passing, and the great individualist entrepreneurs of the twentieth century — William Lever (Lord Leverhulme) and W. R. Morris (Lord Nuffield), for example — are exceptional rather than typical. In general, management and ownership in industry were gradually separated. It became possible after the mid-nineteenth century for the control of vast industrial resources to fall into the hands of a few businessmen who owned little or none of the capital they employed.

These changes in their turn made possible increases in the size of the firm, since there was now no limit to the amount of capital that could be raised, while technical ,advances encouraged the economies of large-scale production. Though in the early nineteenth century many textile factories employed several hundred workers, and though other industries like ship-building and ironmaking tended also to demand large units, the average unit in industry in the early nineteenth century remained very small. Only a small proportion of all industrial workers was employed in factories, and the workshop with half-a-dozen to a score of workers was much more typical. As the nineteenth century developed, the size of the industrial unit grew, and in the twentieth century there are hundreds of factories employing more than one thousand workers and not a few employing over ten thousand workers on a single site.

The growth in the size of the industrial *unit* has been accompanied by an even greater rise in the size of the *firm* in industry. The later nineteenth century saw the extension of *integration* in industry. *Horizontal* integration involves bringing together into one firm several smaller firms carrying on the same process in an industry. *Vertical* integration links together related processes into continuous manufacture. Both these forms of integration were the causes of many of the *amalgamations* of firms that were an important feature of British industry after the 1890's. In this period some of the really big firms of modern industry were founded — United Alkali Co., the major chemical firm around which the Imperial Chemical Industries was built in the 1920's, J. & P. Coats, the cotton sewing-thread monopolists of Clydeside, and Stewarts & Lloyds in the English and Scottish steel industry. The twentieth century has seen the grip of these and similar industrial giants extended into the newer fields of electrical engineering, motor and aircraft manufacture.

3. BANKING

Industry and trade require banking services; since the Middle Ages the growth of business organizations and banking have gone hand in hand. Banks lend capital, offer short-term credit, provide the means of payment in their paper money, hold a firm's cash in safe and convenient keeping, and offer a wide range of subsidiary services to the businessman. The story of how these banking services, so essential to economic development, grew up in the seventeenth and eighteenth centuries has already been told in Chapter 4, section 4. In the early nineteenth century the privileged position of the Bank of England was still unchallenged, its monopoly of joint-stock banking intact; but there had grown up around it two groups of private banks — in London (the *London private banks*), and in the provinces (the *country banks*).

All these banks had contributed to the great spurt of industry, transport and agriculture of the late eighteenth and early nineteenth centuries. The number of country banks increased with staggering rapidity in the early years of the nineteenth century, but their alarming casualty rate in times of crisis or depression indicated the urgent need for action to improve their stability. To serve industry best, banks must be a stabilizing element in the economy; but during and immediately after the Napoleonic Wars banks in Britain went bankrupt so easily that they spread rather than damped down the effect of depressions. There were two basic weaknesses in the banking system of this period which accounted for this instability. First, the Bank of England's monopoly prevented any other bank from having more than six partners; this limited the resources of capital which could be brought together, leaving these banks with inadequate reserves against the sudden drains of cash apt to occur in years of crisis. The second weakness lay in the absence of regulation of the note issue. Economists and bankers were far from certain on what principle the note issue ought to be regulated, but they were coming increasingly to recognize that merely leaving the quantity of notes issued to the discretion of many hundreds of independent banks was unlikely to help cure the chronic instability of the economic system.

A particularly severe crisis in 1825 which caused the bankruptcy of no less than eighty country banks brought matters to a head, and in the following year an act restricted the joint-stock banking monopoly of the Bank of England to within a radius of sixty-five miles from London. This permitted banks outside that radius to have any number of partners or shareholders. The act was followed by another in 1833 which withdrew the Bank of England's monopoly altogether. Hitherto most banks had had but a single office; now, as a result of these acts, an entirely new type of commercial bank appeared — the joint-stock bank with branches. Some of these big branch banks were new companies, like the Manchester and Liverpool District Bank of 1829, or the London and Westminster of 1834; others grew as the result of amalgamations of older family banks: Lloyds and Barclays banks grew in this way.

Though the Bank of England had lost an ancient privilege, it retained a unique position in the banking world. Its notes continued to circulate more widely than those of all other banks; it was the banker to the government; it held the only important gold reserve in the country; it acted as banker to other banks; and the act of 1826 had permitted it, for the first time, to open branches in the main provincial towns. It remained a joint-stock company, subject only to the regulation imposed upon it by its charter which had to be renewed periodically, but it continued to gather slowly the special functions of what is known in the present century as a *central bank*. One of the most important characteristics of a central bank is that it is an instrument of government economic policy; it is the means, that is, through which the government seeks to control certain aspects of the country's economic life. The more, therefore, the Bank of England assumed its specialized functions, the more it became necessary for its freedom of action to be restricted in order that its operations might be guided by the government in the general interests of the state.

It was the Bank of England's note issue, in the main, which was the object of most criticism in the 1830's and 1840's. Opinion on the problem of the note issue was divided. The so-called *Banking School* of thought argued that bankers ought to be free to issue notes according to their own discretion, to allow for variations in the demand for notes, so long as all notes were convertible on demand into gold (as was customary at that time). The *Currency School*, on the other hand, wanted the note issue to be related strictly to the reserves of gold held by the banks. The controversy between these two schools of thought dragged on for some years until it was resolved by Peel in the *Bank Charter Act* of 1844. The primary aim of this act, which represented, in the main, the triumph of the Currency principle, was to bring the note issue throughout the country ultimately into the hands of the Bank of England, and, by determining strictly the principles governing that Bank's issue of notes, to regulate precisely the whole of the note issue. To achieve this end, banks were not permitted to exceed their existing note issues, the Bank of England was to take over the issue of any bank ceasing to issue its own notes, while any banks amalgamating with others were to forfeit their rights of issue. It was not, however, until 1921 that the last note-issuing bank ceased to exist separately. For its part, the Bank of England was to carry on its note-issuing business in a new Issue Department, now to be separated from its Banking Department. All its notes were to be backed by gold reserves, so that increases in the note issue could only be made if the Bank's gold reserve rose. The note issue of all banks in 1844, however, exceeded the existing gold reserves, and, since a sudden reduction in the note issue would have a disastrous effect on the country, the gold-backed note issue was to be supplemented by a fixed *fiduciary* issue (issue on faith, backed by the promise of the government to pay) of £14 million. Finally, in order that the Bank's operations might be made public, it was to publish a weekly return.

The Bank Charter Act of 1844 did not affect Scotland. Scottish banks retained, as they still do, their own note issue. They have, however, subsequently become closely associated with the principal London banks and their note issues have become integrated with the Bank of England's fiduciary issue.

The main object of the Bank Charter Act was to lessen the severity of the fluctuations which periodically rocked the business world. This result was not immediately achieved. In the succeeding three financial crises of 1847, 1857 and 1866 it proved necessary to permit the Bank to exceed the limit to the fiduciary issue set by the Act. But the crisis of 1866, which brought about the collapse of one of London's biggest merchant bankers, Overend, Gurney and Co., proved to be the last major crisis of its kind. With the passing of time, the Bank of England acquired experience and a sense of its new responsibilities which enabled it to use its powers to greater effect in regulating the money market. In the last third of the century, British banking was crystallizing into the familiar structure of the twentieth century. The Bank of England gradually acquired the powers and role of a central bank as one of the principal channels of government economic policy, so that its nationalization in 1946 was merely the logical culmination to its development.

Commercial banking fell increasingly, as a result of hundreds of amalgamations, into the hands of a smaller number of large banks, which, by virtue of their growing experience and immense reserves, were able to withstand the vicissitudes of trade and to collaborate with the Bank of England in oiling the wheels of business at the same time acting as a steadying influence in an erratic economy.

4. THE TRADE CYCLE

As a country becomes more industrialized it tends to become more susceptible to variations in the volume of trade. These variations may be changes in the levels of employment (or unemployment), wages, prices, industrial output, profit or investment. There has never been a time in the history of capitalist organization in this or any other country when there have not been these fluctuations. At first they were associated with changes in the weather which induced periods of good or bad harvests; later the causes became more complex, arising from the very nature of capitalist society itself. A purely agricultural economy is not, therefore, without these fluctuations; but the more industrialized the economy, the more serious their effect. This devastating weakness of capitalism has been to some extent the result of failure to understand the way a capitalist economy works; the work of some twentieth-century economists, notably Lord Keynes, has contributed immensely to the understanding of this problem, and by the mid-twentieth century we are well on the way to curing a disease hitherto thought to be chronic. In the nineteenth century, and until the 1930's, however, this type of fluctuation was the curse of the economy.

The causes of these fluctuations are extremely complex. Each depression, each boom, must be explained separately, for though they have much in common, they are attended by quite distinct historical circumstances. Suffice it to say that, apart from such obvious phenomena as seasons, harvest variations and wars, they arise principally from the fact that the mainspring of a capitalist economy is the profit motive. Businessmen make their decisions, upon which the levels of production and consumption partly depend, according to their expectations of profit. This major element of uncertainty gives rise to alternating periods of extreme optimism and intense pessimism.

Fortunately every down-turn of trade carries with it the seeds of recovery, just as the very nature of each boom generates the succeeding depression. In the nineteenth century boom followed slump with depressing regularity. The pattern repeated itself unfailingly, an unceasing cycle of prosperity and depression. The *trade cycle* dominated British economic history from the eighteenth century to the second World War. A country heavily dependent upon overseas trade, as Britain has been in the nineteenth and twentieth centuries, is even more susceptible to the vagaries of the trade cycle than are countries which enjoy a high degree of self-sufficiency, since a high proportion of its industry is dependent upon the level of demand in foreign markets. This overseas demand may be affected by wars and revolutions, not to mention trade cycles in these foreign countries themselves.

In the nineteenth century the trade cycle repeated itself roughly every ten years. Sometimes the interval between depression and depression was less, sometimes more; but businessmen and economists came to accept an 8 to 11-year pattern as the normal background to existence. The most serious depressions of the nineteenth and twentieth centuries occurred between 1837 and 1843, and between 1929 and 1933. On the other hand there were great bursts of activity, arising mainly from feverish railway construction, in 1836 and 1845–6. The greatest boom of the nineteenth century occurred in the early 1870's, the last years before Britain began to be seriously affected by competition from other rising industrial countries.

For the businessman the fluctuations were not necessarily catastrophic. Admittedly every depression brought its wave of bankruptcies, but the larger firms learned to employ the resources saved during the booms to tide them over the thin years of depression. But this balancing of bad years by good was not within the means of the worker. Even in good years his wage left him with little to save, so that when bad years forced down his wage he was driven to the very border of starvation. And since it is not possible to employ more labour than actually exists, even in a boom, it follows that the much lower levels of activity during depressions involved a great deal of unemployment. Here lay the root cause of much of the immense suffering borne by the British working class in the nineteenth and early twentieth centuries. There was no adequate provision for the relief of poverty arising from the temporary unemployment of the trade cycle. The Commissioners whose recommendation were embodied in the Poor Law Amendment Act of 1834 seemed deliberately to close their eyes to the impact of the trade cycle on the availability of employment in industrial areas. The 'workhouse test' could never meet the problem of periodic mass unemployment which the trade cycle created. The unemployed worker was therefore driven to resort to tramping round the country in search of work, to subscribing to Friendly Societies which operated insurance schemes providing unemployment benefits, or to emigration. Indeed, there is a close relationship between the waves of emigration in the nineteenth century and the recurring depressions. In the remaining chapters of this book the frequent references to this or that boom or slump testify to the importance of this complex phenomenon in modern economic history.

CHAPTER 16

TRANSPORT

1. THE EVOLUTION OF THE LOCOMOTIVE

The immense significance, both economic and social, of the steam engine has been examined in Chapters 10 and 14. Its share in revolutionizing both the economic organization of the country and the life of its people was further extended when the combined efforts of a group of engineers in the early nineteenth century succeeded in adapting it to provide a source of motive power for railways.

The difficulties at first were great. Both Newcomen's and Watt's engines were huge machines, with immense cylinders, which could not conceivably be put on wheels. Thus the first problem was to reduce the size of the machine without making any corresponding reduction in power. This could only be achieved by using steam at higher than atmospheric pressure, which in turn demanded a boiler capable of standing up to higher pressures. Thus it is no coincidence that the man who first experimented with high-pressure boilers — Richard Trevithick (1771–1833) — was the first to build a successful steam locomotive. An engine which employed high-pressure steam dispensed with the condensing power of steam on which were founded all the eighteenth-century developments from Savery to Watt. Watt himself firmly stuck to his condensing engine, with the result that no real progress was made with the steam locomotive until Watt's patent finally expired in 1800. One of the most versatile of the early engineers — William Murdock — had constructed a working model locomotive as early as 1786 but had not succeeded in developing this into a practical full-size machine.

Trevithick had been brought up as a youth amongst the Cornish mines and acquired an early familiarity with the Watt engine. For some years he experimented with a high-pressure boiler, and at Christmas 1801 he put his first steam carriage —

the first 'puffer' (so called from the exhaust release of the high-pressure steam at each stroke of the piston) — on the road near his native town of Camborne. It failed at the first attempt but succeeded partly a few days later. In March 1802 he took out a patent for a steam-driven carriage. In 1803 he ran another steam carriage on several trips between Holborn and Paddington in London. In the following year, Samuel Homfray, one of the great South Wales ironmasters, made a £500 bet with his neighbour, Anthony Hill, that he would produce a steam-driven locomotive to run on one of the cast-iron tramways of the district. It was Trevithick, of course, on whose locomotive he relied to win his bet, and on 21 February 1804, Trevithick set his locomotive on the rails driving it successfully for the full 9¾ miles of the line. The bet was won, and railway history was made. In the summer of 1808 Trevithick built a circular track on the site now occupied by Euston station in London, and gave rides to the public for 6d. a trip on a train drawn by his steam locomotive.

At the time, however, the significance of Trevithick's achievement was not realized, and for several years little progress was made, while Trevithick himself turned his attention to other branches of engineering. Trevithick's locomotives, however, had demonstrated one important point on which doubt had been expressed. This was that the engines could haul useful loads by the adhesion of the wheels on the smooth rails. Some early experimenters had believed that a rack and pinion motion would be necessary if any useful load was to be drawn. John Blenkinsop had taken out a patent for this device in 1811.

At the other end of the country, on the Northumberland coalfield, two other engineers who saw the possibilities of steam power on the colliery wagon-ways of the north-east persevered in the quest for the steam locomotive. In 1813, William Hedley, an engineer at Wylam colliery, built the famous *Puffing Billy*, which ran successfully for almost fifty years. Not far away, at Killingworth colliery, George Stephenson (1788–1848) designed and produced another successful locomotive. This engine drew a train of eight loaded wagons weighing thirty tons at a speed of four miles an hour. Many years' experience of both stationary engines and his own early locomotives secured Stephenson the post of engineer to the company formed in 1821 to build a railway between Stockton and Darlington in the neighbouring county of Durham. Edward Pease, the principal promoter of this railway, had thought at first of using horses to draw the trains, but Stephenson convinced him of the advantages of steam locomotion. Stephenson built his *Locomotion* for this railway. His unique experience and great success on the Stockton and Darlington railway stood him in good stead some years later when, in 1829, the owners of the Liverpool and Manchester Railway, then almost completed, announced that their choice of a locomotive would be determined by a public trial. Stephenson's *Rocket* competed with three other engines. The verdict was in no doubt, the *Rocket* proving faster and more powerful by far than its rivals. The triumph of the *Rocket* at the Rainhill trial of 1829 proved to be the final victory for the steam locomotive, for after this occasion no nineteenth-century railway company seriously considered using any other form of power.

2. THE EARLY RAILWAYS

It is most important to distinguish clearly between the invention of the steam locomotive and the development of the rails on which it ran, for the railway itself had been in use for over two hundred years before the steam locomotive was developed in the first quarter of the nineteenth century. The first railways were known as *wagon-ways* and were used to convey coal from the pit-heads to the nearest water transport. The coal wagons on these wagon-ways were horse-drawn and the rails on which they ran were made of wood. The first wooden wagon-way which historians have succeeded in tracing was constructed in 1605 and conveyed coal from Sir Francis Willoughby's colliery at Woolaton to the adjacent town of Nottingham. Wooden wagon-ways, however, were used much more extensively in the Tyne valley from the early seventeenth century, and in South Wales. In both these areas wagon-ways connected collieries several miles distant from the nearest rivers with water transport, for the lie of the land enabled the heavily-loaded coal wagons to run down to the rivers by gravity, leaving the horses to draw only the empty wagons back up the hill. In Chapter 10, section 4, the part played by these wagon-ways in developing the coal-mining industry is more fully discussed.

For well over a century there was no important technical development in connection with the wagon-ways, though there was a steady spread of their use in the mining areas until there were extensive networks involving hundreds of miles of track in the north-east and in South Wales. Wood was obviously an unsuitable material for the rails and the life of a wooden rail must have been short. In 1767, the Coalbrookdale ironworks, the scene of the important discoveries in iron-making of the Darbys, produced experimentally some cast-iron rails. These were laid down on a wagon-way used for carrying coal and iron from the company's works at Ketley to the River Severn. Evidently they were successful, for in the next three years the Coalbrookdale Company produced about 800 tons of cast-iron rails, most of which must have been sold to other users of wagon-ways. This was an important development, for the steam locomotive would have been useless without its 'iron road'. Moreover the smoother carriage provided by the iron rail encouraged the development of railways — still horse-drawn, of course — for passenger traffic. Early in the nineteenth century quite a number of *tram-roads*, as they became called, were built intended to cater for passenger transport as well as for the carriage of freight. The high cost of horses and forage during the French Wars (1793–1815) was probably the most important cause of this development. The best known of these was the Swansea and Mumbles line of 1804, which has the distinction of being the oldest passenger-carrying railway in the country.

Though, as has been seen, several engineers were experimenting with steam locomotives during this period, none of the railway companies was yet convinced that these locomotives had reached the stage at which they would provide a safe and reliable means of traction. The first railway company to adopt the new steam locomotive was the Stockton and Darlington railway, projected in 1821 by Edward Pease, a Darlington Quaker, and his partners. This railway, some twelve miles in length, ran its first train in 1825, in which year another more important railway was projected. This was to connect Liverpool to Manchester, a distance of thirty-five miles. These two towns had been linked some fifty years earlier by the Duke of Bridgewater's canal, and it was the high charges of this canal company which persuaded a group of Liverpool businessmen to consider

Constructing the entrance to the Edge Hill tunnel on the Liverpool to Manchester Railway, 1831

he construction of a railway. There was considerable traffic between the two towns, occasioned by Manchester's demand for raw cotton, mainly imported through the port of Liverpool, and he export of Lancashire's growing cotton production to many parts of the world. Work began in 1826 under the direction of George Stephenson and continued for four years in the face of severe technical difficulties. Near the Manchester end of the line here was the extensive bog of Chat Moss and it was no mean achievement to provide a firm base for the rails over this treacherous ground. At the Liverpool end of the line it was necessary to cut a deep cutting through solid sandstone rock. These difficulties were conquered by 1829 and in that year the Rainhill trial described in the previous section was held to select the best available locomotive. In the following year, the railway was opened throughout its length, but the splendid ceremony was marred by an accident which resulted in the death of he former President of the Board of Trade, William Huskisson.

During the years when the Liverpool and Manchester railway was becoming a reality, and the Rainhill trial had satisfied a doubting world that the steam locomotive would revolutionize land transport, other railways were being projected. In he ten years following the opening of the Stockton and Darling-

Railway construction in the 1800's : horse-runs employed in the

ton line, no less than fifty-four railway lines were planned and secured parliamentary approval. Amongst these early railways were the Leicester and Swannington line for the carriage of coal, the Leeds and Selby, the London and Birmingham, and the Grand Junction linking the Liverpool and Manchester to Birmingham. Thus the ten years from 1825 to 1835 saw a beginning of the creation of Britain's railway network. At first the progress was modest and unhurried, but suddenly it became a mad craze. Scores of new lines were projected. There was no shortage of investors willing to furnish capital (though for many years returns on capital invested in railways were frequently very small and sometimes non-existent), and in 1836 and 1837 Parliament gave its approval to thirty-nine new lines — about half the number projected — with a total mileage of almost a thousand miles. The pace, however, was too fast. The country could not muster the resources to build at such a rate, and though the construction of the lines projected in 1836 and 1837 went on steadily during the following years, for a few years the number of proposed new lines fell sharply. In 1840 no new railway acts were passed by Parliament. By the early 1840's, however, most of the lines projected in the 'railway mania' of 1836–7 were completed and the summer of 1843 saw the completion of nearly two thousand miles of railway line in Great Britain.

Two thousand miles, however, is but a small fraction of the milage of the railway system of Britain as we know it today, and many decades of brisk activity were to be needed to complete the work. After the first of the great booms in railway building in the 1830's, there was, as we have seen, a pause in the early 1840's. These were years of depression in many branches of economic activity in the country, but in 1845 there was a renewal of enthusiasm for railway building. The new boom, which lasted until 1847, produced almost five thousand additional miles of railway line in Great Britain, and by the end of the 1840's the main framework of Britain's network of railways may be said to have been completed. Most of the subsidiary lines remained to be constructed, and there was continuous activity in railway building for the next forty years. When, in 1886, some 16,700 miles had been laid down, the railway system had reached completion, and there was little new construction

Railway excavation in Camden Town, 1839

after that date. Once the main-line system had been established an elaborate network of branch lines was constructed, while round the larger towns innumerable suburban lines were built to radiate like the spokes of a wheel. London's electric underground system was begun in 1890, and was developed rapidly before 1914. Apart from the extensive network of main and suburban lines in south-eastern England which were amalgamated after the first World War to form the Southern Railway, electricity has never been used extensively on British railways, and the development of diesel locomotives after the second World War has made it unlikely that the use of electricity will be very widely extended in the near future.

The 1840's saw the beginning of the process of amalgamation that has characterized all phases of the development of the British railway system. In its early stages this was mainly the work of George Hudson, the 'Railway King'. In the boom of 1836–7 Hudson had promoted the York and North Midland Railway. He had gone on to create the Midland Railway by the amalgamation of three separate companies to provide a continuous route from the Midlands as far north as Darlington, controlling 179 miles of line. In 1846 a further group of companies joined to create the London and North Western Railway which, by controlling 379 miles of lines, provided a continuous route from London to Birmingham and Manchester. Further amalgamations followed as railway construction proceeded, and though Parliament sanctioned the creation of more than one thousand separate railways during the nineteenth century, by 1914 the process of amalgamation had reduced the number of companies to eleven. After the experience of government control of the whole system during the first World War (1914–18), a further reduction in the number of companies was made by the creation of the 'Big Four' — the Great Western, the Southern, the London, Midland and Scottish, and the London and North Eastern. In 1948 nationalization completed the process by reducing British railways to a single organization.

3. Problems of the Early Railways

The first railways, built in the North of England mainly under Stephenson's direction, had been constructed to the standard gauge of 4 ft. 8½ in. Stephenson had determined the gauge in response to a request from Edward Pease that the width of the tracks should equal that of the carts in the district. Stephenson measured the width of the wheels of no less than one hundred carts and found the average to be 4 ft 8½ in. In the South of England, however, another great engineer, Isambard Kingdom Brunel, planned the Great Western Railway on the broad gauge of 7 ft. 6 in. This railway, carrying main lines from London to Bristol in the West and Birmingham in the Midlands, raised a conflict — the 'Battle of the Gauges' — that was of vital importance for the future of the British system and which ultimately had to be resolved by a parliamentary decision. The importance of the struggle was revealed in the 1840's when extensions of the broad gauge in the Midlands were proposed. These would have involved the Great Western acquiring control over the Grand Junction Railway, one of the earliest railways, linking Birmingham to the Liverpool and Manchester Railway. Other standard gauge lines in the Midlands and North resisted the threat of the broad gauge and the absorption by these other lines of the Grand Junction in 1846 produced the London and North Western Railway Company. By this amalgamation the broad gauge was prevented from spreading northwards, though it remained throughout the Great Western system for many years. It was gradually abandoned in favour of the standard gauge between 1868 and 1892.

One of the earliest railway companies — the Liverpool and Manchester — had come into existence primarily in order to reduce the cost of transport provided until then by canals. Prior to the construction of railways many canals had held almost a monopoly of the transport of goods on certain routes and there were many people who felt that the canal companies were using this monopoly to exact unjustifiably high rates. Thus, from the start, there was a strong element of competition between canal and railway. Both were expensive to construct and both could only justify the heavy expenditure of capital by long periods of profitable operation. Yet after 1830 the advance of the railways meant a struggle to the death, and the superior speed of the railways tipped the balance strongly against the canal. The first effect of any railway which competed against a canal was a reduction in freight rates, and this reduced profits.

The Erewash Canal in Nottinghamshire, for example, reduced its rate for coal from 1s. a ton to 4d. a ton in the 1840's, while the Grand Junction Canal from London to Birmingham, directly threatened by the new London and Birmingham Railway, cut its coal rate from 9s. 1d. to 2s. 0¼d.

The railways from the start adopted an aggressive attitude towards the canals, for canal competition reduced railway profits in the same way that railway competition threatened the canals. Railway companies bought out the shareholders of canals, and by acquiring control in this way either closed down the canals or raised their freight rates so that they no longer offered any threat to the railway. Between 1845 and 1847 nearly one thousand miles of canals passed into the hands of the railways in this way. By the end of the nineteenth century the greater part of Britain's system of artificial waterways had passed into the control of the railways. A few canals escaped the clutches of the railways, and one or two even recovered their independence from the railways later in the century. For some freights, the canals were more suitable than the railways, and a very few canal companies even succeeded in increasing their profits in spite of the coming of the railways. But apart from these exceptions, the canals generally were dealt a blow by the railways from which they never recovered. Thus in the twentieth century only a small fraction of Britain's canal system remains open to traffic, the rest having succumbed to the superior advantages of rail transport.

Parliament was not slow to appreciate that the absorption of canals by the railways threatened to create even more dangerous monopolies of local transport than the canals on their own had provided. From the early days of the railways there was a strong body of opinion in the country in favour of parliamentary control over the railways, while there was even a small group who felt that only by state ownership could a satisfactory control be exerted. As early as 1839 a parliamentary committee investigated the question of railway rates after complaints had been made against monopolistic practices by the London and Birmingham Company. This led to an act of 1840 which gave the Board of Trade powers to investigate the accounts of railway companies as well as to inspect the safety of railway lines. This act was replaced by the more important act of 1842 which further extended the Board's powers of supervision and inspection. In 1844, moreover, Gladstone, then President of the Board of Trade, succeeded in persuading Parliament to pass an act which greatly increased the state's powers of interference with the independence of the railway companies. The act recognized that the railways were of importance to the nation and that it was therefore in the nation's interest to make certain demands on the railways. It brought into being the 'parliamentary train', by insisting that each new railway line (the act did not apply to railways already in existence) should provide at least one train a day in each direction which would stop at all stations and convey passengers for not more than one penny per mile in third-class coaches provided with seats protected from the weather. More important as an indicator of the importance Parliament attached to the railways, was the provision in the act for the government to buy for the nation all railways built after the act, after they had been operating for twenty-one years or more. The terms on which the government should 'nationalize' these railways were very advantageous to the companies concerned, but no government ever availed itself of this section of the act and the railways remained in private ownership for a further century. Though no government in the nineteenth century was prepared to go to the extreme of taking over control of some or all of the railways, Parliament continued to be alarmed by the absence of any real competition with the railways. Commissions were appointed both in 1846 and 1878 to consider the problem of the control of railway fares, and eventually an act of 1894 made it illegal for railway companies to raise their fares above their 1892 levels.

4. THE ECONOMIC AND SOCIAL CONSEQUENCES OF RAILWAY BUILDING

The construction of the railways in the mid-nineteenth century had involved the employment of many scores of thousands of workers, for the excavation of cuttings, the driving of tunnels and the building of embankments was a slow and laborious business when there were no tools bigger than a pick and a shovel, and when every foot of earth had to be carried in a wheelbarrow. In a time of rising population and periodic acute unemployment this was an advantage not to be scorned. The railways also provided a vast new market for the products of the iron industry, for rails, locomotives and rolling stock consumed thousands of tons of iron yearly. The railways also became an important consumer of coal, and provided a rapidly growing market for the mines. The works and repair centres of the larger railway companies provided employment for such large numbers of men of a wide range of skills that new towns were created at railway centres like Crewe and Swindon. The population of Crewe, for example, which in 1841 had been a mere 203, grew to nearly 18,000 by 1871. The populations of other towns like Darlington and Rugby were greatly increased by the employment created by the railways.

The value of the railways, however, lay more in the stimulus they afforded to other industries and to agriculture. By providing a quick service for perishable foodstuffs like milk and market garden produce, they enabled farmers in areas previously remote from the vast new towns to profit from the growing urban demand. The reduced cost of transport lowered the price of agricultural produce and increased its sale. Thus it became practicable for farmers in counties as far distant from London as Norfolk, Dorset and Herefordshire to specialize in milk production for the London market. Even a county as remote as Aberdeenshire was able to develop a valuable trade in the fattening and slaughtering of imported store cattle for the London market. The railways made possible the growth of the fresh-fish industry; not only were consumers in inland areas able to improve their diet by the substitution of fresh for salted fish, but the fishing industry itself developed during the second half of the nineteenth century into a large-scale industry based on a few main ports, each organized for rapid distribution of large quantities of fresh-caught fish. Grimsby, Hull, Fleetwood and Aberdeen owe their development as fish markets almost entirely to the coming of the railways. Similarly, it is scarcely possible to exaggerate the significance of the coming of the railways for industrial growth in Britain. The coal industry probably owes more than any other industry to the growth of the railway system. Before the 1830's, apart from the very limited local markets, almost all the coal mined had to be transported by water. For this reason only those coalfields near the coast could hope for large markets, except those like, for example, Shropshire and South Wales, which had succeeded in attracting a coal-consuming industry like iron-making. The railways, therefore, immediately opened up the inland coalfields, permitting a very big expansion of output and a considerable growth in the consumption of coal for domestic heating and cooking, thus contributing to a rise in living standards. Later in the century railways made possible the opening up of new iron ore-fields. In the 1850's and '60's, for example, a closely-woven network of railways opened up the iron ore mines of the Cleveland Hills of North Yorkshire. Towards the end of the century the vast reserves of ore in Lincolnshire and Northamptonshire were made available for the British steel industry by the invention of the basic process of steel-making (see Chapter 18, section 1), but their utilization depended upon the railways bringing in coal from distant coalfields.

Socially the railways did much to revolutionize many people's way of life. The railway created the suburb and assisted in making towns healthier and pleasanter. So long as people had to live within walking distance of their daily work, towns remained crowded and congested. Though in the mid-twentieth century we may regret that our sprawling suburbs cover such vast areas, the rapidly growing urban population of the nineteenth century had to be housed, and the railway, by facilitating suburban spread, at least prevented urban housing from becoming denser and, therefore, unhealthier. Another social achievement of the railways in nineteenth century Britain was the development of the seaside resort. Brighton, Southend, Blackpool, Morecambe, the Ayrshire coast towns, and a host of similar resorts grew only after the coming of the railways. In Yorkshire the example of the new-found prosperity of Scarborough and Filey encouraged more than one railway company to construct new branch lines to seaside villages in the hope of developing them into resorts and thereby attracting traffic. At first, in the mid-nineteenth century, only the middle classes were able to afford the luxury of annual holidays, but the habit began to spread to the working class towards the end of the century, and became fairly general by the mid-twentieth century in all sections of the population. In the field of education, the growth of the many boarding schools was possible only after the arrival of the railways.

5. Shipping

The principal changes that affected British shipping in the nineteenth century were in two directions — the change from wood to steel as the building material, and the change from sail to steam as the means of propulsion.

Since the sixteenth century, when the new long overseas trade routes had demanded more and larger vessels, the raw material for shipbuilding had been permanently in short supply. Though English oak provided the framework for the wooden hulls, deck-boards, masts and spars had all to be imported, and a shortage of timber for naval shipbuilding remained a constant worry to English governments in the seventeenth and eighteenth centuries. Since oak trees only grew to a certain size, moreover, the size of ships was limited, for keels and stern-posts had to be made of single timbers. Thus the largest ships, even in the early nineteenth century, seldom exceeded 1600 tons, and the usual size for a cargo vessel was merely a few hundred tons. The use of iron and steel in shipbuilding made possible the construction of ships many times larger than the wooden vessels. By the 1930's, liners were being built up to 80,000 tons, and after the second World War oil tankers of 100,000 tons were being planned.

In 1787 the Midlands ironmaster, John Wilkinson, built a canal barge entirely of iron, which astonished his contemporaries by floating. This demonstrated that iron was a practical material from which to build ships. Wilkinson's idea was not rapidly adopted by shipbuilders largely because the technique of iron manufacture still made the production of large thin plates of wrought iron suitable for shipbuilding expensive. Developments in the iron industry following Cort's invention of puddling and rolling made the production of plates and girders for shipbuilding practicable. In the first two decades of the nineteenth century iron canal barges in imitation of Wilkinson's were built, and in 1822 Aaron Manby built an iron steamship in sections at his works at Tipton in the Black Country, transported the sections to London, and set it on the Thames. This proved to be the beginning of a very rapid spread in the use of iron in shipbuilding. At first the iron ships were small, being used mainly for river navigation, and many British-built iron ships plied on French rivers at this period.

A strong prejudice against iron ships remained, and few sea-going iron ships were launched before 1850. In the 1850's, however, passenger vessels began to be built normally of iron, and after 1870 few wooden ships were built. The most remarkable venture in iron shipbuilding of the nineteenth century was the construction of the *Great Eastern*, launched in 1858. This great vessel of nearly 19,000 tons was almost 700 feet long, 83 feet across the beam, and constructed entirely of iron. Powered both by paddle wheels and screw, she achieved an average speed of 14 knots on her first Atlantic crossing in 1860. She had accommodation for no less than 4,000 passengers, though carrying only twenty lifeboats. Though the ship was never a commercial success, and after 1865 was used as a cable-laying vessel, her construction nevertheless was a triumph of engineering, and it was 1899 before a larger vessel put to sea.

After Bessemer's invention of the cheap steelmaking process in 1856 (see Chapter 18, section 1), steel plates, lighter and stronger than wrought iron plates, became available for shipbuilding, permitting further increase in the size and carrying capacity of vessels. But the shipbuilding industry was slow in adopting steel, and as late as 1882, twenty-six years after Bessemer's invention, only 100 out of a total of nearly 800 ships under construction in British yards were built of steel. It was not until the very end of the nineteenth century that steel became the universal material for shipbuilding.

The story of the change from wood to steel in shipbuilding is thus a long one — of almost one hundred years. The adoption of steam power in the place of sail was almost as long-drawn-out a process. The starting-point, of course, was Watt's invention of the rotary steam engine (see Chapter 10, section 3). Watt's engine, however, was far too bulky to be useful as a marine engine, and the steam-driven vessel had to wait until the development of the high-pressure boiler had reduced the size of a steam engine to manageable proportions. The first boat to be propelled successfully by steam alone was built by William Symington and made its maiden voyage on the Clyde in 1804. It was driven by paddle-wheels. The first steamship to run commercially was Henry Bell's *Comet* of twenty-eight tons, which ran a regular service on the Clyde from 1812. In the early nineteenth century the relatively low pressure used in steam engines involved a high consumption of coal in proportion to the power produced, and this restricted the distance over which steamships could run, for the greater the distance the greater the quantity of coal that must be carried. However, improvements to the marine steam engine were steadily being made, and in 1819, the *Savannah*, a sailing vessel assisted by steam-driven paddles, became the first steamship to cross the Atlantic, averaging six knots, taking twenty-seven days, and using her steam paddles for eighty-five hours on the crossing. It was not until 1838 that a vessel — the *Sirius* (703 tons) — crossed the Atlantic entirely under steam power.

All these early steamships were driven by paddle-wheels, but the future of steam navigation lay with the propeller. Francis Pettit Smith produced the first successful screw-propelled vessel on the Paddington Canal in London in 1837, and in the following year the *Archimedes*, of 237 tons, demonstrated the superiority of the propellor over the paddle-wheel. Thereafter there was a gradual transition to the use of the propellor in steamships. The first propellor-driven steamship on the Atlantic run was the *Great Britain* which crossed to America in 1845 in fourteen days. The *Great Eastern* of 1858, described in a previous paragraph, employed both propellor and paddle-wheels.

The early steamships offered the advantage of speed and regularity — there was no more waiting for favourable winds. Yet their high coal consumption reduced the quantity of cargo they could carry, and for some decades their use was confined to the passenger traffic of the Atlantic service and European waters. Over the longer runs — to the Far East, India and Australia, for example — the sailing vessel, not needing to occupy valuable cargo space with coal fuel, was able to operate more cheaply. Two further developments were necessary before the steamship could drive out the sailing vessel — the establishment of coaling stations on the principal sea routes of the world, and the development of the compound marine engine. The former was achieved gradually at points like Gibraltar, Suez, Aden and Singapore in the second half of the nineteenth century. The latter was a slow process of development. The principle of the compound engine involved making use of the steam exhaust from the cylinder in a second cylinder at a slightly lower pressure than the first. An important advance was made with Lord Dundonald's invention of the tubular boiler in 1848, which produced the higher steam pressures that in turn made possible the compound engine. The first compound engines were used in ships in the 1860's. The resultant saving of nearly 60% in fuel consumption permitted steamships to compete with sailing vessels on the China tea run.

In spite of these improvements, and of the opening of the Suez Canal in 1869, which considerably shortened the voyage to the East for steamships, sailing vessels continued to hold their own against steamships in the 1860's and 1870's on many routes. This was partly due to the development of the iron sailing *clipper*, the ultimate stage in the development of the sailing vessel. These vessels combined a high cargo capacity (made possible by new techniques of iron ship construction) with the extensive use of steam winches which cut down the crew required to operate them. These advantages reduced the freight cost on clippers to a point at which steamships were unable to compete until the last years of the nineteenth century.

Though the improvement in steel-making after 1856 enabled steel boilers to be made capable of pressure three times as great as those commonly used in the 1850's, the development that finally gave the steamship the decisive victory over sail was the *triple-expansion* marine engine, first employed in the *Aberdeen* of 1881. This type of engine used three cylinders successively driven by steam at decreasing pressures. The economy of fuel thus achieved at last drove the sailing vessel off nearly all the sea routes of the world.

The heyday of the triple-expansion engine was short, for in 1884 Charles Parsons (1854–1931), a young Newcastle engineer, took out his patent for the turbine. This revolutionary use of steam immediately opened up vast possibilities. The turbine ran at high speeds and produced far greater power in relation to fuel consumption than did the formal steam engine. Parsons first applied his turbine engine to marine propulsion in 1884, when he built a small experimental vessel called the *Turbinia*.

After unsuccessful efforts to convince the Admiralty of the value of his invention, Parsons dramatically demonstrated the virtues of his engine by appearing among the naval vessels drawn up for review at Spithead on the occasion of Queen Victoria's Diamond Jubilee in 1897. The tiny vessel achieved the incredible speed of 34·5 knots, and the future of the turbine was no longer in doubt. The Navy launched its first turbine destroyer in 1900, and in 1904 the *Virginia*, the first turbine-driven Atlantic liner, took the water. Early in the new century the introduction of the geared turbine made the turbine economically attractive for cargo vessels.

The most recent advance in shipbuilding has been the adoption of the diesel engine. First successfully developed in 1897 by Rudolf Diesel, a German engineer living in Paris, it was not until 1912 that the diesel engine was employed in ships. The advantage of this type of engine was economy of both fuel and labour costs in running. In 1930 two new transatlantic liners, the *Brittanic* and the *Georgic*, were equipped with diesel power, since when there has been a steady increase in the proportion of diesel-powered ships launched.

The technical progress outlined in the foregoing paragraphs produced, in the space of a century, a revolution in transport of immense economic and social significance. International trade over long distances in bulky goods such as grain, iron ore, coal and, ultimately, petroleum, became possible. By facilitating the interchange of the surplus commodities of all countries of the world, the steamship was probably the most important single factor in sustaining the living standards of the rapidly growing population of the world, and of raising that of many countries. In Britain it transformed shipbuilding into a major industry and concentrated it in half a dozen centres. The demand from the shipbuilding industry was a major factor in the expansion of the steel industry in the second half of the nineteenth century, while the demand from steam shipping created an important new market for the coal-mining industry.

6. MOTOR TRANSPORT

Though the invention of the internal combustion engine has revolutionized transport, its history is still relatively short. The

earliest petrol-driven motor car had been produced in 1887 by
the German, Daimler, but it was not until 1896 that the first
motor cars were assembled in England. The year coincided
with the removal of the obligation of drivers of 'horseless
carriages' (steam-driven before 1896) to be preceded by a man
on foot to warn pedestrians. (Before 1878 the man had been
obliged to carry a red flag.) Once here, the motor car multiplied rapidly, and within eight years well over 20,000 motor
cars were licensed. The petrol-engined car was immediately
adapted to replace the horse omnibus that had filled the busy
streets of London and other towns for over fifty years. By 1907
one-third of London's nine hundred buses were motor-buses
built by Daimlers, Leylands, Crossleys, Maudslays and others.

The rapid increase in the number of motor vehicles on the
roads in the period immediately before 1914 created a number
of problems. The government expressed its concern at the
growing density of motor traffic on busy roads like that in
Kingston Vale, Surrey, where no less than eighty-two motor
vehicles passed every hour in 1911! Though English roads had
undergone steady improvement during the nineteenth century,
they were not for the most part provided with the smooth, hard
surfaces essential for modern motor traffic. The need to make
some new and adequate provision for road surfaces capable of
sustaining fast-moving motor traffic induced the government in
1909 to create the *Road Board*, with access to the *Road Fund*,
provided from the proceeds of motor taxation. Almost all the
Road Board's expenditure at first went on the improvement of
road surfaces, but later it turned its attention to the building of
new roads. By 1914 it had planned the first of the new approach
roads to London — the road which, though the first World War
delayed its completion until 1927, became the Great West
Road. After the first World War the number of motor vehicles
continued to increase steadily. From just under one million
motor vehicles of all kinds in 1922, the number rose to $2\frac{1}{4}$
million in 1930. To handle the growing problem, the Road
Board was transformed into the Ministry of Transport in 1919,
and many new major roads were constructed during the 1920's
and 1930's.

More people, however, were affected by the introduction of
motor buses than of cars. During the nineteenth century horse

buses and horse-drawn trams, running on rails, provided the
only forms of public transport in the big towns. Most of these
were provided by private companies, though some town corporations, following the example of Manchester and Leeds, initiated
corporation tramway services, particularly after the introduction of electric trams in the 1890's. After 1900 there was a
rapid extension of electric tramways, and in the first seven years
of the new century the mileage was increased from 1,000 to
2,250 miles. By the 1920's, municipalities were beginning to
tear up the tram-lines as trams gave way to the more popular
motor-buses. Some towns, like London, had already acquired a
large fleet of motor-buses before 1914, and made little use of
electric trams. Others, to their cost, had equipped themselves
lavishly with tramways, and clung to these, in some cases until
the 1950's, in the face of competition from the newer buses.
In 1920, 48 town councils operated a total of 649 buses; by 1929
the numbers had risen to 100 corporations running between
them over 4,700 buses.

By the 1950's the vast increase of motor traffic had become
one of the country's major problems; but during its first half
century the petrol engine had contributed to make many
important changes in the nation's economy and the life of its
people. By emancipating industry from its dependence upon
water or rail transport, businessmen were able to locate their
factories more conveniently near centres of consumption. Light
industries rapidly grew up between the wars alongside the main
roads leading out of the big towns. While many millions of
people made use of motor cars to travel about the country on
pleasure or business much more widely than hitherto, it was the
country people, living often in areas relatively remote from
railways, whose lives were most enlivened by the coming of the
bus. Finally, just as the railways had mortally wounded their
predecessors, the canals, so the motor car reduced the importance of the railways, robbing them of much of their goods
traffic and causing the closure, by the 1950's, of many formerly
busy branch lines.

CHAPTER 17

OVERSEAS TRADE

1. THE SECOND BRITISH EMPIRE

The unsuccessful outcome of the War of American Independence (1775–83) had lost Britain her first overseas empire. For a century and a half the thirteen colonies on the American mainland had constituted the wealthiest and most valued part of the Empire, and the whole body of regulation concerning colonial trade reviewed in Chapter 7, section 3, had related principally to the American colonies. Their loss in 1783, however, still left Britain with important overseas possessions — Canada, won from the French during the Seven Years' War (1756–63), many West Indian islands, and some valuable trading stations in India. In 1770 Captain Cook's re-discovery of Australia had opened up possibilities of the colonization of an entire new continent, though until the end of the eighteenth century the only British settlers were convicts sent there by Pitt after the loss of the American colonies had closed that channel for transportation.

The defeat of France in 1815 brought further additions to the British Empire which were ultimately to be of some importance to the development of overseas trade. Holland, fully occupied with her own problems of recovery, was glad to accept £6 million for the Cape of Good Hope colony which Britain had occupied ever since the French invasion of Holland in 1793. Malta, which Nelson had captured from the French (who in turn had taken it from the Knights of St. John) in 1798, joined Gibraltar as an invaluable naval base (and later, coaling station) in the Mediterranean. One or two of the French West Indian islands were likewise transferred to British rule.

Apart from India, where British power was exercised through influence over native princes rather than by direct rule, the Empire was of but small significance in British overseas trade at the end of the Napoleonic Wars. The West Indies provided a useful market for some British manufactures, exporting in return substantial quantities of sugar. The suppression of the slave trade in 1807 had ended the lucrative triangular trade route on which the fortunes of Bristol and Liverpool had been built in the eighteenth century, and the abolition of slavery in 1833, by increasing the cost of production of sugar in the islands, dealt the remaining trade of the British West Indies a severe blow, in spite of £20 million compensation paid by the British taxpayer to the former slave-owners.

Since the loss of the American colonies in 1783, then, Britain's trade with her empire was of secondary importance only, pride of place being held by European, Mediterranean, South American and Far Eastern markets. Nevertheless, important developments were already afoot in the early years of the nineteenth century which promised to alter the pattern of Britain's overseas trade very considerably before the century was out. In India, the trading monopoly of the East India Company was abolished in 1813 and the trade thrown open to all. At the same time, British control was being steadily increased. Lord Hastings, as Governor-General, reduced the Gurkhas of Nepal and the Marathas of Central India to British rule. Under the governorship of Lord Bentinck between 1828 and 1835, the foundations of the modern British civil government were laid. Between 1824 and 1886, Assam and Burma were brought under British rule. In the 1840's, Sind and the Punjab were annexed. With the suppression of the Indian Mutiny in 1857, virtually the whole of India was under direct British rule. From 1845 onwards, aided by British government guarantees for payment of interest on capital borrowed, the Indian railway system was constructed. Amongst the aims of railway construction in India in the third quarter of the nineteenth century was the opening up of the interior to British trade, and the export of India's basic raw materials such as cotton and jute.

Equally significant developments were taking place further east in Australia and New Zealand. Though the first settlements in Australia in the 1780's had been solely of convicts, very soon there was a steady flow of free emigrants, and by 1815 there were the beginnings of large-scale capitalist sheep-farming on which Australia's growing prosperity in the nineteenth century was mainly based. The first shipment of Australian wool to

England were made in the 1820's, and by the 1840's this had
become an important trade, providing a substantial part of the
raw material for the English woollen industry. The discovery of
gold in Australia in 1849–51 drew large numbers of emigrants
to that country. Few of these actually found a living in gold-
mining, but this sudden spurt in population provided a valuable
stimulus to Australia's general economic development. The
settlement of New Zealand came rather later. Edward Gibbon
Wakefield, a reformer who had taken an active part in encouraging settlement in Australia, formed a New Zealand Association in 1837 which provided the first British settlers there.

The economic development of Britain's other large colonies —
South Africa and Canada — came more gradually. In South
Africa, European settlement had been in the hands of the Dutch
Boers who chose farming rather than trade. Though the British,
in conflict with the Boers from time to time, steadily extended
their control over South Africa by the annexation of Natal in
1843, of Basutoland in 1868, and of the Boer republics of Transvaal and Orange River finally (for the third time) in 1902, it
was really the discovery of diamonds at Kimberley in 1871 and
gold in the Rand at Johannesburg in 1884 that drew out large
numbers of British settlers and many millions of British capital.
Not until the last quarter of the century was Britain's trade
with South Africa of great importance. Similarly, in Canada,
though French rule had been ended in 1763, British settlers
were not numerous in the early nineteenth century. The
Hudson's Bay Company's business in furs, begun in the late
seventeenth century, still carried on in the nineteenth, though it
never formed more than a minute proportion of Britain's total
trade. As the extreme east of Canada had been settled mainly
by the French before the nineteenth century, the British settlers
of the nineteenth century moved further up the St. Lawrence,
founding the colony of Ontario and pushing further west to
Winnipeg and the great prairies later in the century. Though
Canada already exported some wheat to England early in the
nineteenth century, it was the construction of the Canadian
Pacific Railway between 1872 and 1885 — 'the spinal cord of
the new Canadian nation' as it has been called by one historian
—that caused Canada to leap into importance in British overseas
trade.

The opening up of Africa to British trade came mainly from the 1880's onwards. The British army entered Egypt in 1882 and Britain remained the effective ruler of Egypt until after the second World War. In 1898 the conquest of the Sudan followed the construction of a railway southwards from Egypt. British merchants had been trading in West Africa since Hawkins had opened the slave trade in the sixteenth century: in the unsettled conditions of intermittent tribal warfare, however, trade was unlikely to expand without more stable government. In the general scramble by European countries for African colonies in the 1880's, Britain emerged with Sierra Leone, Nigeria, Gambia and the Gold Coast (now Ghana), and the Royal Niger Company, chartered by the Crown in 1886, opened a new era in British trade to West Africa. To the north of the Boer territories, Cecil Rhodes, Prime Minister of the Cape Colony in the 1890's, dreamed of an expansion of British rule which would ultimately link Egypt to the Cape in a single expanse of 'red on the map'. His British South Africa Company acquired trading rights over the vast territories now called after him, and the addition of Tanganyika (a former German colony) in 1918 created an enormous tract of British territory in central and east Africa whose economic development, however, had to wait mainly till the twentieth century.

2. THE DEVELOPMENT OF OVERSEAS TRADE

One of the most significant results of the industrial changes of the late eighteenth and early nineteenth centuries was the increase in industrial production far beyond the immediate needs of the home market, leaving an ever-increasing surplus available for export. These growing exports, in their turn, provided the means of purchasing more foodstuffs and raw materials from abroad. In this way it became possible not merely to maintain the standard of life of the rapidly expanding population, but even to improve it. This sequence of cause and effect helps to explain why, in the nineteenth century, Britain's overseas trade consisted mainly of the exchange of manufactured exports for imports of foodstuffs and raw materials, and why it has continued to grow, not only absolutely but also relatively to the population.

Early in the nineteenth century food imports accounted for little more than one-quarter of all imports; by the twentieth century they accounted for over 40%. Within this group, there was an almost complete changeover during the nineteenth century. At the beginning of the period, sugar and wines comprised almost two-thirds of these imports, but by the twentieth century meat, grain and dairy produce were the most important foodstuffs. Imports of grain, of course, grew steadily throughout the nineteenth century, particularly after the repeal of the corn laws in 1846 and later after the opening of the American wheatlands by railway construction in the last third of the century. Meat imports grew rapidly after the adoption of refrigeration in steamships during the 1880's, while imports of butter, cheese and eggs — a sign of rising standards of living in the urban workers — became significant from the 1870's. Technical changes in industry accounted for the fifteenfold expansion between the 1820's and the 1930's of imports of raw materials. New industries required new raw materials often unobtainable in this country — rubber, aluminium (made from bauxite) and chemicals, while the enormous expansion of older industries exhausted Britain's raw material supplies and led to the growth of substantial new trades. Many of Britain's iron ore-fields, for example, were exhausted in the late nineteenth century, and from 1870 ore began to be imported, mainly from Spain and Scandinavia, so that by the 1930's well over half Britain's output of pig iron was made from imported ore. Supplies of home-grown wool were inadequate by the middle of the nineteenth century, and were increasingly supplemented by imports from Australia.

Another change in the nature of Britain's overseas trade during this period, perhaps more significant in the long run, was the growth of imports of semi-manufactured and manufactured goods. Early in the nineteenth century Britain, the leading industrial country, supplied the world with manufactures. As other countries industrialized during the century, their goods first replaced British manufactures in their own home markets, later competed with British exports in other foreign markets, and finally found their way into Britain. Some of these, of course, were specialized products not made in this country, but many of them, like steel and textile products, competed directly with the home industries. Imports of iron and steel products multiplied tenfold between the 1870's and 1914 and grew still more in the 1920's. It was the rapidly growing imports of cheap cotton goods from Japan and India, of chemicals and metal manufactures from Germany, and of jute goods from India which contributed to the demand for tariff protection in the inter-war period.

Britain has never had any very large agricultural surplus to export in modern times, and, with the single exception of coal, her exports in the nineteenth and twentieth centuries have always consisted predominantly of manufactures. Exports of manufactures comprised 78% of all exports in 1815 and 72% in the inter-war period of the twentieth century. From the second half of the nineteenth century coal exports have accounted for most of the remainder, having grown from 3 million tons in 1850 to 77 million tons in 1913. Coal exports suffered severely from foreign competition between the two World Wars of the twentieth century, and though a series of trade treaties, particularly with Scandinavian countries in the late 1930's, led to some improvement in exports, they never recovered their pre-1914 level. For the first decade after the second World War the immense growth of British industry consumed all the coal that could be produced at home, even requiring some imports from the United States in one or two years, and only small quantities of coal necessary to earn foreign exchange were exported.

Early in the nineteenth century textile goods accounted for over three-quarters of all manufactured exports, and of these, cotton predominated heavily. This preponderance of cotton was undermined steadily in the nineteenth century by the growth of the engineering industries, so that by 1914, textiles only accounted for half the exports, the other very diverse half including a wide range of machinery, iron and steel goods and chemicals. This pattern was not seriously altered between the wars, except that cotton exports fell heavily (cotton piece goods exports falling, for example, from 3·6 million square yards in 1929 to 2·2 million square yards in 1932). But after the second World War a quite different pattern began to emerge with the rise of the motor and aircraft industries. In the late 1950's these accounted for 12% of total exports, and with other forms of machinery and steel manufactures made up a substantial part of the export trade.

These changes in the nature of overseas trade have been accompanied by some significant changes in its direction. Trade with Europe, for example, has declined in relative importance, as more distant markets have appeared. Exports to Europe, which accounted for 55% of all exports early in the nineteenth century, had fallen to 35% in the 1920's. Political and geographical changes help to explain the growth of the trade with other continents. Britain's early recognition of the independence of the former Spanish South American colonies in the 1820's led to a growth of trade with those countries. The United States remained an important market and source of imports until their adoption of high tariffs late in the nineteenth century restricted trade. But it was the growth of the Empire itself which produced the most important new trades. In the later nineteenth century, India steadily consumed about 40% of all Britain's cotton textile exports, until the rise of her own cotton industry in the twentieth century reduced these imports to a small fraction of their nineteenth-century level. Australia and New Zealand, whose colonization only began effectively in the first half of the nineteenth century, became important markets in the second half. By the mid-nineteenth century, 30% of Britain's exports went to the Empire. This proportion had risen to 40% by 1930, and the adoption of Imperial Preference at the Ottawa Conference (see section 5 of this chapter) increased this still further to 44%. The industrialization of some Commonwealth countries since the second World War has led to some slight decline in the Commonwealth's share of the trade.

3. THE FREE TRADE MOVEMENT

British overseas trade in the early nineteenth century was subject to many regulations as well as duties on both imports and exports. Regulation had been imposed mainly during the sixteenth, seventeenth and eighteenth centuries in the belief that it was both desirable and possible to guide trade in directions more likely to achieve the ends of economic policy (see Chapter 7); duties were imposed for two reasons, either to produce revenue for the government, or to restrict undesirable trades. Since the publication of Adam Smith's *Wealth of Nations* in 1776, and even earlier, both statesmen and economists were coming round to the view that any form of restriction was theoretically unsound and likely to reduce the country's wealth; but though the younger Pitt between 1784 and 1793 had made a start with the reduction of the tariff, the urgency of the government's need for revenue after 1793 led to the raising rather than the lowering of customs duties. When the war was over in 1815, and when the economy slowly and painfully began to recover from the financial strains of the post-war depression, Huskisson at the Board of Trade was able to take up, after an interval of some thirty years, the work of freeing British trade begun in the 1780's by William Pitt.

At the Board of Trade between 1823 and 1827 Huskisson made numerous important modifications to the tariff and to trade regulations, the general effect of which was to reduce the hindrance to trade. He effected very considerable reductions to customs duties by removing prohibitions and prohibitively high duties. He fixed a maximum duty of 30% on imports of manufactured goods. Most important of all, he designed an important modification to the 1815 Corn Law (see Chapter 19, section 1), which, by decreasing the duty in proportion as the price rose, contrived to give protection to the farmer without prohibiting altogether the import of grain, as the 1815 Corn Law had tended to do. This *sliding scale*, though devised by Huskisson, was actually introduced in 1828 by the Duke of Wellington's ministry. Huskisson also made some important modifications to the Navigation Laws (see Chapter 7, section 4) by making concessions to foreign countries in return for similar concessions by them in favour of British shipping. These *reciprocal trade treaties* helped to encourage trade, particularly with Europe and with the former Spanish South American colonies, whose independence Canning (Foreign Secretary in Lord Liverpool's ministry from 1822–7) had been the first to recognize in 1823.

Another group of trade restrictions was being gradually removed at this period. These were the trading monopolies of the old chartered trading companies, most of whose rights originated in the sixteenth and seventeenth centuries. The Levant and Royal African Companies gave up their rights in

1821, while the greatest of all the companies, the East India Company, was deprived of its exclusive trading rights with India in 1813, though it retained its monopoly of the China trade for a further twenty years. Only the relatively unimportant Hudson's Bay Company contrived to retain its trading rights and is the only one of the old chartered companies still trading today. Other steps to 'liberalize' trade included the removal of the prohibition on the export of machinery and of the emigration of skilled artisans in 1824 and 1825. The Navigation Laws were not finally repealed until 1849.

The Whig government of the 1830's was too concerned with problems of constitutional and social reform to show much interest in overseas trade, an indifference which seemed to be justified during most of that decade by the steady expansion of both industry and trade. Between 1837 and 1842, however, the country's industry declined into what was probably the most serious depression of the nineteenth century, and the urgent need of some measure to re-invigorate the economy persuaded Peel, the Prime Minister of the Conservative government which came into office in 1841, to make substantial reductions of the tariff. Peel was persuaded by his young Vice-President of the Board of Trade, William Gladstone, that the increase in trade which would result from a radical reduction of customs duties would not only prove a valuable stimulus to economic recovery but would more than compensate the government for its initial losses of revenue. In his 1842 budget, therefore, Peel made sweeping reductions to import duties, leaving a maximum of 5% duty on imported raw materials, of $12\frac{1}{2}\%$ on semi-manufactured goods, and of 20% on fully-manufactured goods. He also removed completely the remaining duties on manufactured exports. To compensate the government for the resultant loss of revenue, Peel re-imposed the Income Tax at 7d. in the £. This tax, first levied in 1799 (see Chapter 12, section 3), had been swept away by the flood of popular (middle-class) hatred after the Napoleonic War. Though its revival was intended to be a purely temporary measure, and although Gladstone, when Chancellor of the Exchequer in 1853, had planned to dispense with it, the tax remained to become by the twentieth century the mainstay of government revenue in peace and in war.

The 1842 budget clearly contributed to the recovery of trade and industry from 1843, and this encouraged Peel, once again assisted by the young Gladstone, now President of the Board of Trade, to make a second onslaught on the tariff. In 1845 he swept away all the remaining export duties, removed the excise on glass (an *excise* is a tax on goods produced in the country, as distinct from a *duty*, which is a tax on goods imported or exported), and destroyed most of the remaining import duties, leaving only some on luxuries like wine and tea for revenue purposes, or because of the insistent opposition of vested interests to their removal.

In spite of the immense change Peel had made to the tariff in the short space of four years, one overwhelmingly important duty remained. The refusal of the government to remove the import duty on corn imposed by the Corn Law of 1815 (and modified in 1828) more than cancelled out the popularity which the budgets of 1842 and 1845 had brought. The corn laws between 1815 and 1846 had aimed to restrict or prohibit imports of grain at times when low grain prices indicated relative plenty in Britain. Those who opposed them believed that there were ample supplies of cheap grain being produced in other parts of Europe which were being withheld from the British consumer, who was thus having to pay consistently more for his bread than he would had there been no corn laws. In fact it is doubtful, nor is there any means of knowing exactly, whether bread prices really would have been lower without the corn laws, and there may be some significance in the fact that organized opposition to the corn laws did not appear until twenty-three years after the 1815 law, and then mainly as a political device to bring together dissident elements in the political Radical movement. It seems that opposition to the corn laws was the only cry which would rally working-class and middle-class Radicals, rebel Whigs and rebel Tories.

It was therefore with aims half political and half economic that a group of Manchester free traders founded the Anti-Corn Law League in 1838. For some years the League made very little progress, their meetings being broken up by Chartists who resented this counter-attraction to their own movement, whilst the steps towards free trade taken by Peel's budgets of the 1840's took some of the ground from under their feet. The

League, however, was led by a distinguished free trade poli-
tician, Richard Cobden, at this time Member of Parliament for
Oldham, Lancashire, and it slowly developed an effective
propaganda machine. Not all the League's methods of winning
over voters to their cause would pass today as 'honest' practice,
but by 1845 these methods had built up the League into a
formidable organization whose persistence was at last beginning
to wear down the resistance of members of the government.
Though the Irish potato famine of 1845–6 proved to be the
decisive factor in converting the government to *repeal* (cancellation of statutes) the corn laws, the work of the League was so
effective that the government would probably have been forced
at least to modify the laws seriously before long. Peel had
already in 1842 modified the sliding scale of 1828 in a way
which effectively reduced the level of duties and hence encouraged increased imports, but in 1845 the desperate need of
the starving Irish peasantry for immediate cheap food, combined with a disastrously poor harvest in Britain in the same
year, forced the government's hands, and in June 1846 the laws
were repealed, leaving only a nominal duty of 4s. a quarter, a
duty that was to be reduced to 1s. in 1849.

The price of the repeal of the corn laws was a split in the
Conservative party. Peel was unable to carry all his party with
him on this issue, and had pushed repeal through the House
of Commons only with substantial support from a section of
the Whig opposition. The 'rebel' Conservatives, led by the
young Disraeli, immediately took their revenge on their leader
and secured his defeat on a question of Irish policy. Though
Peel retired from politics in 1846 and died four years later after
a fall from his horse, the impetus he had given to the free trade
movement was carried on by the small but extremely able group
of 'Peelites' led after Peel's death by Gladstone. The Peelites
joined in Lord Aberdeen's coalition government in 1853–5 as
well as in Lord Palmerston's Liberal ministry of 1859–65. As
Chancellor of the Exchequer in both these ministries, Gladstone
was able to complete Peel's work by removal of the last obstacles
to free trade. His budget of 1853 removed most of the remaining
duties on semi-manufactured imports and fixed a maximum
duty of 10% on manufactured imports. He also lowered some
of the few remaining duties on imported foodstuffs — tea

cocoa, fruit, eggs and butter, making good the loss of revenue by renewing the income tax. His budget of 1860 completed the work by removing the remaining duties, leaving only forty-eight commodities on which now purely revenue duties remained. In the same year he sent the free trader Richard Cobden to France to negotiate a trade treaty with France. By this treaty England agreed to reduce the duties (some of the few remaining revenue duties) on French wines and brandy, in return for which France reduced her tariff on some of Britain's most important exports to France — coal, iron, machinery and some textiles.

Thus by 1860 Britain had removed all artificial hindrances to trade which it was in her power to remove, except those on a limited range of goods, mainly luxuries, which were retained as a source of revenue to the government. This was done without any serious injury to Britain's industries, since before 1860 Britain's lead in industry was so marked that it was not in the power of any foreign manufacturer to compete effectively with any of this country's major industries in the home market. Free traders in Britain, known collectively as the *Manchester School* since cotton manufacturers predominated in the movement, believed that free trade would be not merely the means of enriching nations, but would help also to banish war and discord between nations by binding them more closely together with the bonds of trade. Cobden thought of free trade as 'the means, and I believe the only means, of effecting universal and permanent peace'. 'Free trade', he wrote, 'by perfecting the intercourse and securing the dependence of countries one upon another, must inevitably snatch the power from the governments to plunge their people into wars.'

Cobden's prophecy proved to be wrong, if only because few other nations followed Britain's example. Free trade suited the nation with the lead in industrial development; it did not recommend itself to nations whose industrial revolutions had to be made in the face of competition from cheap British manufactures. In the second half of the nineteenth century Britain found herself almost alone in allowing unrestricted imports; and as other countries, particularly Germany and the United States, became industrialized, Britain's isolation increasingly threatened the prosperity of her own industries. The Cobden

Treaty and Gladstone's budget of 1860, the coping stones of the free trade edifice, were followed within a generation by a growing clamour for protection.

4. THE MOVEMENT FOR TARIFF REFORM

Competition from newly-industrialized foreign countries became more and more a serious threat to British industry in the 1870's and 1880's. Foreign manufacturers were able to export their goods to Britain free of duties, whilst at the same time enjoying a protected home market, since they retained what in many cases were substantial tariffs against the produce of British and other manufacturers. The apparent unfairness to British manufacturers of this state of affairs led to the formation in 1881 of the *Fair Trade League*, which advocated that this country should place duties on imports from foreign countries equivalent to those placed by these foreign countries on imports from this country. The Fair Trade League won some support for two or three years, but made no impression on government policy. The free trade gospel, as it had been preached by the Manchester School, was too firmly entrenched, and few could be found to support the idea of a return to protection. Even in the depth of the serious depression of the mid-1880's, when a Royal Commission studied 'the Depression of Trade and Industry', only a small minority of the Commissioners were prepared to recommend any departure from the general principles of free trade.

The competition did not ease, however, and some of our competitors, particularly the United States in the McKinley Tariff of 1890, raised their tariffs substantially, so that when in the early years of the new century, the Conservative statesman, Joseph Chamberlain, launched a campaign for *tariff reform*, the case for the revival of some measure of protection looked stronger. Chamberlain, who was Colonial Secretary in Salisbury's and Balfour's governments between 1895 and 1903 saw tariff reform as a means of achieving his own major political aim of strengthening the bonds of the British Empire. During his period at the Colonial Office he had already done much to make both imperial statesmen and peoples more conscious of the unity of the Empire by summoning Imperial

Conferences at which the leading ministers of the Empire came together in London to discuss their common interests. Trade, Chamberlain believed, should also help to weld together the separate units of the Empire. Britain could do much by giving some kind of preferential treatment to imports from the Empire. *Imperial Preference* in trade would be given by allowing imports from the Empire into this country at lower rates of duties than imports from foreign, non-imperial countries. This was clearly not possible without a tariff, and so Chamberlain advocated a a moderate return to protection, in order that some of the duties might then be waived in favour of imperial countries.

But, even with so powerful an advocate, tariff reform evoked little enthusiasm in Britain in the early twentieth century. Chamberlain found little support even in his own party, and for this reason, as well as to free himself so that he could devote his energies entirely to the propagation of the idea of tariff reform, he resigned from the Colonial Office in 1903. For three years he toured the country trying to arouse interest in his grand imperial design, but everywhere he found that the prospect of dearer imported food robbed him of support.

Unfortunately for the movement, a serious illness in 1906 put an end to Chamberlain's political activities, but not before his movement was put to the test of a general election. His political opponents, the Liberals, made great play in the election campaign of the 'big loaf' which they claimed Liberal free trade policy would guarantee, while those Conservatives who stood for tariff reform on Chamberlain's lines would give the electors a 'small loaf'. With the issue crudely but cleverly over-simplified by the opposition in this way, the electorate voted overwhelmingly for the 'big loaf', and the Liberals were returned to Westminster with the largest majority they had had since 1868. Chamberlain's tariff reform movement had split and weakened the Conservative party, had given new life to the wilting free trade idea, and had killed any prospect of even limited protection until after the first World War.

5. The Return to Protection

During the first World War it became necessary, for the first time since the Navigation Laws were repealed in 1849, to introduce some government controls over foreign trade. These controls were mainly concerned to limit the use of scarce shipping. To achieve this aim, the Chancellor of the Exchequer, Reginald McKenna, introduced in 1915 a series of duties on the import of cars, cycles, clocks, watches, films and musical instruments. These *McKenna duties*, as they became known, were to be removed after the war, since the general virtues of free trade were still not seriously questioned. When the war ended, however, they were not repealed, though a small preference was given to imperial imports of these goods. The thin end of the wedge of protection had at last been driven in. A further blow against free trade was struck in 1921, when protection was given to certain industries which had begun during the war to manufacture goods previously supplied by Germany. Under the artificial protection of the war, the manufacture of optical glass, of certain electrical instruments and of some chemicals had begun in this country, and the *Safeguarding of Industries Act* of 1921, by placing a 33⅓% duty on imports of these and a long list of minor articles, aimed to save these infant industries from destruction by renewed German competition.

The Safeguarding of Industries Act authorized the granting of similar protection to other industries if they could prove that unfair foreign competition was damaging them. A few new duties were added during the 1920's under this clause, but when, in 1927, the steel industry applied for protection, the government, still protesting that, in principle at least, it supported free trade, refused protection on the grounds that to concede it to so important an industry would be as good as to admit the desirability of general protection. Free trade was coming under increasingly heavy fire; even in Manchester, the citadel of free trade, cotton merchants, watching the trickle of Indian and Japanese textile imports into this country grow to a steady stream, were themselves beginning to clamour for a protective tariff. It seemed unlikely that free trade would survive another serious depression.

That depression began slowly in 1929, gathered disastrous momentum in 1931, and reached its nadir in 1932. The catastrophic decline in the demand for industrial goods produced a renewal of a clamour for protection which no government could resist. Nothing could be done about the decline of overseas markets, but the home market at least could be preserved for British producers by keeping out imports from foreign competitors. In November 1931, Mr. MacDonald's National Government introduced a temporary measure — the *Abnormal Importations Act* — which imposed high, even prohibitive, duties on imported manufactures for a period of six months. Before this period expired, the act was replaced early in 1932 by the permanent *Import Duties Act* which declared a general 10% duty on most manufactured imports. An important and influential body — the *Import Duties Advisory Committee* under the chairmanship of Sir George May — was set up to consider in detail any changes to the levels of duties which might be thought necessary. Later in the year an Imperial Economic Conference was held at Ottawa, at which Britain agreed to allow imports from countries in the Empire at lower (preferential) rates of duties, realizing at last Joseph Chamberlain's dream of Imperial Preference. Unfortunately, in 1932 the seriousness of world depression, with its accompaniment of bitter trade rivalry, was not conducive to an atmosphere of friendly economic collaboration which Chamberlain had hoped would result from the establishment of Imperial Preference.

The Import Duties Advisory Committee set to work immediately, and its first recommendation (adopted without delay by the government) was for a substantial rise in the level of import duties, which were now to range from 20% to 33%. Amongst the industries to benefit from this change was the steel industry which secured the highest rate of protection against foreign competition. The Committee worked continuously until the outbreak of war in 1939, considering many hundreds of applications from individual industries for changes in the tariff, and recommending many alterations, both upward and downward, some of which, like the removal of the duty on imports of semi-finished steel in 1937 to meet the needs of rearmament, were to have considerable effect on economic conditions. Though many modifications to the duties laid down in the 1932 act were made, the general principle of protection was now firmly accepted, and Britain emerged from the second World War in 1945 with a moderately high level of tariffs, tempered only by a system of Imperial Preference which served to expose industries like cotton and jute to the competition of commonwealth countries (India, Pakistan and Hong Kong) which enjoyed the advantage of cheap labour. Since the second World War, Britain's participation in the *General Agreement on Tariffs and Trade* (G.A.T.T.) has led to some reduction in the general level of duties.

CHAPTER 18

INDUSTRIAL DEVELOPMENT

1. IRON AND STEEL

The foundation of all modern industrial economies is an iron and steel industry; British industries were able to develop rapidly during the nineteenth century because of the prior development of the iron and steel industry. The inventions of the Darbys and Cort, by making available for the production of iron the vast resources of Britain's coalfields, had enormously accelerated the growth of the industry, with the result that the output of pig iron grew from 250,000 tons in 1806 to 650,000 tons in 1830 and one million tons by 1835. Another important advance was made in 1828 when a Scot, Robert Neilson, invented the *Hot Blast Process*. Instead of using the bellows (operated since 1776 by steam power) to produce a blast of cold air for the furnace, Neilson heated the blast to several hundred degrees centigrade. The result was an immense saving of fuel. In a few years, Scottish smelters were able to reduce the amount of coal necessary to smelt a ton of pig iron from 7 tons to 2½ tons. The Scottish ironmasters were quick to take advantage of Neilson's invention, and in fifteen years Scottish pig iron production rose from a mere 37,500 tons to half a million tons. For a time, English reluctance to adopt the hot blast process gave the Scottish producers an overwhelming advantage, for the English producers could not compete with Scottish prices. Growing demand, however, gave scope to producers in all areas, and there was a steady increase in output, punctuated only by the periodic severe depressions to which this industry was particularly susceptible.

But if iron production was facilitated and cheapened by technical improvements, steelmaking scarcely advanced at all. In spite of the superiority of steel over iron for almost all purposes, there were no important technical improvements in its manufacture in the first half of the nineteenth century. As the demand for steel grew, its production in Sheffield, Birmingham and Newcastle increased slowly, but only a minute proportion of all iron was converted into steel even as late as 1850. Moreover, even in ironmaking, the puddling process, though an immense advance on the old forging process, had severe limitations. By the middle of the century, the advances in iron smelting and the steadily growing demand particularly for railways and shipbuilding made some improvement in the processes of refining and steel-making essential.

Henry Bessemer (1813–98), a professional inventor, turned his attention to this problem in the 1850's, and in 1856 gave details of a new process of steelmaking. He showed that by forcing air through molten iron taken directly from the blast furnace the impurities and the carbon in the pig iron were rapidly burnt out, producing molten steel. By this radical new *pneumatic* method, many tons of steel could be produced from molten iron in a mere twenty minutes. If his invention were to be adopted widely, the large-scale production of cheap steel would now become a commercial proposition. Unfortunately, there were two weaknesses to the new *Bessemer* process. The metal produced in the *Bessemer converter* proved to be brittle and commercially valueless until Robert Mushet, a metallurgist, discovered that the addition of a small quantity of manganese to the molten pig iron remedied this fault. Mushet has never had due recognition of his share in this invention, though Bessemer acknowledged his debt to him by personally paying a substantial pension to his widow.

The other weakness was not so easily remedied. Even with Mushet's improvement, the Bessemer process could not make good steel from iron containing phosphorus. Since most of Britain's iron ore was phosphoric, this was a serious weakness. It led to the rapid exhaustion of the one non-phosphoric ore-field in the country — Cumberland — and to the growth, after 1870, of imports of iron ore from Spain, and, later, from Sweden. Another important development — the *open-hearth* method of steelmaking invented by Siemens in 1867 — did nothing to solve the problem of making steel from phosphoric iron. The open-hearth furnace burnt out the impurities in pig iron by means of a flame playing on the surface of the molten metal. It had two advantages over the Bessemer process — that it was easier to regulate more exactly the quality of the finished steel, and that it made possible the extensive use of scrap in steelmaking.

It was not until 1878 that Sidney Gilchrist Thomas, a Post Office clerk, assisted by his cousin, Percy Gilchrist, a chemist, solved the problem of the phosphorus. They found that by lining the steel furnace with dolomite limestone, the phosphorus was extracted from the pig iron, and good steel produced. Moreover, the phosphorus and other waste drawn out of the furnace as a slag was a good fertilizer and thus a valuable by-product of steelmaking. The *Thomas* or *basic* process (so called because of its employment of a basic substance — dolomite) should have acted as a valuable stimulus to the British steel industry. Steel production, which was still less than one-quarter of a million tons in 1870, averaged a little more than two million tons a year in the 1880's, though at this time pig iron output was running at about eight million tons a year. Progress in the steel industry, after an initial stupendous burst in the great boom of the early 1870's, remained very slow, thanks to growing steel industries in other rapidly-industrializing countries. However, the last twenty years before the first World War saw a resumption of development, and steel output doubled during this period.

Apart from the adoption of the electric arc furnace during the first World War, there have been no major technical innovations in steelmaking since the Thomas process, though immense strides have been made in the rolling and finishing of steel, and in the economies of large-scale production. But the technical changes of the nineteenth century have produced some major shifts in the location of the industry. Firstly, for some thirty or forty years after Bessemer's invention in 1856, steelmaking depended upon imported ores. This encouraged the growth of steelmaking centres near the ports of import — in South Wales, on the north-east coast near Middlesbrough, and in the Scottish Lowlands. Secondly, the steady, albeit slow, adoption of the Thomas process from the last years of the nineteenth century, combined with the exhaustion of most of the older ore-fields in England, encouraged the use of the important fields of low-quality phosphoric ore in north Lincolnshire and Northamptonshire. In the twentieth century the advantages of location near these sources of ore has led to the establishment of major new steelmaking centres at Scunthorpe and Appleby-Frodingham in Lincolnshire (now also using ore imported through the newly-built port of Immingham) and at Corby in Northamptonshire. With one exception, industrial inertia or the availability of imported ore has retained the industry in its principal nineteenth century locations — in Staffordshire, the Yorkshire-Derbyshire-Nottinghamshire coalfield, south Lancashire, the north-east coast (Cleveland), Cumberland, and the Scottish Lowlands. The exception has been in South Wales, where the exhaustion of the local ore has driven the industry, in part at least, from the inland valleys to the coast. Much of the expansion in steel production which has taken place since the outbreak of the second World War has resulted from the construction of immense new steel works on the coast near Port Talbot.

Both World Wars have stimulated steel production, but the period after 1930 has seen the most impressive development of any period in the history of English steelmaking. Output has doubled in the twenty years since 1939, and British steel has remained cheap in comparison with costs in other steel-producing countries. Undoubtedly the ever-growing demand from the motor, engineering, shipbuilding and tinplate industries has made this possible, but the focusing of the attention of the government on the need to foster so vital an industry has played its part too. When granting a substantial tariff protection to the steel industry in 1932, the government insisted on the formation of the British Iron and Steel Federation which has done much to revive and reorganize the industry in its first quarter-century of existence. Since the second World War, not least during the brief period when the industry was nationalized, successive governments have made capital available for the development of the industry.

2. COAL

Technical developments in many fields widened the demand for coal during the nineteenth century. Some of these sources of demand were entirely new, like that from the railways and steamships after 1825; other sources of the new demand derived from the expansion of existing markets, from the immense growth of iron and steel manufacture, or for domestic heating from the greatly increased population. In addition, there was a steady growth in the coal export trade, particularly in the second half of the century, when the extension of steam navigation led to the establishment of coaling stations in all the main ports of the world.

The British industry was able to meet this steadily rising demand for coal because technical improvements in drainage, ventilation, winding and transport made deeper mining possible. By the beginning of the nineteenth century most of the coal easily accessible near the surface had already been extracted, and though there were immense reserves of coal still available, deeper and more extensive mining was necessary to obtain it. Most of the problems of drainage had been solved by James Watt's improvements to Newcomen's steam pump, but great strides were made in the improvement of both steam engines and pumping equipment during the century. Though by about 1830 most mines were employing steam engines for their winding gear (to raise coal and men to the surface), there were still a few pits, mostly in Scotland, where the coal was carried both underground and to the surface on the backs of women and children. Vertical metal guide rods for the smoother running of the cages began to be introduced in

In a coal mine in the mid-nineteenth century

Pit-head at Church Pit, Wallsend, mid-nineteenth century

the 1830's. Another most important innovation which increased
the safety of mines was wire rope, first made in 1834 and introduced widely into British mines in the 1840's. Ventilation, and
the related problems of safety, were slow to find satisfactory
solutions. Urged on by a series of disastrous explosions in
Yorkshire and Lancashire mines in the late 1840's, Parliament
passed an act in 1850 by which inspectors were appointed who
took an active and effective part in improving mine ventilation.
After some experiments during the 1850's, steam-driven fans
were introduced during the 1860's. The later decades of the
nineteenth century saw the first experiments with mechanical
cutting of coal, but the technical problems associated with
mechanical cutting are immense, and while mining labour
remained cheap, as it did until the 1940's, there was little
incentive for mine-owners to equip mines with mechanical
cutters. As a result, British mines tended to lag behind mines in
other countries in the use first of mechanical cutters, and later
in the twentieth century, of mechanical conveyors underground.
This was less true of the Scottish coalfield where the thinness
and steep inclination of many of the seams made the use of
machinery more economic.

These technical developments, combined with the creation of
the British railway system, permitted an immense growth in the
output of coal during the nineteenth century. British coal pro-

duction, which had been 30 million tons in 1836, had risen to 84 million tons in 1861 and to 185 million tons in 1891. Though the older coalfields of the north-east, South Wales, the Scottish Lowlands and the Midlands played their parts in this increase, in the long run the rise of other newer coalfields was more significant. In particular, an important new area was being opened up in South Yorkshire around Doncaster, and beginnings were made with an entirely new field in Kent, near Dover. In the north-east the trend was steadily away from the inland area to the coast, and some workings even penetrated from the coast under the sea.

A maximum output of 287 million tons (of which 77 million tons was exported) was achieved in 1913. The industry was never again to produce so much coal. Labour shortage and shipping restrictions led to some decline during the first World War, and for a brief two years after the war the English industry enjoyed a seller's market. For most of the rest of the period between the wars the industry suffered drastically from seriously declining markets. Electricity was now beginning effectively to compete with coal both in the home and in the factory, and though much of the electricity was made from coal, it used the fuel more economically. Since just before the war there had, too, been a rapid trend of conversion of steamships from coal- to oil-burning. At this time, also, the governments of some foreign coal-producing countries, particularly Poland, subsidized their exports so that they were able to oust British coal from Continental markets like the Scandinavian countries. In general, industry was becoming more conscious of the advantages to be derived from fuel economy; the steel industry, for example, steadily reduced the quantity of coal necessary to make a ton of pig iron by improvements in blast-furnace design and operation. The British coal industry found itself in the 1920's and 1930's saddled with declining markets and antiquated equipment. With no serious problems of selling coal before 1914, the industry had been slow to equip itself with mechanical cutters and conveyors. Underground haulage was out-of-date and expensive, too little use was made of electricity, and amenities like pit-head baths for the miners seriously deficient.

The mine-owners' answer to the problem of shrunken

markets was to attempt to reduce costs by lowering wages and increasing the length of the miner's daily shift. Naturally the miners resisted this treatment, and though the government several times intervened in attempts to keep the peace, labour relations in the industry deteriorated. A Royal Commission under the chairmanship of Lord Sankey in 1919 had made several recommendations favourable to the miners, including increased wages, a shorter working-day (seven hours) and the nationalization of the mines. Though some of these recommendations were accepted, labour relations remained bad, and a long strike in 1921 decided very little. Unemployment in the industry grew — from 6·9% of the miners in 1924 to 28·3% in 1930. The attempt of the Samuel Commission of 1925–6 to solve the problems of the coal industry, and its disastrous result in the miners' and general strike of 1926, are described more fully in Chapter 20, section 5. The *Mining Industry Act* of 1926, which gave effect to the recommendations of the Samuel Commission, conceded much to the mine-owners and next to nothing to the miners. It made some half-hearted proposals for voluntary amalgamation of mines, in the hope that larger and more economic units would emerge, but few amalgamations resulted. The Labour government of 1929–31 made a more determined effort to restore the fortunes of the industry, but its *Coal Mines Act* of 1930, though it introduced schemes for restricting output, minimum prices and compulsory amalgamations, achieved little. Coal output fell from 244 million tons in 1930 to 207 million tons in 1933.

From that lowest point there began a recovery. With a slight set-back in 1938, this recovery continued until 1958. In the 1930's the recovery was due rather to the general revival of trade than to any specific measures of government assistance. Trade agreements with Ireland and the Scandinavian countries, by which these countries agreed to take British coal in return for exports of foodstuffs, proved a valuable stimulus to recovery. In the later 1930's re-armament stimulated demand for coal from the heavy industries. During the second World War it proved essential to maintain coal output, and coal miners were exempted from military service to permit this. The immense expansion of industry since the second World War served to maintain the demand for coal until 1958 in spite of the cost of the expensive modernization of the industry's equipment since nationalization (1948), much higher labour costs (war-time labour shortage at last forced the industry to pay a good wage to the miners), and the increasing substitution of other fuels.

3. ENGINEERING

During the eighteenth century very few skilled craftsmen were engaged in what could strictly be called 'engineering'. This was because of the relatively limited use made of metals and because machine-making for the most part seldom called for the services of the specialist craftsman. The 'engineer' of the eighteenth century was the millwright (the word 'mill' meaning at that time any piece of power-driven machinery). It was the development of the steam engine that gave birth to the engineering profession and industry; in particular, it was the work of the great industrial partnership of Boulton and Watt that gave the impetus to the new industry by developing techniques for the construction of large numbers of steam engines. Other technical advances during the late eighteenth and early nineteenth centuries, such as the invention and widespread use of complicated machinery in the textile, iron and flour-milling industries, broadened the scope of the infant industry.

During the 1820's and 1830's other factors contributed to the development of the industry. The coming of the railways immediately created a demand for locomotive engineers and some firms like William and John Galloways of Manchester were established to specialize in locomotive manufacture. The rapid growth of the textile industries led to the foundation of Lancashire's highly important textile machinery industry. Typical of this branch of the industry was the small business for the making of carding machinery started by Henry Platt in Oldham in 1821. He was joined by the brothers Mather in 1830 and their partnership grew into one of the country's major engineering firms specializing in textile machinery but also manufacturing a wide range of other engineering products. Developments in roadmaking and shipbuilding also contributed to the technical advance and diversification of the engineering industry. Some of the great bridges of this period — Telford's Menai Bridge, and Robert Stephenson's tubular railway bridges at Conway and Menai, for example, demanded not only advanced theoretical knowledge, but also the use of powerful hydraulic machines for raising and testing. There is little need to point out that the adoption of the steam-engine for marine propulsion, and the design of iron and steel ships were the major factors underlying the separate development of the marine-engineering industry. Perhaps the most significant advances after the 1820's were the evolution of the lathe and other machine tools, and the introduction of standardized parts. Joseph Whitworth, who founded a great engineering business in 1833, was the real pioneer of the use of gauges and templates for standardizing parts on mass-production processes. Few ideas have contributed more to progress in engineering than Whitworth's standard gauges for screws.

On these sure foundations the British engineering industry developed during the later nineteenth century. The technical advances which marked its progress are too numerous to describe, and the most striking aspect of the industry's history in this period is its diversity. Great progress was made in the design and manufacture of locomotives, railway rolling-stock, bridges, marine engines, and hydraulic power. The production of cheap steel by the Bessemer process after 1856 revolutionized the engineering industry by making available to it a new, hardwearing but flexible, basic raw material. Similarly, fundamental changes in the demand for, and nature of, armaments in the half-century before 1914 led to the growth of a new and important section of the engineering industry, involving the production of small-arms at Birmingham and Enfield, Middlesex, of armour-plated warships, of gun turrets and other forms of munitions.

The last years of the nineteenth century witnessed the birth of yet another new branch of the industry — electrical engineering. Though some of the earliest experiments in the use of electricity had been made in Britain, this country was slow to follow these up. In the 1880's private companies began to undertake the provision of electric light in the principal towns, and the construction of electricity-generating plant, begun at this time, led quickly to the growth of the electrical engineering industry manufacturing generating-plant, switch-gear, and electric motors.

From the early days of the engineering industry, production for export had always been an important feature. In the last quarter of the nineteenth century Britain's lead in the export of machinery began to be challenged by Germany and, after the first World War, by the United States. However, though Britain did concede the lead in engineering exports to Germany and the United States, this trade remained an important one, and exports in the late 1920's comfortably exceeded those of the years before the first World War. Though the products of the engineering industry defy classification, it is nevertheless clear that this industry has emerged from the second World War as one of Britain's three or four most important industries, and it has continued to retain its high share of the export trade.

4. COTTON

By the end of the first quarter of the nineteenth century, the cotton industry was firmly established as Britain's major industry, having overtaken the woollen industry early in the century. This revolution in industry had been accompanied by, and in part caused by, a series of important technical improvements in the spinning and weaving processes. Since 1830 there have been few changes in the processes of textile manufacture. Such improvements as have been achieved have successively increased the productivity of labour without radically altering the basic methods of production. This made possible a slight reduction of the labour force employed in all branches of textile manufacture in the period before 1914, during which time there was a substantial growth in the output of the industry. The most important of these inventions — significantly an American one — was the ring-spinning method introduced in America about 1830, and adopted gradually in this country during the second half of the century. A 'self-acting' mule, a labour-saving improvement to Crompton's eighteenth-century invention, had been invented in 1825, but was adopted only slowly.

After the astonishing growth of the cotton industry in the late eighteenth and early nineteenth centuries, it is not to be wondered at that it grew more slowly later in the nineteenth century; other industries needed, and succeeded in attracting, the capital and initiative which the cotton industry had claimed earlier. Moreover, between 1861 and 1865 the industry suffered a severe set-back; the American Civil War cut off its main source of supplies of raw cotton. During the resultant *Cotton Famine* there was much unemployment and hardship in Lancashire and Clydeside. Nevertheless, the industry enjoyed a renewed burst of expansion early in the twentieth century. Between 1905 and 1907 no less than ninety-five new spinning mills appeared, and the output of yarn rose by 25% in the twenty years before 1914. While the Lancashire industry continued to grow in the nineteenth century, its only rival in Britain — the Clydeside industry in Scotland — failed to maintain its earlier momentum. With an output perhaps one-third of Lancashire's in the 1820's, the Scottish industry never recovered from the two blows of the financial crisis of 1857 and the Cotton Famine of the 1860's. By the twentieth century all branches of the cotton industry (except the thriving sewing-thread industry at Paisley near Glasgow) were concentrated in south-east Lancashire.

The English cotton industry had reached its peak in 1914. After the first World War it began a decline which has continued unhindered ever since. There are many reasons for this failure, but by far the most important is the decline of the export market. Cotton manufacture tends to be the first industry many countries turn to in the early stages of industrialization, and one by one, most of Britain's major export markets for cotton goods have developed their own cotton industries. The most serious loss was the Indian market; in 1913 India bought 3,000 million yards of British cotton cloth — 40% of the exports of cotton goods; at the end of the first World War these exports had fallen by over two-thirds to 900 million yards, and by 1936 to a mere 400 million yards. By the 1950's Britain was importing more cotton goods from India than she exported to India. In addition to this loss of export markets, Lancashire cotton producers have also found the home markets invaded by foreigners — Japanese imports in the 1920's and 1930's, and Indian and Hong Kong imports in the 1940's and 1950's. Inevitably, too, the industry has lost ground to the new chemical-fibre industry; for many purposes rayon, nylon and terylene replaced cotton during the second quarter of the twentieth century.

The cotton famine in Lancashire
above: Crowded streets and empty mills
below: A soup kitchen

There was virtually no answer to this decline of both export and home markets except to specialize in the production of the finer qualities of cloth which Lancashire's competitors could not yet produce, and to invest in the most up-to-date productive machinery in order to keep down costs. Lancashire succeeded in the former, but has been slow to follow the latter course. The two most important developments in the twentieth century — the automatic loom (which enables a single weaver to control with ease a large number of looms), and electric drive for spinning and weaving mills — have been slower to enter Lancashire's mills than they have the mills of other countries. Moreover, the framework of British society has not encouraged two- and three-shift working in an industry whose labour is mainly female, so that this opportunity to reduce cost has been forfeited. Since Imperial Preference is an essential part of the country's tariff system, the cotton industry has continued to suffer defeat in the home market from Commonwealth competitors.

5. SOME NEW INDUSTRIES

The century following the Great Exhibition saw the relative, and in some cases absolute, decline of the industries whose superiority the Exhibition had asserted. To take their place new industries gradually arose. In the mid-twentieth century some, at least, of Britain's major industries have histories of barely one hundred years; some, like the important aircraft industry, histories of less than fifty years. The century from 1850 to 1950, in other words, has witnessed a major transformation in the industrial structure of Britain; and most of this transformation has taken place since 1918.

Of these newer industries, the heavy chemical industry is today one of the most important. It was founded in the eighteenth century mainly on a process of making soda (an important raw material of soap) invented in 1791 by a Frenchman, Nicholas Leblanc. The *Leblanc* process made soda from salt, and the infant chemical industry grew up in south Lancashire at Liverpool and St. Helens, and on Tyneside in the north-east. Though there was slow expansion, there was no great change in the nature and location of the chemical industry, and in 1864, out of 84 soda manufacturers, 38 were on Merseyside and 19 on Tyneside. In the 1860's, a Belgian chemist, Solvay, developed the commercial manufacture of soda by the *ammonia* process. This cheaper and more efficient process only slowly displaced the older Leblanc process in Britain, for the latter produced a valuable by-product — bleach — with a ready market in the Lancashire textile industry. But in the 1890's, the ammonia process overtook its rivals, and the chemical industry grew rapidly, doubling the employment it provided between 1891 and 1911. In the decade before 1914 some progress was made in the production of dyestuffs from coal-tar, but in this branch of the industry, as in the adoption of electrolytic methods of alkali and chlorine manufacture, this country lagged behind its more progressive Continental rivals.

A period of immense and rapid growth in the chemical industry began in 1919. There was expansion of the Lancashire and north Cheshire works, and with the establishment of Brunner Mond's works at Billingham in south-east Durham in 1923, the foundation was laid of what was to become, within a quarter of a century, one of the largest industrial units in the whole country. In 1926, Brunner Mond's merged with some of the other major firms in the chemical industry — United Alkali, Nobel Industries and British Dyestuffs — to form the Imperial Chemical Industries, Britain's largest industrial undertaking. This firm has been responsible for much of the large-scale development of the modern chemical industry on Merseyside, Tees-side, Tyneside, the Midlands, south Lancashire and elsewhere, though it has always had many smaller competitors. Another major development of the period since 1918 has been the growth of the oil-refining industry in this country. Each of the principal refineries on Southampton Water, the Thames estuary, in South Wales and at Grangemouth on the Firth of Forth, has gathered round it clusters of by-product industries, known collectively as the petro-chemical industry, producing synthetic rubber, plastics, paints and artificial textile fibres.

Rubber-making was first introduced into this country in the 1820's, when Charles Macintosh (1766–1843) and Thomas Hancock (1786–1865) first successfully made a commercial product from a raw material whose properties had been known since the sixteenth century. The most significant technical development, however, came only in 1839 with the discovery by the American, Charles Goodyear, of the vulcanization process. This invention was the basis on which the modern rubber industry was built. The beginnings were small, and British imports of raw rubber did not exceed 2,000 tons anually until the 1870's: they reached ten times that figure by the end of the century. The still-young railway industry proved to be the most important market for the new industry, for the rubber clothing to which the industry's founder gave his name never accounted for more than a small proportion of the total output. By the end of the nineteenth century the industry was firmly established in London, near Bristol, in Birmingham, Manchester, Liverpool, Leeds, Newcastle-on-Tyne, Glasgow and Edinburgh.

In the twentieth century two developments have affected the course of the industry. The rising motor industry created an immense new market, so that by the 1930's rubber tyres formed the major part of the industry's output. Throughout the nineteenth century the industry had been supplied with natural rubber from the forests of Brazil, but the scale of the demand in the twentieth century, mainly as a result of the demand for cycle and motor tyres, led to the development of rubber plantations in the Far East. The raw-material problem has also been affected by the development of synthetic or artificial rubber. First invented in Germany in 1901, synthetic rubber was not manufactured in Britain commercially until the second World War. Since then it has become an essential part of the rubber and chemical industries.

In the early years, few cars were completely built in Britain, and in the first twenty years of motoring many of the cars on British roads (23,340 cars licensed in 1904) were imported. Between 1896 and 1904 there was a considerable industry in the assembly of cars from imported components. Henry Ford's famous 'Model T', the first mass-produced car, for example, first made in 1908, was assembled in Britain from imported parts from 1911. Gradually British makers took to manufacturing more and more of the parts themselves, until they produced complete cars. The modern motor industry in Britain dates from 1918, though the first World War gave it a valuable stimulus. In 1925 the industry was one of those protected by the restored McKenna duties (see Chapter 17, section 5). Between 1923 and 1935 the industry grew at an average rate of 10% each year. This was the period when the motor-manufacturing centres at Oxford, Birmingham, Coventry, Bedford and Dagenham were being built up. Slowly the industry entered the export trade, and imports dwindled to a few thousand cars a year. In the disastrous depression of the early 1930's, the motor industry was one of the few industries which continued to expand; output grew from 239,000 vehicles in 1929 to over 500,000 in 1937. The second World War, like the first, stimulated further growth, and motor manufacture emerged in the 1950's as one of Britain's major industries, employing 450,000 workers, and providing moreover a greater share of the country's exports than any other industry. The steady growth of the industry since the first World War has been accompanied by an immense increase in the size of the firms manufacturing cars, and, of course, by a corresponding reduction in the number of firms in the industry. This is a trend which has been typical of most industries during the twentieth century, but in none has it been more marked than in the motor industry, where technical advances have continually increased the economies of large-scale production.

CHAPTER 19

AGRICULTURE

1. Agriculture under the Corn Laws

During the wars against France, British farmers had
enjoyed considerable prosperity. Population, and with
it the demand for foodstuffs, was growing rapidly, but
at the same time the Napoleonic blockade (the *Continental
System*) reduced imports appreciably. During the eighteenth
century the acreage of land under wheat cultivation was
increased by about one third, and the yield of seed increased by
almost 10%. Until the 1760's, Britain had been, on balance,
an exporter of corn. After that decade, demand from the
growing population turned the trade in favour of grain imports.
Assisted during the war by an unusually high number of bad
harvests, prices of corn rose, not steadily, but in a series of wild
fluctuations, until early in 1812 wheat sold at 155s. a quarter,
having been barely a third of that in 1792 before the outbreak
of war. An exceptionally good harvest in 1813 brought prices
tumbling down to 63s. In the following year the downfall of
Napoleon opened the British ports to grain supplies from the
Continent, and it seemed that the farmers' good days were over.

To make matters worse, during the period of prosperity,
farmers had borrowed money on a large scale to finance
enclosure and to bring under cultivation poorer land not
hitherto used for wheat. The highly profitable nature of farming during the twenty-two years of war from 1793 to 1815 had
led to a marked rise in rents. Rents were normally fixed by
leases for quite long periods — for twenty or thirty years — so
that the burden of high rents during a prolonged period of low
prices depressed the profits of British farming until well into
the 1830's. In these circumstances the legacy of high taxation
after the war added another crushing burden to the farmer.
With the abandonment of the Income Tax in 1816, agriculture
bore more than its share of the weight of taxation, and to this

burden was added those of tithes of medieval origin, and of poor rates. Tithes — the payment of a tenth of the produce of the land to support the clergy of the Established Church — had in most cases long since been commuted to a money payment, but in years of depression these payments were grudged. The adoption of the 'allowance' system of poor relief after 1795 had led, among other causes, to a serious rise in the poor rates. In one Buckinghamshire village it was claimed that the poor rate had risen eightfold between 1793 and 1822.

Sharply-falling wheat prices in 1813 and 1814 gave farmers a taste of what lay in store for them once the seaports were open to renewed imports of foreign corn. High prices during the war had been matched by high costs, and in 1815 the farmers faced a prospect of continuing high costs but lower prices. To meet this threat the agricultural interest used its immense influence in Parliament to secure some restriction on the import of corn. This was achieved in the *Corn Law* of 1815, by which the import of wheat was prohibited when the price in Britain was 80s. or lower (signifying fairly plentiful supplies of home-grown corn), and permitted when the price rose above 80s. (signifying relative scarcity), the aim being to keep wheat at about the relatively remunerative price of 80s. a quarter. In fact, the depression in agriculture was shared by many sections of industry, and the purchasing power of the nation remained low for some years. Corn seldom rose as high as 80s., remaining generally between 50s. and 60s., even falling on occasion to as low as 40s. Modification of the corn laws in 1822 and 1828, by which import was permitted on payment of a duty which varied inversely with the price in the home market, improved the effectiveness of the laws. Industrialists and townspeople believed that the result was to raise the price of bread, and as there were more consumers than producers of bread in the country, it is hardly surprising that opposition to the corn laws grew as the laws became more effective. The story of that opposition has been outlined in Chapter 17, section 3.

By the 1830's, British agriculture was slowly emerging from the acute depression of the period after 1815. Its prospects in the long run were bright, for the steady growth of population guaranteed an ever-rising home demand, while few countries elsewhere in the world had any very large surpluses of agricultural production above their own immediate needs; even without the artificial protection of the corn laws British farmers were relatively secure from competition in the home market. By 1830, moreover, most of the old open-field arable land had been enclosed, so that farmers were free to adopt what new techniques they chose. There still remained quite considerable areas of common and waste land, and enclosure of these continued steadily for another forty years. After the passing of the *Commons Act* of 1876, further enclosure became difficult and little has taken place since.

In addition, during the 1830's, some of the burdens which had oppressed British farmers since the war were gradually being relaxed. New leases took account of the lower price level; the *Tithe Commutation Act* of 1836 reduced this burden on farmers; more important, the *Poor Law Amendment Act* of 1834, by abolishing the 'allowance' system, reduced poor rates. While these changes were taking effect, important improvements in transport were opening up new markets to farmers. Canals serving purely agricultural areas tended to come later than those in the industrial towns, but since 1815 canals and roads, particularly in the south of England, had given farmers in many areas easier access to markets. But it was the coming of railways after 1825 that did most to make the rapidly growing urban markets accessible to the farmer. Perishable foods like milk, fruit and vegetables became attractive, profitable products which could be quickly and cheaply marketed for sale in the towns.

Furthermore, during the 1830's and 1840's, important new techniques of farming were becoming available at a time when, unlike in earlier centuries, the existence of enclosed, separate farms facilitated their adoption. Great strides were made in drainage techniques. James Smith, in Perthshire in the 1820's, showed how trenches loosely filled with stones could be a simple and effective way of improving marshy ground. By the early 1840's machine-made clay field-drainage pipes were coming on to the market, and by 1847 there were pipe-making machines capable of producing 20,000 feet of pipe daily. The 1840's, too, saw the introduction on a large scale of artificial manures. There were useful experiments with bone-dust in the 1830's, and the first use of guano from Peru in the early 1840's. By 1846 over one quarter of a million tons of Peruvian guano was imported annually. Superphosphates, manufactured in this country after 1842, were slower to be appreciated, and their use was still limited in the 1850's. New machinery was slowly coming into use. Steam power was being used for threshing and even ploughing from the 1830's and 1840's, while the seed-drill, though known for well over a century (one was invented in 1701 by Jethro Tull), was coming at last into more general use.

Jethro Tull's seed drill

The low state of agricultural fortunes in the generation after 1815 afflicted the labourers most severely. They were now the most numerous group in the English countryside, out-numbering the tenant and owner-farmers by three to one. Many of these labourers were suffering from periodic unemployment, and from loss of common rights. Wages remained extremely low, the result partly of the Speenhamland system of poor relief and partly of the unprofitable state of farming, and the agricultural workers were as discontented as their industrial fellows. There were serious riots in 1830 whose cause lay primarily in the desperate poverty of the labourers; in this year men actually died from starvation. Crowds roamed the countryside, burning ricks, threatening employers and landowners, and destroying workhouses. But these were spontaneous, unorganized out-breaks, and the government had little difficulty in restoring order with the aid of the military. The workers turned to trade unionism in the hopes of securing a living wage; the fate of the 'Tolpuddle Martyrs' in 1834 (see Chapter 20, section 4) made it abundantly clear that the ruling class was not going to take any chances with agricultural trade unions, and once again the rural workers relapsed into the apathy which poverty breeds. There were faint stirrings again under the impulse of Chartism between 1838 and 1848, but the farm workers have never been in the van of labour agitation in this country. Whether agriculture in Britain prospered or declined, the farm worker in the nineteenth century remained the worst-paid worker. Only in the neighbourhood of large towns were wages higher, and in spite of the efforts of Joseph Arch's National Agricultural Labourers' Union of 1872, agriculture has been one of the few fields in which minimum wages have had to be fixed by law (by the *Agricultural Wages Act* of 1924).

2. 'HIGH FARMING': 1846–73

The corn laws between 1815 and 1846 had probably given wheat farming an artificial stimulus, attracting farmers away from other types of farming for which the land may have been more naturally suited. Though farmers and landowners fought the Anti-Corn Law League bitterly in the 1840's in the belief that repeal of the corn laws would mean the destruction of British agriculture, when repeal came in 1846 (see Chapter 17, section 3), there was no catastrophic fall in wheat prices. Instead, British farming found itself on a mounting wave of prosperity. In the main this prosperity was the fruits of the numerous improvements (outlined in the previous section) which were gradually being introduced in the 1830's and 1840's. It has been suggested also that the removal of protection in 1846 stimulated British farmers to adopt improved methods of farming.

There were no major changes in the nature of farming. The agricultural labour force remained almost stationary in numbers throughout the third quarter of the nineteenth century, at a time when the total population of the country was growing fast; there were more mouths to feed, but agricultural productivity was rising fast. Although imports of wheat continued to grow steadily, prices remained fairly stable, and British wheat farming did not suffer; the acreage of land under wheat increased slightly until the late 1860's.

The sphere of farming which saw the biggest expansion in this period was dairying. Enclosed grazing was at last bearing fruit in the shape of dairy herds bred for milk production along the lines pioneered by Bakewell a century earlier. The output of milk, butter and cheese increased steadily. A French commentator of this period, Leonce de Lavergne, was astonished at the British consumption of milk and milk products. 'The quantities of butter and cheese manufactured exceed all belief,' he wrote, adding that 'the consumption of milk under every form is enormous.' But the explanation of the rise in agricultural output and prosperity lies to a large extent less in the improvement of the standards of the best farmers, than in those of the smaller, backward cultivators. 'The change', wrote James Caird, a noted agricultural commentator, in 1878, 'has not been in any considerable progress beyond what was then the best, but in a general upheaval of the middling and the worst.'

Added emphasis was given to the application of science to farming. The scientific study of soil chemistry had begun with the publication in 1840 of the German, Liebig's *Organic Chemistry in its Applictions to Agriculture and Physiology*. In 1843 the Board of Agriculture established an experimental farm at Rothampstead, five years after the Royal Agricultural Society had been founded. Both these organizations assisted the farmer by the testing and propagation of improved methods. This was the time when the use of artificial fertilizers (nitrates and superphosphates) was spreading rapidly, and although the acreage of root crops for winter cattle feed (turnip, mangold and swede) reached its maximum during this period, oil-cake was also being introduced for stock feeding.

Underlying this more vigorous approach to farming lay a steady rise in prices. During the 1850's and 1860's prices of farm products rose by as much as 40%. This partly reflected a general rise in prices during the third quarter of the century, but also reflected the steadily growing demand for foodstuffs from the ever-increasing urban population. Throughout this period the British farmer enjoyed an artificial protection which the repeal of the corn laws had done little to destroy. There was still no serious competition from abroad; few countries yet had any large surplus of agricultural produce to send to this country. The continent of Europe was frequently distracted by war and revolution, while the still small exports from America were seriously interrupted during the Civil War of 1861–5. The areas of the world capable of immense agricultural expansion — the United States, Canada, the Argentine, Australia and New Zealand — were still undeveloped. The rich wheatlands a thousand miles from the Atlantic seaboard of North America constituted no threat to English farmers so long as there were no railways. The disaster which it had been feared would result from the repeal of the corn laws was delayed until these new lands were opened up by the railway. When this happened, in the late 1860's and 1870's, technical development in shipbuilding had also made ample cheap shipping available, and a flood of cheap agricultural produce was let loose on the British market.

3. FOREIGN COMPETITION: 1873–1914

From the early 1870's, British agriculture was assailed by many new sources of foreign competition. Cheaper long-distance transport accounted for much of this. Improvements in steam navigation, for example, produced a sharp fall in shipping freight rates. The freight rate for wheat from Chicago to Liverpool, which had been 65s. per ton in 1868, fell to 24s. by 1882. The opening up of the Prairies and the wheatlands of North America after the construction of the trans-continental railways in the 1860's and 1870's made possible the cultivation of grain crops on a scale hitherto inconceivable. New railways too, opened up the hinterland of Argentina and Australia. From these countries came a flow of meat, wool and wheat. The invention of refrigeration in the late 1870's enabled frozen meat to be carried half round the world, though the taste for fresh meat in this country ensured a continuing demand for the home-grown product. The new technique of canning was developed at this time, and imports of corned beef and other tinned foods reduced the demand for home-produced foods. Colonial settlement in Australia and New Zealand was beginning to bear fruit in the production of vast quantities of cheap dairy produce; though the consumption of cheese and butter per head of population continued to rise, imports rose even faster, displacing the home-produced article. In the 1880's margarine, a substitute for butter, was first marketed in this country, and its cheapness attracted many who would otherwise have bought butter. Finally, as though to add insult to injury, an unusually prolonged period of bad summers — five of them between 1873 and 1879 — reduced the crops at the very time when lower prices made larger yields more important than ever to the farmer. In 1879 the excessively wet weather caused the loss of three million sheep through sheep rot.

The effect of the sudden appearance of massive foreign competition in the English agricultural market was to drive down prices far below the levels to which farmers had grown accustomed during the 1850's and 1860's. Rents and standards of living had been determined on the expectation of wheat prices in the region of 55s. a quarter; for the last twenty years of the century the average price was less than 33s., and in 1894 it was less than 23s. — lower than it had been for 150 years. The price of wool, under the impact of Australian imports, fell by one half between 1873 and 1886.

The harsh winds of competition blew most keenly on wheat farming, which was concentrated principally in eastern and southern England. Cattle farmers, though they did not really prosper, were less seriously affected; the consumer's preference for fresh meat over frozen meat protected these farmers against the imported product, while the ever-growing urban demand for milk as well as for other fresh dairy products could only be met by the home supplier. Thus the dairy farmer, particularly in the vicinity of the manufacturing areas of the Midlands and the North, felt far less of the impact of foreign competition than did the corn-grower. The unprofitable nature of wheat farming led farmers to turn away from this type of arable farming. In the last thirty years of the century, the acreage under wheat was reduced drastically. The problem was, what was to take its place? There was, of course, no single easy solution to the problem. Generally speaking, the situation was met in a variety of ways — careful economies, for example, in the use of fertilizers, particularly by the medium and smaller farmers; some reduction of labourers' wages, fortunately offset by a fall in the cost of living; an increased tendency towards specialization, including forestry; a significant increase in the acreage of permanent grassland for cattle-farming; a marked growth of market gardening, producing fresh vegetables and fruit for the ever-growing town markets; a sharp fall in rents; and, inevitably, a drift of workers at all levels away from farming. In 1871 there were 1¼ million people in England and Wales employed on the land; by 1914 this had fallen to less than one million, during which period the total population had risen by nearly 40%.

It was not to be expected that the government at this period would take much positive action to assist the farmers in their plight; the prevailing economic policy favoured free trade, and after the experience of the corn laws no government could risk even the suggestion of import duties on foodstuffs. Since protection in the form of a tariff was ruled out and direct financial assistance was not even considered at this stage, there was little that could be done. There were, of course, the usual commissions of enquiry — a *Royal Commission on Agriculture* of 1879–82, and another on *Agricultural Depression* of 1893–7; a Ministry of Agriculture was established in 1889 in place of the old Board, but otherwise little was done. Some minor steps were taken to improve the legal position of the tenant farmer (the *Agricultural Holdings Act* of 1875); several acts were passed for the creation of allotments and small-holdings by parishes and county councils, but the multiplication of small farms was unlikely to furnish the solution to the problem of competition from the immense farms of the New World.

By the late 1890's the British farmer had begun to adjust his ways to the new circumstances. New machines, artificial manures and feeding stuffs were permitting the farmer to produce more with a smaller labour force. With reduced costs and the discovery after years of hardship of the products in which the British farmer still held an advantage over his overseas rivals, it was found that farming could still be made to pay. From about 1896 there was a reversal of the general downward trend in prices; though prices rose only slowly, this held much greater hope for the future. Wages, too, rose slightly during the twenty years before the first World War. In 1892, imports of foreign live cattle were prohibited, a measure which removed sources of both competition and infection of cattle. An increasing mastery over cattle diseases was playing a valuable part in promoting prosperity. But in most other spheres, competition was no less in 1914 than it had been twenty or thirty years earlier. What had happened in the meantime was that British farmers had reconciled themselves to sharing the home market with competitors all over the world and had learned to adapt their methods accordingly.

4. Farming between the Wars

The war of 1914–18 created the need for a vast increase in food production in this country. For the first time since 1846, imports of foodstuffs were artificially restricted, and once again government policy turned to the encouragement of grain production. One result of the decline of arable cultivation since 1873 had been that by 1914 Britain produced only one-fifth of her own needs of wheat. Immediately on the outbreak of war much former grassland was ploughed for grain cultivation, resulting in a 60% increase in the wheat harvest. There was also a comparable increase in the output of potatoes, results which were not achieved without some decline in meat production. The need to encourage these drastic changes in British farming during the war caused the government to intervene in agricultural affairs far more directly and actively than it would ever have considered proper before 1914. But once the initial step of active government regulation of agricultural development had been taken, it proved difficult to withdraw. Since 1917, in fact, when the *Corn Production Act* guaranteed both minimum corn prices and minimum wages for farm workers, government policy has played an important part in the varying fortunes of British agriculture; this is in marked contrast to the nineteenth century when the government had quite deliberately abstained from intervention in this field.

There was cause, too, for government assistance in the inter-war period, for agricultural prices fell sharply in 1920, and with the lapse of war-time controls, farm workers' wages fell drastically. After one of Britain's rare strikes of farm workers in 1923, the Labour government of 1924 re-instated the wage-fixing machinery, and there was some rise in wages. But farming remained at a low ebb. The extra wheat-land cultivated during the war reverted to grass, and only dairy production showed any increase in the first decade after the war. Britain had produced 44% of her food requirements in 1914; in the late 1920's this proportion had fallen to 39%.

The farmers themselves reacted to this return to bad times by renewing their search for the most profitable forms of specialization. An important new departure was the cultivation of sugar-beet. All sugar had been imported before 1914, and to economize in scarce shipping the government had encouraged the growth of beet sugar at home with subsidies. These were continued after 1918, and by 1930 there were 350,000 acres under sugar-beet cultivation in this country, mainly in East Anglia and Lincolnshire, producing one-quarter of the country's sugar needs. There was further concentration on milk and egg production. Mechanization progressed steadily; the number of tractors more than doubled between 1925 and 1937, and combine-harvesters were introduced on the larger farms.

In the 1930's, as part of a much wider policy of economic recovery, the government turned more vigorously to a programme of agricultural assistance. There could still be no question of a protective tariff on imports of many foodstuffs, but for the first time quotas (licences to import fixed quantities) were introduced by the *Agricultural Marketing Act* of 1933 to restrict imports. After 1931 *Marketing Boards* were created for milk, bacon, potatoes and hops. The Boards assisted in marketing and offered guaranteed prices to farmers. The policy of subsidies, which had already borne fruit in the cultivation of sugar-beet, was extended to wheat-growing in 1932 and to meat production in 1934.

The combined efforts of the government and the farmers themselves produced some recovery in British farming during the 1930's; agricultural output increased by one-sixth between 1931 and 1937. Rising food prices stimulated investment in cost-reducing equipment. British farming was once more set on a forward road, in time, fortunately, to permit a renewal of the concentrated effort necessary to feed the country in the second cataclysm of 1939.

CHAPTER 20

WORKING-CLASS MOVEMENTS

1. THE WORKING CLASS IN THE EARLY NINETEENTH CENTURY

Though it will be necessary in this chapter to speak of the 'working class' as though this were a clearly defined social group, in reality those social classes below the upper and middle classes in the early nineteenth century were exceedingly diverse. The early nineteenth century working class, in other words, was a composite group, including such diverse types as the skilled artisan, the unskilled labourer, the Irish immigrant, the village craftsman, the worker in rural domestic industry, the small farmer, the landless agricultural labourer, the women and child workers, a numerous group of both male and female domestic servants, and — an important element in early nineteenth century society — the 'impotent poor' — those whom age, poor health, or inability to find employment threw on the poor law. What would be true of one of these groups would not necessarily be true of another. Together they probably comprised at least four-fifths of the population.

But though there was such diversity amongst them, they had much in common. Weekly wage rates in the early decades of the nineteenth century varied from less than 10s. for the lower-paid adult male worker to as much as 30s. or 40s. for the skilled male worker. Women's wages seldom exceeded half these rates. Though the workers contrived to exist on these wages, even the higher rates left only a small margin above mere subsistence. There could be little saving for old age in an era without pensions. Although by the middle of the nineteenth century $1\frac{1}{2}$ million men were able to afford Friendly Society subscriptions which brought them assistance in sickness and old age, this was barely one quarter of the male working population: the remainder depended upon the still extremely harsh poor law in time of need. Wages, then, seldom sufficed for more than food, a minimum of clothing, and housing. Entertainments were few and holidays non-existent. Leisure was scarce, since hours of work, as they had always been, were long — the twelve-hour day or longer was customary. When the family's income in normal times provided only the barest of necessities, temporarily higher wages in boom periods were all too often spent on drink. Perhaps the most serious aspect of the worker's condition, however, was the insecurity of his employment. Throughout the nineteenth century the persistent fluctuations in trade and industry periodically threw out of employment large sections of the working class. There are no statistics to show the seriousness of this periodic unemployment, but the immense sums of money spent on poor relief, particularly in years of acute depression like 1842, bear ample witness to this aspect of working-class existence in this period.

Economic historians still disagree as to the trend of working-class conditions in the early nineteenth century. According to one view, the benefits of increased industrial and agricultural production were beginning to improve working-class standards of living by the 1830's and 1840's; according to another the thirty years after the end of the Napoleonic Wars in 1815 saw no improvement, and possibly some deterioration, in working-class conditions. The very diversity of the working class itself makes it possible for both schools of thought to produce evidence in favour of their views. On the whole it seems likely that while conditions for the poorer-paid workers did not improve during the first half of the nineteenth century (and for some groups like the hand-loom weavers and the framework knitters seriously declined), a growing class of skilled workers — engineers, builders and skilled railwaymen, for example, — were able to enjoy higher standards of comfort, at least during times of good trade.

It was this existence, at the same period of time, of a rising group of skilled workers whose appetite for better living had been whetted by their first taste of it, together with the vast mass of unskilled workers existing uncomfortably and unhealthily at mere subsistence level, that provided the ingredients for a powerful movement of agitation for social improvements. Between them they produced both the leaders, and the rioting, clamorous, at times rebellious followers. Their problem in the nineteenth century was how to achieve their aim of improvements to their standards and conditions of life and work. They were entirely without political power, for even the Great Reform Act of 1832 had left them without the vote. Very few belonged to trade unions, and the unions themselves were small, short-lived, and bitterly opposed by both employers and government. The task was immense, and the prospects seemingly hopeless. Not surprisingly the early history of working-class agitation is one of almost unending failure. The remaining sections of this chapter will describe some of the ways in which the British working class sought for ways of bringing pressure to bear on those in political power in the hope of thereby securing some improvement in their social condition.

2. THE CO-OPERATIVE MOVEMENT

One method which working-class men believed would open the way to both a fairer share of the country's wealth and a better way of life, was through *co-operation*. There were two kinds of co-operation — in production and in retailing. *Co-operative production* involved communal ownership of the means of production (land, implements, machines, etc.), and the pooling by the members of a co-operative community of the fruits of their labour; after the needs of the community had been met from its own agricultural and industrial production the proceeds from the sale of the remainder would be used for the common good of all. In the co-operative community, all worked for the common good instead of for individual gain, both labour and wealth being shared equitably by all. In co-operative retailing (*consumer co-operatives*) the members of the co-operative society bought collectively and re-sold to themselves the goods ordinarily bought in shops. In this way the retailers' profit was cut out.

The first co-operative stores of the latter kind appeared after 1815. A London Co-operative Society was formed in 1826 with William Lovett, the Chartist leader of a dozen years later, as storekeeper. By 1830 there were 300 such societies, and by 1832 nearly 500. But none of these early co-operative retail societies managed to survive for more than three or four years. The cause of failure was frequently dishonest storekeepers, for these societies were not recognized by law, and the only redress against theft was for individual members to sue for their portion of the loss — a hopelessly impracticable solution. This initial burst of co-operation unhappily failed, and by 1834 all the early societies had ceased to exist.

The pioneer of the early producer co-operative societies was Robert Owen, whose experiences as a capitalist employer at New Lanark had filled him with a burning conviction that the conditions most likely to develop the best in human character could only be produced in co-operative communities, and he devoted the vast fortune earned as a capitalist to experiments in this form of society. He planned 'villages of co-operation' in which between 500 and 1500 people would work communally. Finding little support in England, Owen decided to create his first 'model community' in America. In 1825 New Harmony, a community of 900 people, was founded, but, in spite of its name, the community lacked harmony, and differences between members led to the break-up of the community in three years. Back in England some years later, Owen founded another model community at Queenwood in Hampshire, but it was hardly more successful than the American venture.

After the failures of the first experiments in both producers' and consumers' co-operatives, no fresh attempts were made to revive the co-operative idea for some years. In 1844, however, another band of working-class enthusiasts for co-operation — a group of seven flannel-weavers — pooled their savings to open and equip a co-operative store in Rochdale, Lancashire. The 'Rochdale Pioneers', as they became known, operated their store like any other retail shop, buying their goods in the usual markets, and retailing at normal prices. But instead of the profit going into the hands of an independent retailer, the members shared it between themselves in proportion to their purchases. Though the beginning was small, the Rochdale store prospered, perhaps — in contrast to Owen's grandiose schemes — because of the modest scale and simple principles involved. Its success quickly attracted imitators, and within seven years there were nearly 130 co-operative societies of the Rochdale type. It was a short step from co-operative retailing to co-operative wholesaling, and in 1863 the British co-operative societies created the Co-operative Wholesale Society, which was to buy centrally in bulk on behalf of the individual local societies. The next step, first taken in 1872, was for the Wholesale Society to undertake the production of goods to be sold in the stores. The system of co-operative trading, which plays so large a part today in the production and distribution of consumers' goods, was thus developed in the quarter-century after 1844. Its growth during this period was immense — from 15,000 members in 1851, it grew to nearly half a million in 1875.

3. Chartism

Co-operation was only a way of mitigating some of the minor evils of nineteenth-century society, or at best an escape from them. For the great mass of the working population some more direct, decisive and sweeping action was the only hope for improvement. The actions of the government after 1815 — of instituting corn laws, of suppressing freedom of the press, of speech and of meeting, and of the use of physical force to prevent the expression of working-class opinion (as at Peterloo) — had convinced the working class that there was no hope of effective action in improving living and working conditions from existing governments. Their only hope lay in a government with a very different approach to social problems: their need, in other words, was to bid goodbye to governments which, as Lord Liverpool said in 1819, insisted that 'the people of the country ought to be taught that evils inseparable from the state of things should not be charged upon any government'. They wanted a government which would take an energetic and active hand in the improvement of social conditions.

Only a very small minority genuinely believed that radical changes in the nature of society, such as were envisaged by Owen's model communities, were desirable; the great majority were willing to accept the forms of capitalist society, providing this society recognized their simple human needs. Since in the early nineteenth century the working class was denied the right to participate in both national and local government, either by voting in parliamentary and borough elections or by sharing the freedom to stand as a candidate for election, it is not surprising that moderate working-class opinion favoured the entry of the working class into political power by means of an extension of the franchise (the right to vote) and the creation of conditions in which it would be possible for the working-class man to become a Member of Parliament.

For these reasons there was enthusiastic working-class support for the Whig agitation in favour of Parliamentary Reform, and when, in 1830, the Whigs were returned to power, after nearly fifty years of unbroken Tory rule, with Parliamentary Reform as their first aim, hope ran high. But the changes introduced by the Whigs' Reform Act of 1832 were a bitter disappointment and disillusionment to the working class, for the act added less than a quarter of a million voters to the existing 400,000, and the working class continued to be excluded from power. To add insult to injury, most of the 'Whig Reforms' of the few years following the 1832 Reform Act added fuel to the fires of working-class discontent. The abolition of slavery in 1833, admirable though it was, did not affect the British working class; the Factory Act of the same year fell a long way short of the aims of the Ten-Hour Movement whose agitation had led to the introduction of a factory reform bill in the first place; the Poor Law Amendment Act of 1834, by harshening the conditions under which poor relief would be granted, was bitterly opposed by the industrial workers; and even the Municipal Corporations Act of 1835, on the whole one of the most beneficial reforms of the nineteenth century, was suspected as being a means by which the hated Whigs intended to strengthen their grip on local government.

The working class was thus driven into agitation for further and much more far-reaching political reform. It only needed one of the recurring trade depressions to accentuate their misery. This arrived in 1838, and in that year the London Working Men's Association, which had been founded two years previously by William Lovett and others, drew up a 'Charter' embodying six political demands. These demands, which were for annual election of Parliaments, for manhood suffrage, for the payment of Members of Parliament, for equal political representation, for the abolition of the property qualification for Members of Parliament, and for voting by secret ballot, had long been voiced by middle-class and working-class radicals, but in the special circumstances of the year 1838, they carried a particular appeal. Other working-men's groups joined the London association to call a National Convention of workers' representatives from all over the country.

The Convention of the movement now known, from its charter, as 'Chartism', met in London early in 1839 and agreed, as a first step, to present the Chartist demands (the 'Six Points') in a petition to Parliament. Discussion over what action should be taken in the event of Parliament rejecting the petition revealed a wide rift in the movement, which in the end proved fatal. On the one hand were the 'moral force' Chartists, who believed in pressing by all legal means for the desired political reforms and who recommended the working class to prepare themselves by education and political discussion for the day when political power would be theirs. Opposing them, the 'physical force' Chartists advocated a demonstration of the strength of the working class by marches, mass demonstrations, and, if necessary, by riot and rebellion. The former, led by William Lovett, repudiated violence; the latter, led by Feargus O'Connor, the owner of the Leeds newspaper *The Northern Star* which was the movement's mouthpiece, and by Julian Harney, a youthful, fiery agitator, knew that pious hopes and the presentation of petitions would achieve nothing. In the event, Parliament rejected the 1839 petition by a huge majority, and the Convention broke up when it became clear that the cleavage between the two extremes was irreparable.

There followed a period during which the 'physical force' Chartists organized many meetings and demonstrations, and even, in November 1839, an armed rising at Newport. The latter was to have been part of a much larger rising, but failure to co-ordinate led to the Newport Chartists, under John Frost, marching on their own; they were easily surrounded and defeated by a small contingent of soldiers. With some slight recovery of trade, Chartism waned after 1840, but with the return of mass unemployment in the acute depression of 1842, the movement revived. Another petition was presented to Parliament, with the same lack of success as before; Harney worked ceaselessly to stir up enthusiasm, particularly amongst the miners and metal-workers of the north-east and the Scottish Lowlands, while O'Connor waged a weekly propaganda war in *The Northern Star*. But once again the movement

The Chartist demonstration at Kennington Common, 10 April, 1848

died away as inevitably and as fruitlessly as it had done in 1840. Renewed depression and the occurrence of rebellion in almost every other European country in 1848 led to a final resurgence of Chartism. A third petition, alleged to contain $5\frac{3}{4}$ million signatures, but in fact containing less than 2 million, many of them forged, was presented to Parliament after a mass meeting on Kennington Common. Like the earlier petitions, it was rejected. Though the Chartist leaders continued for some years to whip up enthusiasm, they found few supporters. Chartism was dead, and working-class energies were directed into other channels.

Why did so promising, widespread and popular a movement fail? Mainly because of the fatal division between the 'moral force' and the 'physical force' sections. With no general agreement on the best means to achieve the ends, strength was wasted in dispute. Moreover, there were powerful counter-attractions during the ten years when Chartism flourished. The Anti-Corn Law League, for example, founded in the year the Charter was drawn up, offered the much more tangible bait of cheap bread. The Anti-Corn Law League was effectively organized, was strongly hostile to Chartism, and, unlike Chartism, was ultimately successful. From the mid-1840's, both the trade unions

and the co-operative societies offered a programme more calculated to appeal to the better-paid, skilled worker, who seldom
took the side of violence. Chartism throve on depression and
languished in times of good trade; the later 1840's witnessed a
substantial rise in the incomes of large sections of the working
class, and it was in this decade, too, that town councils began
to get to grips in a more determined way with the problems of
health, sanitation and water supply.

Probably the most effective cause of the failure of Chartism
was the determination of the government and of the middle
classes to suppress it. Though the army in England was small
and dispersed, it was used most effectively to prevent agitation
from growing beyond purely local movements, and to disperse
any meeting which threatened to turn into a riot. The government imprisoned leaders and made extensive use of spies to keep
one step ahead of the agitators. When danger threatened,
middle-class civilians were enrolled as special constables; when
the third petition was presented after the Kennington Common
meeting in 1848, 150,000 special constables were on the alert in
London to preserve law and the old order. Lacking a truly
effective national organization, Chartism could not overcome
this determined opposition.

4. THE TRADE UNIONS TO 1868

While the early attempts to found co-operative societies were
being made in the 1820's, another struggle was taking place to
secure the repeal of the laws of 1799 and 1800 against 'combinations' of workmen, or trade unions. Francis Place, a London
craftsman who had been an active trade-union worker before
the Anti-Combination Laws had driven the unions underground, began an agitation for the repeal of these laws in 1814.
However, it was only after 1822, the year in which he enlisted
the support of Joseph Hume, a Radical Member of Parliament,
that his campaign looked like having much success. In 1824,
Place and Hume secured the appointment of a parliamentary
committee to investigate the laws relating to trade unions. By
adroit management of this committee's investigations, Place
and Hume succeeded in securing a favourable report, and in
the same year, 1824, the Anti-Combination Laws were repealed.

At the same time the prohibition of the emigration of skilled artisans, which had been in force since 1719, was withdrawn. Contrary to Place's expectations, the repeal was followed by a wild outburst of strikes in many parts of the country, by Glasgow cotton workers, by seamen on the north-east coast, by Sheffield cutlers, and by coopers and shipwrights in London. Parliament was alarmed, and in the following year limited the freedom granted in 1824 to associations for the purpose of regulating wages and hours of work only. The right of working men to associate specifically for the purposes of negotiating collectively with their employers was firmly established, and has remained the foundation stone of the law regulating relations between employer and worker.

No sooner had the trade unions secured the right to exist than the serious financial crisis of 1825 spread a depression throughout the country which damped down any effective trade union activity. A fresh start was in the late 1820's, and for about five years the efforts of trade union leaders were concentrated on building up nation-wide unions. Though the efforts of these national unions were primarily directed towards securing improvements (or preventing deterioration) in the working conditions of the trades concerned, there was the underlying aim of uniting these national unions into a single national *trades* union which would wield such enormous power that it would be able to take over the control of industry and dictate social and economic policy to the government.

The first of the effective national unions in one trade was the National Union of Cotton Spinners formed by John Doherty in 1829. Doherty, who had started as the leader of the Manchester spinners, went on to establish a National Association for the Protection of Labour in 1830, with 150 constituent trade unions drawn mainly from the textile industries of the North. This scheme, and others like it of the same period, collapsed through failure to co-ordinate the operations of the many members. The last and greatest effort to create such a national organization was made by Robert Owen in 1834. In that year he founded the Grand National Consolidated Trades Union which attracted more than half a million workers in a few weeks. A general strike was planned which was to force the government and the employers to surrender control to the workers. Once again, however, local and sectional strikes broke the unanimity and discipline of the movement, and when the government prosecuted many leaders under the conspiracy laws, the movement disintegrated as quickly as it had grown. Later the same year six Dorsetshire agricultural workers who were attempting to form a union were prosecuted for the administration of illegal oaths and were sentenced to seven years' transportation to Australia. This savage punishment of the *Tolpuddle Martyrs* reflected the determination of the governing classes of the time to use every weapon available to them to suppress trade unionism.

The failure of the Grand National Consolidated Trades Union and the conviction of the Tolpuddle Martyrs effectively discouraged the wilder hopes of trade unionists, while the depressed state of trade in the late 1830's and early 1840's gave the movement little opportunity of recovering from this false start. Chartism, co-operation and the Anti-Corn Law League proved for the time being to be more successful counter-attractions. But in some of the skilled trades some small but effective unions were beginning to emerge during the 1840's. In particular a union of machine-makers and millwrights which had grown out of a small Manchester association had acquired sufficient strength by 1851 to attract the amalgamation of many smaller unions of various types of engineers. The resultant Amalgamated Society of Engineers of 1851 endured because its aims were restricted to what was practicable, and because its principles and organization were sound. It became the model on which all effective trade unions of the next generation were built; for this reason the type of trade unionism exemplified by the Amalgamated Society of Engineers has become known as *New Model Unionism*. The Amalgamated Society of Engineers was imitated by the Amalgamated Society of Carpenters of 1860, by the Tailors in 1866 and by several other skilled trades.

The New Model Unions differed from the unions of the decade after 1824 by accepting the capitalist structure of industrial society instead of trying to rebel against it. Accordingly they believed that the interests of their members would best be served by co-operation with the employers. Since they were confined to the better-paid skilled workers, they were able to afford high weekly subscriptions (their one shilling a week union subscription would probably represent six shillings a week in the mid-twentieth century). As a result they quickly accumulated substantial reserve funds with which to sustain effective strikes should the need arise. The wise administration of these funds and the necessary discipline were provided by the appointment of full-time, paid secretaries — an important innovation. Thus, for the first time, effective national control and leadership was exerted. At the same time the New Model Unions carried on well-managed insurance schemes amongst their members — an essential provision for self-respecting workers in the days of the New Poor Law.

Not surprisingly, the permanent secretaries of these unions emerged during the 1850's and 1860's as the real leaders of English trade unionism. Their influence tended to be cast on the side of moderation, but they worked unceasingly for the reform of the law relating to trade unions. Those who resented and suspected their power nicknamed them the *Junta*, after a much-hated group of politicians of the seventeenth century. But it was mainly owing to the efforts of the Junta that the first *Trades Union Congress* (T.U.C.) was called in 1868. This annual meeting of trade unionists to discuss their mutual interests led gradually to the creation of a permanent body which, without exercising any real control or discipline over its member unions, has played an important part since its foundation in guiding and advising, alternately restraining and encouraging, the efforts of individual unions.

5. The Trade Unions after 1868

The trade unions described in earlier sections affected only a fairly narrow section of the working class. In the early 1840's there were probably less than 100,000 regular trade unionists out of a male adult population of over five million; by the early 1870's there may have been a million union members, or little more than 10% of the male working population. Trade unionism had been going through its early, experimental stages, but the durable organizations that emerged in the 1870's were more suited to the needs of the skilled worker than to those of the great mass of semi-skilled and unskilled labour. The latter class could not afford the high subscriptions and did not, until the 1870's, receive the advantages of education; it was naturally less inclined towards peaceful methods and, since it had less to lose, believed more strongly in the need to reorganize the framework of society.

The twenty years after 1867 brought many changes. The Reform Act of that year gave political power to the industrial workers of many towns; the Education Act of 1870 for the first time gave the working class everywhere access to at least elementary education; between 1867, when Karl Marx's *Capital* was first published, and the early 1880's, when the Social Democratic Federation was formed, there had been a re-birth of Socialism; in 1886 the issue of Home Rule for Ireland split the parliamentary Liberal party, through which both working class and middle-class radicals had hitherto operated; finally, the periodic depressions of the last quarter of the nineteenth century produced higher unemployment than those of the third quarter, a trend which affected the unskilled labourers most seriously.

These developments led to an outbreak of unions and strikes in the late 1880's. Ben Tillett formed the Tea-Porters' and General Labourers' Union among the London dockers in 1887, and in the following year, under the guidance of Annie Besant, the women and girl match-makers in London formed a union to agitate for the improvement of their incredibly low wages and poor working conditions. They were successful, as were the London dockers who struck in 1889 for the 'docker's tanner' — a minimum rate of sixpence an hour. These early successes led immediately to the formation of other national unions among the unskilled and semi-skilled workers. A General Railway Workers' Union was established in 1889 to rival the older and more moderate Amalgamated Society of Railway Servants, and between 1888 and 1891 the powerful Miners' Federation was created. These *New Unions* (the movement for the establishment of national unions for unskilled and semi-skilled workers is known as *New Unionism*) contrasted strongly with the older New Model Unions. They did not willingly accept the established, inferior position of the labourer in society and therefore wholeheartedly embraced Socialism. They were anxious to use their great power at the earliest opportunity to improve their position; hence the big increase in trade-union membership up to

1914 was accompanied by many large and determined strikes. And in an effort to increase their effectiveness, the period after 1888 saw a great many amalgamations of smaller unions to form the powerful federations which have come to dominate trade unionism in the twentieth century.

Both the New Model Unions of the 1850's and the New Unions of the generation before 1914 were concerned in the fight for recognition and for a basis of law so that their struggle against the employers could proceed without interference. They wanted, in other words, to fight one opponent — the employers; and not two — the employers and the state. The struggle to secure protection at law was long, and marked by frequent reverses. A series of violent demonstrations by trade unionists in Sheffield against 'blacklegs' (fellow workers who refused to join their unions) — the *Sheffield Outrages* of 1867 — drew attention to the need to clarify the law relating to trade unions. A Royal Commission was appointed in 1867 and its recommendations produced two important new laws in 1871. The *Trade Union Act* of that year protected the funds of unions against embezzlement by extending the laws of the 1840's and 1850's relating to Friendly Societies to cover trade unions. This valuable recognition at law of the corporate nature of trade unions was, however, seriously offset by the *Criminal Law Amendment Act* of the same year which (with the Sheffield Outrages in mind) virtually made all forms of picketing illegal. In the days when trade unionists were almost always in a minority in any dispute, picketing (the prevention or hindrance of strikebreaking by non-unionists or 'blacklegs') was an essential ingredient of successful strike action, and the Criminal Law Amendment Act brought Gladstone's Liberal government, which passed it, a great deal of unpopularity. As a result of determined agitation, and with the help of the Conservatives grateful for the temporary trade-union support, peaceful (nonviolent) picketing was once more legalized by the *Conspiracy and Protection of Property Act* of 1875.

The legislation of 1871 and 1875 provided the background to the development of New Unionism in the 1880's and 1890's, but the spread of trade unionism received a severe set-back in 1901, when a law court awarded substantial damages to the Taff Vale Railway Company which had sued the Amalgamated

Society of Railway Servants, then on strike, for £23,000 damages representing revenue lost during the strike. The *Taff Vale Decision* laid down a principle which, if accepted generally, must have killed strike action and with it trade unionism, since every strike must inevitably and intentionally injure the employers' revenue or profit. The Conservative government of the time showed no inclination to reverse the judgment by new legislation, and it was left to the Liberal government which took office in 1905 to pass the *Trade Disputes Act* of 1906, which gave trade unions extensive protection against actions for damages.

The Taff Vale decision was merely another episode which convinced trade unionists of the necessity of direct action in Parliament by means of a Labour party which would be independent of the other principal parliamentary parties. Much of the unions' effort in the twenty years before 1914 was directed towards the increase of direct Labour representation in Parliament. Members of Parliament were still unpaid, and the unions supported most of the Labour Members. Not all union members, however, accepted Labour party policy, and in 1909 a union official, W. V. Osborne, brought a successful action against his union, the Amalgamated Society of Railway Servants, restraining them from collecting the *political levy*, the small additional weekly subscription by which the unions financed Labour Members of Parliament. The effects of the *Osborne Judgment* were considerably mitigated by the decision of 1911 to concede the old Chartist demand for the payment of Members of Parliament, but the unions continued to press for a reversal of the 1909 judgment. This was achieved by the *Trade Union Act* of 1913, which authorized the political levy on condition that the majority of members of a union voted in its favour and that any member who so wished could 'contract out' of it.

In the period between the two World Wars the disturbed conditions, the high rate of unemployment, and the government's apparent acquiescence in the policy of low wages, inevitably produced discordant relations between unions and employers. More particularly, the severe fluctuations in prices in the period immediately following the Armistice of 1918 seriously affected the purchasing power of wages and gave rise to a great many wage claims and strikes. The low level of

The general strike, 1926

above: A food convoy passing through Poplar, London
below: A bus, immobilized by strikers, being towed away

demand in many industries compared with pre-war conditions left the employers in a difficult predicament which in some cases strengthened their determination to resist the workers' demands. This uneasy situation characterized the period between 1919 and 1926, which was accordingly one of serious labour unrest and militant trade-union activity. One of the industries most seriously affected by the lower level of output and employment was coal-mining. Disappointed by the failure of the government and the employers to carry out the recommendations of the Sankey Commission of 1919 (see Chapter 18, section 2) the miners refused to accept a reduction in wages in 1921 and were 'locked out'. Though they failed to secure support from other unions, the miners stayed out for many weeks, but were driven in the end to accept defeat and return to work on the employers' terms.

When renewed conflict broke out once again in 1925 over wage negotiations, and the Samuel Commission was appointed to investigate and recommend a solution to the problem of labour relations in the mining industry, memories of the defeat of 1921 sharpened the determination of the miners. The Samuel Commission was very much less favourably disposed towards the miners than the Sankey Commission of 1919 had been, and its report in 1926 recommended (amongst other things) lower wages and the discontinuance of a subsidy the government had granted in 1925 to permit the existing wage levels to be maintained temporarily. The miners refused to accept these terms and were once again 'locked out' by the employers. This time the rest of the trade-union movement did not stand by to watch another defeat of the miners. A sympathetic strike was called on 4 May 1926 by the Trades Union Congress, and all transport, steel, printing and building workers came out in what was called the *General Strike* in support of the miners.

At last the hundred-years-old dream of a general strike in defence of the workers' interests had been achieved; but after nine days the general strike was called off by the T.U.C. in the belief that it had obtained satisfactory assurances from the government and the mine-owners. Baldwin's government had skilfully organized both emergency services and propaganda against the strike. Ministers pronounced the strike to be illegal and the Trades Union Congress in London, never entirely certain in its use of so powerful a weapon, seized the first opportunity of calling off the strike. Trade unionists throughout the country were aghast at the decision to end the strike, but accepted the impossibility of continuing without Trades Union Congress support. The miners alone fought on, refusing to submit to the terms proposed by the Samuel Commission. But hunger aided the coal-owners, and slowly and inevitably the miners were forced back to work, to accept reduced wages and, in most parts, an eight-hour day.

The failure of the general strike and of the miners' strike of 1926 proved a serious set-back to the trade-union movement. Insult was added to injury in the following year, when the government passed the *Trade Disputes Act* which made the sympathetic or general strike illegal, legalized the political levy on condition that members specifically 'contracted in' by signing a form for the purpose, and forbade civil servants to join unions affiliated to the Trades Union Congress. Though a Labour government held office from 1929 to 1931, it did not command a majority in the House of Commons and was unable to reverse the hated 1927 act. Not until 1947, when a strong Labour government was in office, were the offending clauses of the 1927 act repealed. In the meantime, the worst depression in history, beginning in 1929 and reaching its climax in 1932, had driven unemployment to such heights that trade-union action was inevitably forced on the defensive. As an emergency measure striking was declared illegal between 1939 and 1950, so that the movement did not really recover from the catastrophe of 1926 for over twenty years.

6. The Rise of the Labour Party

In the 1830's and 1840's the Chartists had felt that the only hope for government action to remove the social evils which afflicted all but the small middle and upper classes was for the preponderant working classes to be effectively represented in Parliament: all the Chartist aims were directed to this end. Chartism failed, and though Reform Acts of 1867 and 1884 gave the vote in parliamentary elections first to town and then to rural labourers, the working man remained excluded, for all practical purposes, from active participation in government on account of his poverty (which prevented him from giving up his wage to become an unpaid Member of Parliament) and of the absence of a political party interested in the problems of working-class existence. Payment of Members of Parliament was resisted by the governing classes until the issues raised by the Osborne Judgment ultimately led to a decision in 1911 to pay Members £400 a year. The greater problem of creating a party which would effectively give the working man a voice in the government of the country was less easily solved.

The working class first entered parliamentary politics in Britain in 1867, at which time two main political parties held the field — the Conservative and the Liberal. The latter had always included a left-wing radical element, and since there was little hope (as there still is today) for any candidate not backed by one of the established parties, the first Members who might be said to have been returned on a working-class vote inevitably entered Parliament as Liberals. These Labour members of the parliamentary Liberal party, known as the *Lib-Labs* or *Trade Union Liberals*, slowly increased in numbers until there were eleven in 1885, but such small numbers were clearly insignificant in a House of 600 members. An early attempt at direct Labour representation organised by the Labour Representation League, a body created largely by the trade unions in 1869, had got two of its thirteen candidates elected in the 1874 election, but no further results were achieved by this body.

In the late 1880's and 1890's, however, changing circumstances increased the dissatisfaction with the meagre results of the working-class franchises of 1867 and 1884. It became clear that the Liberal party, through which Labour representatives had hitherto mainly worked, offered little prospect of genuine social advance. In 1886 the party had split irrevocably over the issue of Irish Home Rule, and it became clear that the main body under Gladstone's leadership was committed to Irish reform to the exclusion of the 'condition of England question'. Joseph Chamberlain, the radical ex-mayor of Birmingham, in whom many of the working class had placed their greatest hopes for social reforms, found himself in a small political minority, turned his main interest towards Imperialism and drifted to the Conservative party. The only other radical leader in the Liberal party, Sir Charles Dilke, was suddenly driven out of politics in the same year after becoming involved in a divorce case. While this attachment to a moderate political party was dwindling from the late 1880's, the very aggressive, militant element of New Unionism was increasing its influence in the Labour movement, the effect of which was to shift the growing movement strongly in the direction of Socialism. And when, in the late 1890's, unions of both older and newer types suffered costly defeats in some large strikes, it was forced upon all sections of the labour movement, particularly the trade unionists, that, other methods having failed, direct participation in government through an independent Labour party was the only hope.

Throughout the 1880's and 1890's three young political associations had been gathering strength, experience and small followings. The earliest of these, the *Social Democratic Federation* of 1881, was a severely socialist party led according to Marxist principles by H.M. Hyndman. Its strength lay mainly in London, and its candidates in parliamentary elections were never successful. The *Fabian Society*, founded in 1884 by George Bernard Shaw, the dramatist, and Sidney and Beatrice Webb, two indefatigable social historians, had quite a different character. Its emphasis was on gradual social reforms, and it believed at first in continued co-operation with the Liberal party. The Fabian Society was an intellectual, not a working-class, group and its association with other Labour bodies was always reluctant. The third party, the *Independent Labour Party* of 1893, proved to be the most important of the three. Its policy may be summed up in the phrase 'Socialism of a mild type'. Its strength lay in the industrial North and the Scottish Lowlands, and it provided many of the leaders of the early Labour party, including Ramsay MacDonald, Keir Hardie and Philip Snowden.

Though these three groups provided many of the ideas and policies of the early Labour party, the overwhelming support for the movement from all over the country came through the trade unions, and the initiative which led to the creation of the parliamentary Labour Party came from the T.U.C. In 1900, after a conference between representatives of the T.U.C. and the three Socialist bodies, the *Labour Representation Committee* was established. The general election of that year came too soon for the new Committee to get to work, and in its first year only two official L.R.C. candidates were elected to Parliament. For the next six years, however, under its hard-working secretary, Ramsay MacDonald, the L.R.C. developed a nation-wide party organization, and in the general election of 1906, after the Committee had renamed itself the *Labour Party*, thirty Labour members were returned. As the same election brought twenty-four Lib-Labs to Westminster, there was at last a Labour section in the House of Commons capable of influencing the work of Parliament, though it would not be strong enough for many years yet to form a Labour government. Between the wars there were two occasions when Labour governments were formed (under Ramsay MacDonald in 1924 and 1929–31) but though Labour was the largest single party in the Commons on these occasions, it was always out-voted on major issues by the combined strength of the two other major parties, and so achieved little. Not until 1945 did the Labour party win a sufficient number of seats to give it an absolute majority over all other parties. Thus the 'Welfare State', the nationalization of major industries, and other long-standing Socialist aims much discussed during the last decades of the nineteenth century were only realized in the mid-twentieth century, long after the early Labour leaders had disappeared from the political scene.

CHAPTER 21

PEOPLE AND TOWNS

1. MORE PEOPLE

The population of Britain in 1831 was, at 16 million, twice what it had been about sixty years earlier, but still only one-third of what it has grown to in the mid-twentieth century. The population had grown at an unprecedented pace in the second half of the eighteenth century, and this high rate was maintained for most of the nineteenth century. The censuses of population, taken for the first time in 1801, and continued at ten-yearly intervals, show the following expansion:

Census year	*Population of Great Britain* (millions)
1801	10·5
1811	12·3
1821	14·1
1831	16·3
1841	18·5
1851	20·8
1861	23·1
1871	26·1
1881	29·7
1891	33·0
1901	37·0
1911	40·8
1921	42·8
1931	44·8
1941	(no census)
1951	48·9
1961	52·7 (provisional figures)

The threefold increase of population during the nineteenth century, quite apart from any other economic change taking place at the same time, transformed the nature of the country.

Instead of being predominantly agricultural, with only one town large by twentieth-century standards, Britain became a country of town dwellers, and as the century progressed, became increasingly dependent upon imported food supplies.

But the great rate at which the population was growing in the late eighteenth and early nineteenth centuries was not maintained. Three distinct periods in the century and a half after 1800 may be discerned, in each of which quite different factors had a bearing on the rate at which population was growing. The first of these, in which the very high rate of growth achieved in the later eighteenth century was fully maintained, lasted until about 1820: the causes of this high rate are discussed more fully in Chapter 8, sections 3 and 4. Between about 1820 and 1890, the rate of growth fell from its earlier very high level, though it continued sufficiently high for the population to more than double during this period. The principal reason for this slight fall in the rate of growth was an increase in the death rate, resulting from the phenomenal growth of the industrial towns during the first part of this period. The provision of decent housing, pure water supplies and sanitation lagged seriously behind the increase of inhabitants of these midland and northern towns, and in some the expectation of life of the working class was lower than had been usual in earlier centuries. Towards the end of the nineteenth century, when municipal councils were beginning to produce some improvement in the health of towns, other changes contributed to reduce the birth rate. This more than offset the fall in the death rate, and from the end of the nineteenth century the rate of growth of population fell again, reaching a very low level in the 1920's. The rate of growth has since remained slight, a low death rate having been matched by a correspondingly low birth rate.

The fall in the birth rate during the late nineteenth century was the result of several social trends all tending to reduce the size of the large Victorian family. Educational advance and factory reform had turned children from economic assets into expensive liabilities, while the rise in living standards of the last quarter of the nineteenth century made possible a much more humane attitude to the health, education and welfare of children. Women, too, began to rebel against the slavery and burden of excessive child-bearing, and advances in medical science made possible the limitation of the size of families. The development of tastes for other forms of spending — on sport, motor cars, domestic appliances and education — increased the desire to reduce the size of the family. Though the middle classes were restricting the size of their families from about the 1870's, working-class families remained commonly very large until the early decades of the twentieth century. The birth rate was halved between 1880 and 1930. Though this downward tendency of the birth rate in the twentieth century was arrested by the 1940's, the death rate has continued to fall very slowly, and it is small wonder that during the 1940's and '50's the rate of growth of population has been lower than in any other nineteenth or twentieth century decade.

2. People on the Move

When population increases over a long period its distribution must alter. Some occupations and some areas are not capable of absorbing a growing number of workers; others are crying out for ever-greater quantities of labour. In nineteenth-century Britain, in spite of the steady expansion of population, agriculture did not provide any additional employment; towards the end of the century, on the contrary, there was even a decline in employment on the land. Ever-growing industries, of course, absorbed the surplus population, but the increasing concentration of employment in industry at the expense of agriculture involved constant movement. With poor living and low housing standards, the working class of the nineteenth century was a great deal more mobile than it has become in the twentieth century. This flexibility, of course, was a great asset in a rapidly-industrializing country, since for industry to produce most advantageously, it must be located where economic factors dictate, and these were constantly shifting.

Steam was the principal source of industrial power in the nineteenth century. Industry, therefore, grew on the coal-fields, and the history of population movements in the nineteenth century is thus one of migrations into the coal-fields, mostly from the nearby countryside. And since the coal-fields lie almost all to the north and west of a line connecting the estuaries of the Severn and the Humber, this meant a heavy concentration in

the Midlands, the North of England, the Scottish Lowlands and
South Wales. The one exception to this general trend was
London, which has never ceased to be an irresistible magnet.
Greater London has retained almost one-fifth of the population
of the country since the eighteenth century.

The quarter-century after 1914, however, revealed important
changes in the structure of British industry. The older industries
like steelmaking, shipbuilding and textiles, heavily dependent
upon the coal-fields, were found to be declining, and their place
was taken by much more diversified engineering and light
industries. Moreover the use of electric power made industry
less dependent on the coal-fields. Industries were freer to
move nearer to their markets or ports of export, and since
London combined both the largest single market and the
country's largest seaport, these tendencies accelerated the
growth of London's population in relation to other parts of the
country. At the same time areas in which the older and now
declining industries were situated — South Wales, the Cumberland coast, Tyneside and the Scottish Lowlands — experienced
a slow drift of population away to more prosperous districts.
As a result, in the 1930's, the situation was that in these
depressed areas population was declining while unemployment
remained high, but in London and the south-east population
continued to grow steadily and unemployment was very low.
Since most house-building between the wars was prodigal of
space, London's sprawl rapidly obliterated square mile after
square mile of the surrounding countryside. All these aspects of
population movement worried the government of the later
1930's and led, firstly, to some attempt to retain population in
the depressed areas by special measures to attract new industrial
development (see Chapter 23, section 3) and, secondly, to the
appointment of a Royal Commission in 1937 to investigate the
Distribution of the Industrial Population (the Barlow Commission).
It was partly as a result of the recommendations of this commission that, after World War II, governments assumed much
greater powers over the location of industry and the spread of
towns. Some of these developments are discussed in section 4 of
this chapter.

These movements of population within the country were
accompanied by equally important movements of people into

and out of the country. During the nineteenth century many parts of the British Empire as well as the United States were peopled from this country. But for the immense outflow of emigrants the rate of growth of Britain's population would have been much faster than it was. Even in 1839, a statistician estimated that there were 1·2 million British people living overseas, of whom the majority lived in North America and only a small proportion in Australia and the West Indies. By the 1870's emigration was at the rate of nearly 90,000 every year, and in the depression of the 1880's reached almost 200,000 a year. Emigration fluctuated considerably according to the state of trade: bad years drove up the flow of emigrants, good years kept people at home. Trade unions used their funds occasionally to assist emigration from areas where there seemed to be a surplus of labour, while the Poor Law Amendment Act of 1834 had authorized the new Boards of Guardians to make grants to assist emigration, though little use was made by them of this power. Developments overseas proved a powerful influence in accelerating or reducing the flow of emigrants. The discoveries of gold in California in 1849, in Australia between 1848 and 1851, in the Transvaal in the 1880's, and the Klondike in the famous *Gold Rush* of the 1890's, attracted immense crowds of immigrants to those countries, few of whom actually found a living in gold mining.

The world-wide depression of the late 1920's and 1930's led to an almost complete cessation of emigration, while the serious decline in the trade of the countries to which the nineteenth-century emigrants had gone led to the return home of many. Thus there were more immigrants to Britain than emigrants from it in the 1930's.

During the nineteenth century the immense outflow of emigrants was partly, at least, offset by an influx of immigrants. The Irish, who had been coming to England in large numbers since the late eighteenth century, continued to come, particularly after the terrible famine of 1845–6. Some Scots crossed the Border — Scottish farmers were found taking over farms in Essex during the difficult years in the last quarter of the nineteenth century, while a whole community of Scottish steel-workers was moved from Clydeside to Corby in Northampton-shire when the steel firm of Stewarts and Lloyds moved their tube works there in the 1930's. But in the second half of the nineteenth century the immigrants were mainly from Central Europe: Jews from Poland, Germany and Russia predominated.

3. Towns

The ebbing and flowing of the tides of population described in the last section occurred to the constant accompaniment of a swelling of the total volume. But throughout the period the population of rural England remained practically unchanged; it was the towns that grew, and the shifts of population described above largely showed themselves when some towns, or groups of towns, grew rather faster than others.

The general character of urban growth was changed in three principal ways during the nineteenth and twentieth centuries. Firstly, the older towns grew until in some areas they merged into one another, forming what a modern town planner has called *conurbations*. Secondly, some entirely new towns appeared, having their origins in small villages, but growing quickly to

Nineteenth-century industrial housing at Burnley, Lancashire

sizeable towns. Thirdly, large and numerous industrial villages grew up close together in clearly defined areas, forming areas of relatively dense population, but lacking the concentrated, commercial centres of towns.

More than a century of growth was required after large-scale modern industry came to an area before the individual towns reached such a size that their suburbs merged with each other. Thus, in most cases, the conurbations did not emerge until the twentieth century. During the nineteenth century there was just persistent expansion, street after street of small red-brick houses being set down as close as possible to the existing streets. Quite early in the nineteenth century the middle-class employers and professional men moved from their houses in the older centre of the town to healthier suburbs perhaps a mile or two out of the town. Before many decades had passed, the advancing tide of small workers' homes swept past the villas of the employers, leaving them as islands, or as a ring of different character from its neighbours. Suburban railway construction in the late nine-teenth century permitted the middle classes to leap further out once again, in some cases sufficiently far for the expense of travel to deter working-class settlement, or beyond the city boundary, where the County Council was reluctant to spend money on housing for town workers. But as housing radiated like ripples from a stone thrown into a pond, and as successive waves of housing development produced bigger and healthier houses with gardens, the land between neighbouring towns was en-tirely consumed, and only a boundary post or a change in the quality of the road surface marked where one town ended and another began. This happened in south-east Lancashire, where Manchester overflowed into Stockport, Oldham, Ashton-under-Lyne, Bury, Rochdale, Hyde, Bolton and Salford; and in the West Riding of Yorkshire, where the twin cells of Leeds and Brad-ford coalesced with Keighley, Otley, Huddersfield, Halifax and Wakefield, encircling and devouring many smaller townships in the process. It happened, too, on the north-east coast, lining the rivers Tyne and Wear solidly with houses many miles deep for ten to fifteen miles inland, and on Clydeside, where Glasgow merged ultimately with Paisley, Dumbarton, Motherwell and Coatbridge. Most of all it afflicted London, which by 1914 stretched in an almost unbroken sea of housing in a vast circle of almost ten miles' radius. By the 1950's the radius was doubled, and many formerly separate towns like Staines, Slough, Croydon and Barking all but lost their identities in 'Greater London'.

New towns appeared during the nineteenth and twentieth centuries from a variety of origins. The railways created some after the 1830's. Crewe and Swindon developed out of important junctions and railway works. Other centres like Darlington and Rugby owed much of their rapid expansion in the nineteenth century to the employment created by their railway centres. Railways also, by opening-up the vast trade in fresh fish, were responsible for the growth of several fishing towns like Grimsby and Fleetwood. Technical changes in industry produced other new towns; the expansion of steelmaking after the 1850's, for example, accounts for much of the growth of Middlesbrough and Barrow-in-Furness, both of which were the smallest of villages before the coming of heavy industry. Royal patronage first made Brighton fashionable as a seaside resort in the late eighteenth century, and it was almost a century before annual holidays became common amongst even the middle classes. Towards the end of the nineteenth century, however, 'wakes' weeks and other forms of working-class holidays began to give the mass of the people the opportunity to relax at the seaside, and resulted in the rapid growth of resorts like Southend and Margate, Scarborough and Filey, Blackpool and Morecambe, Llandudno and Rhyl. Finally, new towns were deliberately planned, firstly as a reaction from the squalor, crowding and dirt of most of the nineteenth-century industrial towns, and later as a means of absorbing the growth of population without adding to the existing, overgrown towns. This aspect of urban development is discussed more fully in the last section of this chapter.

In the twentieth century, though most English people are town dwellers, many of those engaged in industry do not live in towns. The dispersed nature of coal-mining, in particular, has dictated settlement in villages rather than in towns. In the coalfields of Durham and Northumberland, of Ayrshire and Lanarkshire, of the South Wales valleys, and of Yorkshire, Derbyshire and Nottinghamshire, population grew as fast as in other industrial areas in the nineteenth century, but much of the growth occurred outside the towns. The industrial village

The new town, Edinburgh, planned in the late eighteenth century

has been a feature of the English landscape since the Middle Ages, and the industrialization of the nineteenth century strengthened its hold on the British pattern of human settlement.

4. Town Planning

The way towns grew up has almost always been left to chance. There was seldom any attempt made to guide the direction of new streets or suburbs, or to control the number of houses in any given area. Borough councils had neither desire nor power to influence the kind of houses erected, though they were able to improve, widen and pave streets under powers granted to Improvement Commissioners (see Chapter 14, section 2) or corporations after 1835.

Dissatisfied with the squalor which this lack of supervision produced, a few enlightened men in the nineteenth century tried to show how, by planning in advance and by insisting on certain minimum standards, it was possible to create towns, villages and suburbs in which it would be both pleasant and healthy to live. These pioneers could not, of course, re-build the old, chaotic, industrial towns, and their early experiments had to be made on new sites; they were therefore small, and affected only a very small number of town-dwellers. Nevertheless, by drawing attention to the value of town-planning, they pointed the way to twentieth-century developments which are helping to prevent the mistakes of the nineteenth century from being repeated.

In spite of the magnificent example set by the planning of the 'new town' at Edinburgh as early as 1767, the earliest attempt in the nineteenth century to build a planned industrial community on anything larger than the scale of a village was begun by Titus Salt, a Yorkshire woollen manufacturer, in 1851. At a site on the River Aire near Bradford, round an immense new factory, he laid out a new town to house the families of his 3,000 workers. Careful attention was given to the quality of the houses, to drainage, and to the provision of a full range of public buildings — churches, schools, baths and an infirmary. There was a park and several squares which provided open spaces to ensure that the density of population remained low. Saltaire, as the new town was called after its founder and river, took twenty years to build.

Salt's example was followed by two great industrialists of the late nineteenth century. The Quaker chocolate manufacturer, George Cadbury, began the construction of a new factory outside Birmingham in 1879. In 1895 he set to work to lay out a 'model village' for his work-people. Bournville took twenty-five years to complete, but it provided excellent homes in gracious surroundings in a community where the social needs of the inhabitants were also provided for in schools, meeting halls and churches. At about the same time, William Lever (later Lord Leverhulme), the founder of the firm that has become Unilevers, one of the greatest industrial combines in the world, started building Port Sunlight, a small town to house the workers of his soap and margarine factory in north Cheshire. Believing that a successful business depended upon a contented body of work-people, he sought to create a community which would attract and retain workers. In addition to good houses, Lever's town included a swimming-pool, a theatre, schools, churches and clubs. Further south, some new towns were planned to provide an escape from the sprawling mass of London. A movement to create 'garden cities' led to the foundation of Letchworth in 1903, Hampstead Garden suburb in 1906, and Welwyn Garden City in 1920.

None of these pioneer ventures was on a large scale, and none, of course, had any effect on the older towns, which continued in the twentieth century to develop on the same haphazard lines as they had previously. The housing acts of the late nineteenth century gave municipalities some control over the quality of houses, but none over the number or siting of new houses. A *Town Planning Act* of 1909, though ineffective, made a tentative approach to a new field of state action. Not until after the second World War was the question of town planning taken up energetically. The Barlow Commission of 1937–40 (see section 2 of this chapter) had drawn attention to the dangers of the uncontrolled spread of London, and the *Distribution of Industry Act* of 1945, and the *Town and Country Planning Act* of 1947 gave wide powers of control and direction to both central and local government. Instead of the aimless expansion of the older towns, the policy after the war was for the establishment of a number of entirely new towns in areas adjacent to, but entirely detached from, the older towns. In this way Stevenage, Hatfield, Hemel Hempstead, Harlow, East Kilbride and several other *new towns* were born. Though the old towns still suffer from the undisciplined growth of the nineteenth century, the new towns of the mid-twentieth century offer at least a token of better intentions for the future.

CHAPTER 22

SOCIAL LEGISLATION

1. Parliamentary Reform

Throughout the nineteenth century Parliament concerned itself with reform aimed at improving the conditions of life and work. There were acts of Parliament which created an educational system and an administrative framework by which public health services could be provided, which gave powers to local authorities to provide housing, local transport services, libraries and parks, or which protected the workers against exploitation by employers. Great strides were made in these directions but, in the view of those whose health and happiness they were designed to protect, the reforms came too slowly; too often they were too little and too late. So much, indeed, had both the working- and middle-class Radicals despaired of Parliament taking the kind of action they looked for, that their aims had been concentrated on securing political power as the first step towards the social reforms they had ultimately in mind. Earlier chapters have shown how the social disturbances of the few years after 1815 and of the Chartist decade between 1838 and 1848 had resolved themselves into demands for parliamentary reform. Depressed classes everywhere and at all times have turned to political before economic and social advancement.

And in the early nineteenth century there was ample scope for political reform. A mere 400,000 possessed the right to vote in parliamentary elections (the *franchise*) out of a total population of 16 million. There were two kinds of constituencies before 1832 — county and borough. In the former only those owning land valued for taxation purposes at 40s. per year or more (the 'forty shilling freeholders') were enfranchised, while in the latter (some 200 boroughs) there was a wide variety of franchises which produced electorates varying from a mere handful of voters to several thousand. Naturally the smaller the number of voters the greater the possibilities of bribery and corruption, and much of the dissatisfaction with the electoral system before 1832 arose from the extensive corruption. Over three-quarters of the Members of Parliament were returned by the boroughs which owed their representation to their charters of incorporation, many of which dated from the Middle Ages. The pattern of representation, therefore, reflected the medieval distribution of population rather than that of the early nineteenth century. Indeed the new industrial centres, bringing vast concentrations of population to the Midlands and the North, were almost entirely without direct representation in Parliament.

After an agitation lasting intermittently nearly fifty years in which the landmarks had been Peterloo and some serious rioting in 1831–2, the *Reform Act* of 1832 amended the system of parliamentary elections. Many of the smaller boroughs lost their separate representation, and the seats thus gained were used to raise the representation of the larger counties, or to allow the newer large towns like Manchester, Sheffield or Birmingham to return their own members. In the counties some new classes of tenant voters were added to the forty shilling freeholders, and in the boroughs the franchise was standardized at occupiers of properties valued at £10 per annum ('£10 householders'). The effect of these changes was to add a mere 50% to the electorate, which therefore continued to exclude the working classes of both town and country. Since the agitation of the working class had been a major factor in driving the act through a hostile Parliament, the continued exclusion of any section of the working class from political power produced a bitterness which contributed to the violence of the later 1830's and 1840's.

For the next sixteen years after the Reform Act of 1832 political reform remained in the forefront of Radical agitation, but after the final failure of Chartism in 1848 it dropped out of the picture; working-class energies were diverted into other more hopeful channels. When further reform came, in 1867, it was the result of political moves by the leaders of the major parties rather than of pressure from below. Disraeli's *Reform Act* of 1867 made a further re-distribution of seats in favour of the expanding towns, and widened the borough franchise in a way that enfranchised the working class in all existing boroughs. But not all towns were boroughs, and many working-class men in the smaller towns remained without the vote. The electorate was doubled, but the rural worker and the urban worker in small towns and industrial villages remained voteless. Not until the third *Reform Act* of 1884 was the franchise altered to give the vote to the rural worker.

Though by 1884 virtually all men had the vote, the electoral system was far from satisfactory. It was still not practicable for working men to become Members of Parliament (see Chapter 20, section 6), women were entirely excluded, and the distribution of seats still left the industrial towns grossly under-represented. These shortcomings were only rectified gradually. The re-distribution of seats has been a matter of slow adjustment which has tended inevitably to lag behind the constant shift of population. The payment of Members of Parliament in 1911, and the rise of the Labour Party, aided by the trade unions' political levy, have made possible the entry of working men into Parliament. In spite of the violent agitation of the *suffragettes* (women agitators for female suffrage) in the few years preceding the first World War, the enfranchisement of women was delayed until 1918. In that year women over thirty were given the right to vote, a right which in 1928 was extended to put women on an equality with men by giving the right to vote to all over twenty-one.

2. EDUCATION

Until the nineteenth century was well advanced, education was an advantage secured by a very small proportion of the population. True, there were schools in every town and in most villages, but children of parents unable to pay for schooling were seldom able to attend a school. Attendance at school would have had the effect of reducing the family income, because in too many cases meagre earnings forced parents to put their children out to work at an early age.

The problem of educating children who worked a six-day week was tackled by the Sunday Schools, which originally attempted to fill the role of ordinary schools. Reading, writing and arithmetic were taught to children between the ages of about six and ten who attended all day on Sundays. The first Sunday Schools were started in the third quarter of the eighteenth century and the movement achieved considerable success in industrial areas. One of the largest and most successful Sunday Schools was that at Stockport in Cheshire, founded in 1784. By 1825 this school counted over 4,000 pupils, housed in an immense building which had been completed in 1805. The cost of this type of school was defrayed entirely by public subscription.

Societies supported by churches provided a number of primary day schools which taught children up to the age of about ten. The Church of England maintained the *National Society*, and the non-conformist Churches the *British and Foreign Schools Society*. There was also a considerable number of small private schools up and down the country providing elementary education for a few pence a week. In quite a different category were the grammar schools and boarding schools, where for more substantial fees, boys (for there were none for girls, whose time, it was thought, was better spent at home learning the arts of house-keeping) were taught Latin, Greek and, until the second half of the nineteenth century, little else besides.

But all these types of schools together fell a long way short of providing adequate schooling for the nation's children. It was reported in 1833, for example, that of the 12,117 children in a working-class area of Manchester, only 252 attended day-schools, and a further 4,680 attended Sunday Schools. The remainder received no education at all. In the early nineteenth century it was not generally felt that it was the duty of the government to provide for education, and it was not until 1833 that Parliament first voted money for education. Even then the amount was trifling — only £20,000, which was to be spent by the two Church Societies for the building of new schools. This grant was, however, increased from time to time, and from this time onwards serious attention was given to the training of teachers. Quite probably the government would have taken more active steps to provide more schools had not the unfortunate question of religious teaching arisen. The nonconformist churches resented the efforts made by the Church of England to extend its control over the training of teachers, whilst the support of the schools of any one church with taxes paid by members of other churches caused increasing friction. All sects of the Church believed that education necessarily involved instruction in religion; but there agreement stopped for no sect would accept either non-sectarian teaching or instruction according to the dogma of another sect for their own children. In the event, positive action by the government to develop schools in the country was delayed by this *sectarian controversy* until 1870.

In that year Gladstone's government secured the passing of an *Education Act* which laid the foundations of the present system of universal education. The act ordered the setting up of local *School Boards* whose duty it was to provide schools in all districts where they were needed, with the object of providing elementary education for all between the ages of five and ten. To pay for these new schools and their maintenance, the School Boards, which were to be elected locally, were empowered to levy a local education rate. The School Boards were also to assist the maintenance, but not the building, of church schools. An important clause in the act prohibited denominational teaching (religious teaching according to the beliefs of any one church) in schools established by School Boards. The School Boards did not immediately achieve all that was hoped of them, but in spite of dilatoriness by some Boards, and positive obstruction by a few, the provision of schools had advanced so far by 1880 that it was then possible for the government to make attendance compulsory for all. At first a very small charge was made in 'Board' schools, but by 1891 this type of education was given free.

Still the religious problem dogged the development of education, for the 1870 Act had only required the School Boards to set up schools where none had existed before, and with the assistance of state grants from 1833 onwards the Church Societies had secured strong footholds in many districts. Ill-feeling was caused when rate-payers found themselves paying taxes to support schools run by churches other than their own.

Not until 1902 did the government assume fuller responsibility for the national system of education. By the *Education Act* of that year, the School Boards were abolished, and the provision of education made the responsibility of county and borough councils under the general supervision of the Board of Education. Councils in the larger towns and counties were to elect Education Committees to be responsible not only for primary, but also for secondary, education. Some smaller boroughs and urban district councils were given control over primary education only. The new Education Committees were granted some control over church schools. In extending state control over secondary education, the government was not only making possible important developments in that direction, it was also giving legal authority to experiments in secondary and technical education which had already been made by some of the more progressive of the School Boards.

Once the principle of state provision of universal compulsory education had been firmly established, rapid strides were made in the improvement of the educational services. The provision of school meals was ordered by an act of 1906, whilst medical examinations were instituted by another of 1907. There was a steady extension of secondary education, aided by the act of 1907, which provided Free Places in secondary schools for children from 'elementary' schools. The 1918 *Education Act*, designed by the historian, H. A. L. Fisher, then President of the Board of Education, marked another important stage in the development of the educational system. The act forbade exemptions from the school-leaving age of fourteen which had been widespread and placed strict limitations on the employment of children of school age. It planned a system of 'continuation schools' which young people between the ages of fourteen and sixteen would attend part-time for further education. Lack of money prevented the execution of this section of the act. These developments were accompanied by a considerable broadening of the curriculum in all types of schools, to include science, handicrafts and physical education.

While the number of pupils after 1918 taking advantage of the facilities for education beyond the minimum school-leaving age continued to grow steadily, the provision of schools and classes suitable for this type of education by local authorities increased only very slowly, though some authorities showed much more enterprise than others. The reduction of grants to education by one-third in 1921 had temporarily halted progress in this direction. The Labour government of 1924, however, appointed a committee to consider the whole question of 'post-primary' education. The *Hadow Report* of 1926, as this committee's report is known, though not followed up by any new legislation, influenced and encouraged local authorities in the

Boys of the same age in a school in Bermondsey, London,
in 1894 (above) and 1924 (below)

development of 'secondary education'. The tri-partite division of secondary education into grammar, technical and modern, as well as the selection tests at the age of 'eleven-plus', which were subsequently reinforced by the *Education Act* of 1944, stem from the Hadow Report. Following the committee's recommendations, local authorities have dropped the term 'elementary' and, aided by the *Education Act* of 1936, have reorganized their schools to provide 'primary' education up to the age of eleven and 'secondary' education to the official school-leaving age and beyond.

The century after 1830 saw important progress, too, in the sphere of 'further' education (i.e. all forms of university and adult education). There was a rapid growth in the 1820's and 1830's of Working Men's Institutes and Mechanics' Institutes, where, for very small fees, working men were able to attend evening courses of lectures in a wide range of technical and cultural subjects, and where periodicals, newspapers and books were available in reading-rooms and libraries. The universities, catering still almost exclusively for those who could afford them, underwent a period of drastic change. Until the early nineteenth century, there had been only two universities in England — Oxford and Cambridge — although there were four in Scotland. In the nineteenth century the increase of population combined with the rising standard of education led to the growth of many new universities. These new foundations were mostly established in the newer manufacturing towns like Manchester, Birmingham, Leeds, Liverpool and Sheffield, though the two earliest were in the older centres of Durham and London. Like the older grammar schools and the new secondary and technical schools, the universities in the late nineteenth century broadened the scope of their teaching enormously. Science, hitherto almost completely neglected in the older universities, made rapid strides, whilst History and Modern Languages were added to the Arts Faculties.

The great advances in education in the nineteenth and early twentieth centuries resulted from the work of two types of men — those who produced the new ideas, and those who created the administrative system which put the ideas into practice. Neither group could have achieved substantial progress without the other. The former group included great names like Thomas

Arnold, whose example at Rugby paved the way for the modernization of the Public Schools; Edward Thring, the Headmaster of Uppingham in the second half of the nineteenth century, who led the way in broadening the curriculum of secondary education by introducing such subjects as drawing, carpentry and science; and Margaret McMillan, who, in the early years of the present century, pioneered the development of nursery education. Nor should the influence of such foreigners as Pestalozzi and Froebel be ignored. Their influence on the development of methods of infant teaching can be seen in most English schools to-day. The first of the great educational administrators was Sir James Kay Shuttleworth. On being appointed secretary to the newly-formed education committee of the Privy Council in 1839 he became the first of a long line of distinguished civil servants who have shaped the course of British educational progress. He was followed later by Sir Michael Sadler and Sir Robert Morant, the latter of whom designed the Education Act of 1902.

3. THE RELIEF OF POVERTY AFTER 1834

The New Poor Law of 1834, bitterly opposed though it was when first introduced, brought into being an administrative organization which survived unchanged in its essentials until 1929; but in the intervening century so many circumstances affecting the relief of poverty changed that the Poor Law as administered by the local Boards of Guardians was itself radically transformed. Some of the general economic trends, for example, only made the problems of poor relief more acute. The increasing susceptibility of the economy to fluctuations, and the growing dependence upon overseas trade (itself particularly subject to severe fluctuations), created recurring periods of heavy unemployment. As the expectation of life increased, so the problem of providing for the aged became greater. To offset these trends, there was probably some increase, at least for some sections of the working class, in the level of incomes. This in turn permitted a steady growth of *Friendly Societies*, by which members paid a weekly subscription which entitled them to benefits in the event of unemployment or sickness, or covered the cost of a funeral. Acts of Parliament of 1793, 1829 and 1846 had recognized and protected the Friendly Societies, while the Trade Union Act of 1871 extended this protection to trade unions. In the 1840's about one-quarter of all workmen were members of Friendly Societies. The New Poor Law aimed to cater for all classes of paupers — the sick, the orphans, the aged, as well as the workless. As the nineteenth century progressed, many new local government authorities were created whose activities bordered on those of the local Boards of Guardians. These included the Municipal Corporations brought into being after 1835, School Boards after 1870, County Councils after 1888, and Urban and Rural District Councils after 1894. By the early twentieth century these had taken over many of the social services formerly carried out by the Guardians. But the innovation which most vitally changed the work of the Guardians was the introduction of old age pensions in 1908, and of health and unemployment insurance in 1911.

These changes affected the question of who was to deal with certain aspects of the problem of poverty as well as how they were to be handled. They did not in any way reduce poverty. Towards the end of the nineteenth century two social investigators — Charles Booth in London and Seebohm Rowntree in York — revealed the existence of widespread serious poverty, and in 1905 a Royal Commission was appointed to consider the problem of the Poor Law. The Commission included many well-known social thinkers, including Charles Booth and Beatrice Webb of the Fabian Society. Unfortunately, though the commissioners agreed in condemning some aspects of the Poor Law, they differed in many of their main recommendations. This want of agreement gave the government the excuse to take no action, and the Guardians retained their responsibilities for a further twenty years. Not until 1929 did the *Local Government Act* transfer to county and borough councils the duties of the Guardians.

Between the two World Wars, unemployment was much higher than hitherto. Not only was there seldom less than one million unemployed, even in the best years, but in years of depression the number approached three million. Here was a problem of a scale and a nature which the Guardians were totally unfitted to handle. Indeed by this time the Guardians were concerned with little more than the aged poor, whilst the unemployed worker was assisted by an ever-growing apparatus of insurance. When unemployment insurance was first introduced in 1911, it gave relief payments for not more than fifteen weeks in any one year. This benefit was raised to include two periods of sixteen weeks in 1921, but when many of the unemployed were workless for years at a stretch, this system clearly did not meet their needs. 'Transitional' benefits were introduced to fill in the gaps, and by 1934, when an Act of Parliament brought some order into the complications of the 'dole', over one-third of payments to the unemployed took the form of 'transitional' payments, which since 1931 had been subject to the 'means test'.

Long before the Boards of Guardians were abolished in 1929 the official attitude to poverty had changed decisively. The designers of the New Poor Law of 1834 believed that poverty was a moral, not an economic, problem, and, by assuming that work was available for all, believed that if relief was made unattractive, the problem would solve itself. This attitude died long before the law that embodied it, but it is a disconcerting reflection on the social organization of the wealthiest country in the nineteenth-century world that no attempt was made to change the system of the relief of the unemployed until the twentieth century. Not until 1944, when the wartime coalition government published a White Paper (statement of policy) on *Employment Policy*, did any British government declare that the avoidance of unemployment was to be the first aim of its economic policy. Two years before this a report entitled *Social Insurance and Allied Services*, written and largely devised by Sir William Beveridge (an associate of the Webbs), was published by the government. This outlined a comprehensive scheme of social services which should give all men the *Five Freedoms* — Freedom from Want, Disease, Ignorance, Squalor and Idleness. Between 1945 and 1948 the *Beveridge Report* was translated into practice in a series of acts of Parliament. The 'Welfare State' of the 1940's was a far remove from the New Poor Law of a century earlier.

4. FACTORY LEGISLATION

One of the ways in which the state was required to intervene arose out of the new forms of organization of industry. The early

factories, described in Chapter 14, section 1, brought large
numbers of workers, mostly women and children in the early
stages, together under a single roof. Power was given to
employers to affect the lives of hundreds if not thousands of
workers for good or evil. Where the employer accepted this
grave responsibility to create acceptable working and living
conditions — as did Robert Owen of New Lanark, Jedediah
Strutt of Derby, or Samuel Oldknow of Marple — the transition from the older small-scale domestic industry to the newer
factories and towns was accomplished without serious harm to
the lives and comfort of the working people; but where this
power was wielded by employers devoid of social conscience,
intent only to make profits quickly, untold misery and degradation resulted. In the textile industries, which first turned to
factory organization, the latter type of employer predominated,
particularly in the smaller mills. To make matters worse, the
new textile machines demanded a high proportion of children's
and women's labour. It soon became difficult to recruit
sufficient child labour in the areas in which the textile factories
were springing up, and two birds were killed with a single stone
by making use of the cotton mills to employ the pauper children

Factory children in the early nineteenth century

of large towns like London, Birmingham and Bristol. The children, separated from their parents, were officially 'apprenticed' to their employers, but *pauper apprenticeship* of this kind was a travesty of the old medieval tradition. The pauper apprentices were housed near or in the mill, and worked for the long hours customary amongst all types of workers at this time (up to 13 or 15 hours a day), so that they easily and frequently became victims of every kind of disease and deformity.

The plight of the factory children attracted the attention of a small group of philanthropists. Some of these were themselves cotton-mill owners — like Robert Owen or Sir Robert Peel (the father of the well-known Prime Minister) — who endeavoured to set examples as humane employers; others, like Richard Oastler, an estate manager in the West Riding of Yorkshire, saw the textile industry from outside. They saw that only a rigidly-enforced law would prevent this type of abuse of the powers of employers, and accordingly devoted their energies to securing laws which would prevent the exploitation of the labour of those unable to stand up for themselves in the hurly-burly of nineteenth-century industrial life.

The early tentative factory legislation has been described in Chapter 13, section 4. One effect of the 1802 act had been to turn employers away from the employment of pauper apprentices, which was subject to restrictions, towards the employment of 'free' (i.e. non-apprentice) child labour. The factory reformers therefore turned their attention next to securing restrictions on the exploitation of all kinds of child labour. The first really effective *Factory Act* came in 1833, mainly the outcome of the agitation of *Short-time* or *Ten-hour Committees* organized in the textile districts by Richard Oastler. The lead given by the *Ten-hour Movement* in 1831–2 was taken up in Parliament by Lord Ashley (later to become the Earl of Shaftesbury) who introduced a 'ten-hour' bill in 1833. Realizing that they could not withstand the clamour of the moment for factory reform, the government appointed a Commission to enquire into the question of children's employment. On the basis of the report of this Commission, the government introduced and passed its own Factory Act, less far-reaching than Ashley's original bill. This *Factory Act* of 1833 applied, like its

Women coal-bearers — probably early nineteenth century

predecessors, to textile mills only, prohibited the employment of children under nine, restricted the hours of those under 13 to nine a day or forty-eight per week, and of those between 13 and 18 to twelve hours a day or sixty-nine per week, and required that every factory child should receive two hours' schooling a day. But if the 1833 act disappointed the Ten-hour Movement, it instituted an effective system of inspection: four full-time factory inspectors were appointed with powers of prosecution, and for the first time the laws restricting the employment of children were enforced fairly efficiently.

The 1833 Act was a great advance on the earlier factory acts. So too was the *Collieries Act* of 1842, which prohibited the employment of women and girls underground and required that winding gear (the machinery for raising and lowering the cages for miners and coal) should not be in the charge of anyone of less than fifteen years of age. But the factory acts so far had always fallen far short of the demands of the reformers. After its failure in 1833, the Ten-hour Movement temporarily declined as working-class energies turned against the New Poor Law or to Chartism. It was revived, however, in the early 1840's, and

Ashley introduced another Ten-hour Bill. Once again this was greatly modified by the government before becoming law as the 1844 *Factory Act*. This act prohibited the employment in textile factories of children under eight, and fixed the working day for children at 6½ hours, thus permitting two shifts of children within the long adult working day as well as increasing the time available for the children's education. All dangerous moving machinery was to be fenced to prevent accidents. Once again the Ten-hour Movement had failed to secure its objective, but the successful culmination of the work of the Anti-Corn Law League in 1846, and the advent of a new government in the same year, renewed prospects of success. In 1847, at last, a *Factory Act* was passed which imposed a maximum of ten hours on the working day of both women and children in textile factories.

There have been many factory acts since the successful conclusion to the work of the Ten-hour Movement. These have been concerned with two main developments — the extension of the existing regulations to industries other than textiles and to workshops as well as factories, and the gradual building-up of a comprehensive body of regulations concerning safety and sanitation. Hand-in-hand with this creation of factory law has gone the growth of the factory inspectorate, a highly skilled body of men familiar with the problems of enforcement in every industry, whose work, specialized knowledge and recommendations have been instrumental in bringing modern factory law to its present state of thoroughness and efficiency.

5. Public Health

The factory acts were concerned with the improvement of working conditions. Public health legislation dealt with living conditions. The range of services covered by the expression 'public health' includes the provision of paved streets, street scavenging, drains, sewers, a pure water supply and the regulation of house-building to ensure minimum standards of space and cleanliness. Until the mid-nineteenth century, the creation of healthy living conditions in towns was not considered to be the province of the central government. Various local authorities like parish vestries, manorial courts, borough councils and the sessions of the county Justices of the Peace existed to take whatever steps they considered necessary in these matters, and

Parliament was always willing to co-operate by granting special powers or by creating Sanitary or Improvement Commissions. The work of these Commissions has already been reviewed in Chapter 14, section 2. Useful though this was in many towns, the Improvement Commissions laboured under many difficulties, not the least of which were inadequate technical knowledge of sanitary engineering and grossly insufficient sources of revenue. Inevitably they fought losing battles against the rising flood of squalor in the new towns. The new municipal corporations after 1835 were able to acquire fairly extensive powers by private acts of Parliament, but only limited use was made of these powers in the first decades of the existence of the new town councils.

Though many medical men, notably Thomas Percival and James Kay of Manchester, as well as foreign visitors like Friedrich Engels, publicized their horror at the disgusting condition of British towns in the first half of the nineteenth century, the first report to lead to government action was published in the summer of 1842 by the Poor Law Commission, on *The Sanitary Condition of the Labouring Population of Great Britain*. Edwin Chadwick, now Secretary to the Poor Law Commissioners, instigated this enquiry on the principle that the prevention of poverty (much of which arose from the ill-health engendered by insanitary living conditions) would in the long run be cheaper than its cure by poor relief expenditure. The report led ultimately to the passing of the *Public Health Act* of 1848, which created a central Public Health Board (in imitation of the central Poor Law Commission of 1834) and authorized the election of local Boards of Health. In towns where the death rate was particularly high the central Board could order the establishment of a local board. But neither central nor local boards had much power and the act was very ineffective. The central Board itself, of which Chadwick was the Secretary, was allowed to expire in 1854, and responsibility for public health lay once again with the frequently indifferent local authorities.

There were many attempts in the quarter-century after 1848 to remedy social evils affecting public health, but these either created new local authorities or overwhelmed the existing inadequate bodies with a host of additional duties. One of the most successful of these new authorities was the Metropolitan

Board of Works, created by an act of 1855. This Board, which was ultimately supplanted by the London County Council, made immense strides in sewerage, slum clearance and the preservation of commons. After the *Royal Sanitary Commission* of 1869 had enquired into the administrative tangle, a new central authority, the Local Government Board, was created by the *Local Government Act* of 1871. This Board assumed the supervision of all local public health work, but as the powers of the local authorities remained unchanged, there was little real improvement in the health of towns. The *Public Health Act* of 1875 attempted to remedy these deficiencies. The duties of local Urban and Rural Sanitary Districts (created in 1872) were enumerated. These authorities were to provide a comprehensive service of sewerage, drainage, scavenging and water supply as well as enforcing minimum standards of sanitation in new housing. Several of the larger towns had appointed Medical Officers of Health long before the 1875 Act — Liverpool as early as 1847 — and had a good record in the field of public health long before 1875, but throughout the nineteenth century — both before and after 1875 — the state of British towns remained a disgrace to the nation.

Whether compelled by legislation or acting on local initiative, local authorities worked continuously for the improvement of public health services in their towns, yet conditions improved only very slowly and in some towns scarcely at all during the century. Good work was too often cancelled out by rapidly growing populations. British towns were still hideously unhealthy in the early twentieth century. This was, however, not so much due to local neglect, as to the failure to provide housing fit for humans. By the end of the nineteenth century the basic public health services essential to life in a modern industrial town had come into existence, and the public health problem had become mainly a housing problem. How the nation has tackled the problem of housing in the last hundred years is discussed in the next section.

6. HOUSING

Until the last third of the nineteenth century no authority, either local or central government, had ever considered that the control of housing lay within its sphere of action, still less had there been any suggestion that local or central governments should themselves build houses. Only when the line of housing beside a road was considered to make the road too narrow were local authorities empowered to order the alteration of houses. Not until 1868 was any attempt made to give town councils power to deal with housing in their areas from the point of view of public health. The *Artisans' Dwellings Act* of that year empowered councils to investigate the condition of houses, to condemn and demolish insanitary houses if they judged this to be desirable, and to compensate owners accordingly. The act was never intended to sweep away large numbers of unhealthy houses and the limits to the amount of compensation that could be paid severely restricted the usefulness of this first venture into a new field of legislation. A second *Artisans' Dwellings Act* of 1875 proved to be much more important. This act gave councils powers to deal with whole slum *areas*; the earlier act had been concerned with individual houses. The new act gave powers for the condemnation and demolition of insanitary housing, and required councils to submit reconstruction schemes for the areas affected to the recently-established Local Government Board. Once again there was no suggestion that councils themselves should re-build houses in these areas; it was assumed that the sites would be handed over to private builders. The really important innovation of empowering local authorities to *build* houses themselves came only in 1890, but the number of houses and flats built before 1914 by local authorities was fairly small.

During the first World War, Britain's soldiers had been spurred on with the promise that after the war they would return to 'homes fit for heroes' — a rash promise, since even in the most favourable circumstances many years of strenuous building would have been needed to replace the worst of the oldest housing. Immediately, by the *Addison Act* of 1919, the government prepared for the first time in history to assist the finance of house-building. Local authorities were ordered to survey the housing needs in their areas, and prepare and carry out housing schemes. Government grants were offered to subsidize the rents of houses built by local authorities, while private building was to be encouraged by a substantial subsidy on each house built. The economy campaign during the depression of 1921 caused these subsidies to be reduced, but a new act — the

Wheatley Act of 1924 — paved the way for a vast expansion of municipal housing by offering a subsidy of £9 per house for 40 years on all council houses. Over half a million council houses were built in the next nine years under this act, but a further economy campaign in the depression of the early 1930's cut off this subsidy completely in 1933. By the 1930's, however, housing policy had become focused on slum-clearance: the *Greenwood Act* of 1930 required local authorities to take steps to clear their slums, and offered a subsidy which depended upon the number of families re-housed in slum-clearance schemes.

As a result of these inter-war subsidies, over a million new houses were built by town and county councils in the period 1919–39. During the same period, private builders built nearly three million houses, one-seventh of which were aided by subsidies. This immense burst of house-building, therefore, re-housed nearly half the population of the country. Since most of this housing was in areas not previously built up and consisted of two-storey houses, there was a vast spread in the geographical area covered by towns. Nevertheless there still remained after the second World War a large number of houses condemned as unfit for human habitation long before the war, and the work that had started so vigorously between the wars has had to be resumed with unremitting zeal since 1945.

7. MUNICIPAL ENTERPRISE

Towns which housed many hundreds of thousands of inhabitants found themselves faced with heavy responsibilities. While the smaller towns of the eighteenth and earlier centuries could leave to the individual or to private enterprise the problems of water supply and street lighting, the vast increase in the population of towns during the nineteenth century raised the scale of these problems far above that which could be tackled in the old way. The Municipal Corporations Act of 1835 created effective town councils and gave them access to powers to provide reasonable amenities in their towns; the Public Health and Housing Acts, as has been seen, added further obligations.

These acts, however, simply laid down minimum standards which the government considered municipal authorities ought to adhere to. It is to the credit of British municipal government in the nineteenth century that many town councils went a great deal beyond these minimum standards in certain directions, taking a pride in the municipal achievement, and catering on a much broader front for the needs of their citizens. Powers to undertake these extra tasks — the right to levy local rates and to purchase land for these purposes — were sought and obtained by towns individually by private acts of Parliament.

The first need of any town was for an ample supply of pure water. Until the nineteenth century most towns left the supply of water to private companies who expected to make a profit out of the business, and the inhabitants, on the whole, were accordingly ill served. Until the formation of a private Waterworks Company in 1809, Manchester, for example, with a population then of well over 100,000, drew water only from some local wells or from rivers of questionable purity. For a generation private companies continued to meet the needs of the towns in what was clearly an inadequate way, but by the 1840's, armed with a new sense of responsibility imposed by the act of 1835, the municipal corporations began themselves to take a hand in the task of providing an adequate supply of pure water. Few big towns could provide this from near at hand, and most were driven quite long distances in their search for valleys suitable for damming for reservoirs. In 1847, Manchester Corporation received powers which enabled it to construct extensive reservoirs in Longdendale, a Pennine valley some 15–20 miles to the east of the town. This, like similar schemes in other cities, involved the corporation in immense labour in the construction of a network of water mains to supply houses throughout the town.

The continued growth of towns gave the corporations no rest, and there was endless activity until well into the twentieth century, when the population of the larger towns became fortunately stabilized, to construct new reservoirs even further from the centres of consumption. By the end of the nineteenth century Liverpool had undertaken schemes to pump water from its reservoir in the remote Vyrnwy valley in central Wales, Birmingham from the Elan valley almost one hundred miles away in Central Wales, and Manchester from Thirlmere and Haweswater in the Lake District. London's problem was even more acute since its distance from mountain valleys ruled out that possible source of fresh water. It resorted to extensive pumping from artesian wells and to drawing water from the rivers Thames and Lea, constructing expensive storage reservoirs between the 1890's and the 1940's. As a result of these vast undertakings after 1850, virtually every town house in the land today has its own abundant supply of piped fresh water.

Although gas lighting was first invented by William Murdock in the last years of the eighteenth century, it was slow to come into widespread use. Like other amenities, it was at first left to private enterprise to profit from its sale, and it was many decades before town councils accepted the obligation of meeting the needs of its citizens in this respect. In London the famous Gas Light and Coke Company, established in 1812, had three gasworks by 1822 and supplied gas for street- and house-lighting through 126 miles of mains. By this time there were already similar gas companies at work in Edinburgh, Manchester and other towns. Once again, it was just a question of time before this service passed into municipal control. In Manchester this occurred very early, for even before the city acquired its municipal corporation in 1838, the Police Commissioners, who provided most of the effective government in the town in the period of its rapid growth, had undertaken the supply of gas locally as early as 1817. Another smaller Lancashire town, St. Helens, was supplied after 1832 by a private company, and it was not until 1878 that this company handed over its works to the town council. But in many towns private companies were allowed to carry on, and even by 1914 two-thirds of all gas consumed was supplied by the companies and only one-third by municipal undertakings. Between the wars the corporations continued to take over private companies, until in 1948 the whole industry was nationalized.

By the time that it first became practicable, in the 1880's, to supply electricity for street- and house-lighting and for industrial power, the larger town councils had developed a much broader sense of their responsibilities, and they mostly did not hesitate to go straight into this new field, without leaving it to private enterprise to show the way. An act of 1882, which first established the principles under which private companies might be granted concessions by boroughs for house- and street-lighting, had insisted on such rigorous provisions that few companies ventured into the field. After a second act of 1888 had relaxed some of these conditions, many companies appeared — twelve in London, for example, in 1889 and 1890. Big cities, with experience in the management of large-scale enterprise, entered the field at about the same time. Manchester, for example, secured powers to provide electricity in 1890 and within a few years was distributing electricity to thousands of consumers in all parts of the city. The problems associated with the supply of electricity, however, called for organization on a scale larger than even the biggest towns could provide, and in 1926 the Central Electricity Board was created to co-ordinate and control the generation of electricity throughout the country. Its activities rapidly increased the output of electricity, and between 1923 and 1937 the number of consumers of electricity increased from 2 million to 9 million, their electric cookers, vacuum cleaners, wireless sets, refrigerators and heaters adding much to the comfort and pleasure of human life.

CHAPTER 23

BRITAIN BETWEEN THE WARS

1. DEPRESSION

As the first World War was coming to an end in 1918, businessmen looked forward to a great expansion of trade. The war had caused such disruption to European industry that it was assumed that an interval of many years must elapse before European needs could be met as they had been before the war, and during this period British industry could not fail to enjoy boom conditions. For almost two years after the armistice of November 1918 this prophecy appeared to be true, but in the summer of 1920 prices began to fall, demand for all kinds of goods declined, and stocks began to accumulate. To make matters worse, the government withdrew the price guarantee it had inaugurated towards the end of the war for wheat and coal, and, in 1922, in its anxiety not to squander the taxpayer's money needlessly, reduced state expenditure on education, the health service, the police and the armed services.

The depression which Britain entered in 1921 was never really relieved before 1939. There were times between the wars when slow recovery was initiated, but the economy never recovered to the state of bounding expansion it had enjoyed in the best years just before 1914. Unemployment rose from 690,000 in December 1920 to over 2 million in June 1921, when nearly 18% of all insured workers were out of work. The older, heavy industries were hardest hit, and by the end of 1921 over one-third of all shipbuilding and steel workers were unemployed. Though these industries slowly climbed the uphill path of recovery during the 1920's, mass unemployment remained a feature of the country throughout the inter-war period. Few of the older industries ever achieved again the high levels they had reached in 1913 or for a few months in 1919–20.

Even after some years of progress, there were still nearly 1·2 million workers unemployed in 1929. In that year a serious depression in America began to affect European markets. With a renewal of the fall in prices of all kinds of commodities, demand fell off again. For two years Britain contrived not to be seriously disturbed by this turn for the worse in world trade, but in 1931 the slow downward trend steepened. British trade and industry were hit by the worst depression ever experienced. Between 1929 and 1932 prices fell on the average by 30%, and unemployment rose to a peak of just under 3 million — roughly one worker in five — early in 1933. The depression was most severe in 1932 and 1933; thereafter, partly as a result of a general recovery of world trade, and partly as a result of measures taken by the government and by industry itself, there was a slow recovery. Even this recovery, however, received a set-back in 1938, and it is by no means certain that, had war not broken out again in the autumn of 1939, there would not have been another serious depression in the late 1930's. As it was, there were still $1\frac{1}{4}$ million workers unemployed in 1937, the highest point of recovery in the 1930's.

The economy, therefore, failed to function normally after 1918. There were wild fluctuations in prices, in employment, and industrial output, but even in the relatively good years the level of demand for the products of British industry was far below what was necessary to employ those wanting work. Fluctuations, even quite serious ones, there had always been in the centuries before the first World War; but in those earlier centuries the years of good trade had always strained the economy to the limit, each return of the trade cycle driving output to successively higher levels. Now the fluctuations remained, were indeed more acute than before, and there seemed no prospect of the capacity of industry ever being fully utilized. The phrase 'excess capacity' was always on the lips of businessmen and economists. What had changed? Why had so large a proportion of Britain's workers whose skill and hard work had given Britain her industrial leadership in the nineteenth century to suffer the miseries of worklessness and idleness — some for years on end? These questions are discussed in the next section.

2. CAUSES OF DEPRESSION

Britain's position in the world was changing rapidly in the late nineteenth century. From being in the early nineteenth century virtually the only country with an advanced industrial economy, she became by the early twentieth century merely one country among several. The United States, Germany, France, Belgium and Japan were all industrializing rapidly in the half-century before the first World War. Countries in the early stages of industrialization tend to have a high rate of growth which is not easily maintained in the more advanced stages of industrialization. In the years when a country's railway system is under initial construction, for example, or when its merchant marine is being converted from wood to steel, the demand for the product of the steel industry causes its output to expand prodigiously every year; but after the completion of these early stages of transport development, the demand for steel is merely for replacement or for the normal rate of expansion, and so the rate of growth of the steel industry must fall unless new markets are continually being found. Thus it happened that in the early twentieth century Britain inevitably fell behind in the race for industrial leadership; first — towards the end of the nineteenth century — her rate of growth fell behind that of her rapidly progressing industrial competitors, and then — in the early years of the twentieth century — her industrial output was actually overtaken by both Germany and the United States, so that from first place Britain fell back to third.

Another feature of nations undergoing industrialization is that as their industry grows, they tend to export an increasing proportion of their output; in many instances they need to provide for growing imports of foodstuffs and raw materials. This leads to increasing competition in world export markets. It was inevitable under these circumstances that Britain's share of the world's export trade should fall. So long as world demand for manufactures was growing rapidly, as it was before 1914, it remained possible for Britain's *share* of world trade to fall while the actual quantity of her exports increased: but when, between the two World Wars, the volume of world trade only grew very slowly, or even fell, the continued decline of Britain's share of world trade involved a reduction in the physical volume of Britain's exports.

The trouble arose largely from the fact that, until the last quarter of the nineteenth century, Britain's lead in industry had enabled her to capture a share of the world export trade which it could never have been possible for her to maintain. Her textile, steel and engineering industries supplied countries all over the world which sooner or later turned to the production of these goods themselves. In the first instance Britain merely lost the export trade to the countries which began to meet their own needs for these manufactures. Later, as industries in these countries expanded, they produced in excess of their own requirements and began to compete with British exports in the diminishing number of countries still importing these goods. Some countries, anxious to expand their industries, even went to the length of offering subsidies on goods exported. A good example of these trends is the rise of the Indian cotton industry. In the late nineteenth century India had taken 40% of Britain's cotton exports — probably one-third of her whole output of cotton cloth. After 1900 India turned to manufacturing cotton herself, and her imports from Britain began to fall. She had taken 2,000 million square yards of cotton cloth in 1900, but by 1918 these imports had fallen to 900 million; they fell further to 416 million in 1936 when India was already competing with Britain in other world markets. By the 1950's India was exporting to Britain more cotton goods than she was importing from her.

Another rather more complex development also accounted for Britain's trading difficulties in the inter-war period. Throughout the nineteenth century Britain had consistently lent large amounts of capital to overseas countries, and by the second half of the century the incoming interest payments on these loans were beginning to provide Britain with a useful source of foreign exchange — a substitute for export earnings — which permitted Britain to enjoy the luxury of a disparity between imports and exports: she was able to import more than she exported, using the earnings from her overseas investments to pay for the excess imports. To this form of income from abroad was added the earnings of the extensive British merchant navy, and by 1914 Britain's imports exceeded her exports by almost 30%. Then, during the first World War, Britain was obliged to sell a considerable proportion of her overseas assets in order to pay for food and raw materials at a time when she could spare neither resources nor shipping for exports. Adjustment after the war was therefore particularly difficult. There were insufficient earnings from abroad to meet the bill for imports. Imports must be cut down or exports increased; unfortunately the whole structure of British industry was geared to the pre-1914 relationship between imports and exports. It was proving very difficult even to maintain the existing level of exports, while at the same time the structure of British industry and agriculture dictated the existing level of imports of foodstuffs and raw materials. This *balance of payments* problem remained throughout the inter-war period, and was only partly solved in 1931 by changing the value of the pound in relation to other currencies. As a postscript, it might be added that further heavy sales of British assets during the second World War raised the same problems again after 1945, but on this occasion British industry successfully met the challenge by a striking rise in the level of exports.

For several reasons, therefore, Britain's main need between the wars was to increase her exports, or at least to recover the lost ground in this field. But here, too, she was doomed to be thwarted, since the uncertain economic position of many countries was leading them to erect tariff barriers to trade in the hope of fostering the growth of their own industries. Despairing of finding markets in an increasingly competitive world, countries fell back on preserving the home markets for the products of their own industries. This reaction was, unfortunately, infectious, and many of the raised import duties of the 1920's and 1930's were simply retaliatory. British exporters found themselves squeezed out of one market after another, while at home the government clung tenaciously to the doctrine of free trade. Not until 1931 did the government accept the view that Britain too must protect its home market for British producers (see Chapter 17, section 5).

A great deal of discussion has raged over the question of the effect of changes in the rate of exchange during the 1920's on the predicament in which British industry found itself. Before the first World War the pound sterling and most of the other currencies of the world were related to the price of gold bullion in such a way that it was never possible for exchange rates to vary widely. During the war, however, for technical reasons, it had been necessary for Britain to depart from this *gold standard* of currency valuation, and after the war the question arose as to how soon it would be possible to revert to the normal pre-war practice of the gold standard. Since the former gold standard had been associated with Britain's leading financial position in the world, there was a strong body of opinion in favour of a return to the gold standard at the old valuation. Eventually, in 1925, this school of thought had its way. Some economists consider that the new valuation of the pound was too high, with the result that the return to the gold standard raised the price of British goods overseas; others, however, have argued that stability of exchange rates was the most important goal in 1925, that in achieving this the 'return to gold' in 1925 promoted rather than retarded British recovery, and that Britain's difficulties between the wars cannot therefore be explained in terms of the high valuation of the pound in 1925.

In all these adverse circumstances, the only hope for British industrialists lay in their making the most strenuous efforts to modernize their equipment with a view to reducing costs. With a few honourable exceptions it cannot be said that this was their response to the challenge. This was truest of the old, heavy industries. In coalmining, for example, a high proportion of coal was still cut by hand, while inadequate use was being made of the latest advances in underground transport. In the cotton industry, the decline in markets was so great that there was little incentive to invest in new equipment when the outlook was so unpromising. In general, the level of profits was so low that the supply of industrial capital, about half of which in normal times came from ploughed-back profits, dried up. In these circumstances the best hope was believed to lie in measures to raise the level of profits in manufacturing industry. This would involve scrapping a lot of the older, less efficient, units in industry, and guaranteeing minimum prices for those that were left. This drastic remedy was one of those tried in several major industries in the 1930's, and, with other measures, is discussed in more detail in the following section.

3. How the Depression was Fought

Broadly speaking, then, British industry sought to solve its own problems between the wars by three main expedients — by amalgamations, by closing down the smaller, older, worst-equipped units, and by re-equipment. Amalgamations generally aimed to secure the economies of large-scale production mainly through the integration of all the processes of production in an industry. Already before the first World War had ended one of the new industrial giants — the United Steel Companies — emerged in 1918. This firm brought into one huge organization companies producing iron ore, coal, pig iron and a wide range of steel products, in sites as widely dispersed as Cumberland, Yorkshire and Lincolnshire. In the chemical industry the immense combine of Imperial Chemical Industries appeared in 1926, while in the margarine and soap industries Lever Brothers annually absorbed scores of smaller firms before joining hands with its Dutch rivals, Van den Berghs and Jurgens, in 1929 to become Unilevers, one of the largest international manufacturing combines in the world. The railways, too, had reduced the number of companies to 'the big four' in 1921. On a smaller scale there were similar groupings of firms in the coal, cotton and engineering industries.

The elimination of 'excess capacity' — plant which, it seemed, must remain redundant in view of the reduced demand for the products of industry — was assisted in some instances by organizations set up by the government, but in the shipbuilding industry, the shipbuilders themselves collaborated to create an association known as National Shipbuilders' Security in 1930 which was to buy up and pull down redundant shipyards. The shipbuilders each contributed towards the cost of this operation, which succeeded within four years in reducing the capacity of British shipyards from 2·4 to 1·4 million tons. One of the shipyards eliminated in this way was Palmers' of Jarrow in Durham — 'the town that was murdered'. The shipyard had been the largest employer of labour in that town, and its closure resulted in unemployment there rising to 73% in 1935. In the steel industry, as a result of the recommendations of the Import Duties Advisory Committee (see Chapter 17, section 5), the British Iron and Steel Federation was formed, which took in hand the question of re-organization. This inevitably resulted in the closing down of several older works in Scotland, Tees-side and South Wales.

But the reaction of British industry to depression was not

entirely defensive and restrictive. Some industries displayed a strong determination to recover their former leadership by substantial schemes for re-equipment and re-building. The steel industry, in particular, undertook plans involving heavy capital expenditure at a time, in the early 1930's, when the prospects, in the short run at least, looked particularly discouraging. Colville's in Scotland, Richard Thomas's in South Wales, and United Steel in north Lincolnshire, all embarked on extensive re-equipment, with the result that in the late 1930's the steel industry was able to respond to the demand arising from the re-armament programme with an increase in output from 7 million tons in 1933 to 13 million tons in 1939.

The invigorating reaction of the steel industry in the 1930's to the depression was not, however, typical of the other older industries. Coal, cotton and shipbuilding, in particular, languished. Since these industries employed large numbers of workers and were all concentrated in clearly defined areas, the social repercussions of depression raised urgent problems which the government could not ignore. With the drastic turn for the worse in 1931, the government, for the first time in Britain's modern industrial history, accepted the necessity of action in many fields to promote industrial recovery. Previously, governments had consciously abstained from interfering in industrial matters, and when times were more prosperous, this attitude had won the undeviating approval of industrialists themselves. A drowning man, however, will clutch at a straw, and in the 1930's few groups clamoured more loudly than the industrialists for government action. The steps taken by the so-called 'National' government of the 1930's may be divided into those calculated to create the conditions generally favourable to industrial recovery, and measures concerned with the relief of particular industries.

In the first class was the return to a protective tariff in 1931 and 1932 (see Chapter 17, section 5), after nearly a century of free trade. This only helped to preserve the home market and, so far as it provoked retaliatory tariffs in other countries, may even have contributed to the decline of overseas markets. But the tariffs proved to be useful bargaining counters when negotiations were opened with other countries in attempts to destroy some of the restrictions that were strangling world trade in the 'thirties. In 1935, for example, the British Iron and Steel Federation was able to strike an agreement with the European Steel Cartel (an association of all steel producers in Germany, France, Belgium and Luxembourg), which, by mutual lowering of tariffs, led to a substantial increase in Britain's exports of certain types of steel. Similarly there was an important series of trade agreements between 1932 and 1935 in which Britain was able to secure important concessions from other countries in return for tariff reductions. The most important were with Argentina, the Scandinavian countries, Poland, Germany and Russia, as well as one of 1938 with the United States. The east coast and Scottish coalfields derived considerable benefit from these agreements, recovering important contracts, for example, with the Scandinavian railways.

In the monetary field, the decision to abandon the gold standard in 1931 reduced the price of British goods to overseas buyers, but because world demand was so deficient in that year it was some years before its effect was felt. In a further attempt to stabilize the conditions for overseas trade, the government set up in 1932 the Exchange Equalization Account. The Bank Rate (an official rate of interest which is closely followed by many other rates of interest in the capital market) was reduced to 2% in 1931 and kept at that low figure throughout the 'thirties, partly in the hope of stimulating investment in industry.

In the acutely depressed areas with concentrations of older industries, some more specific action seemed called for. A famous report on 'Investigations into the Industrial Conditions in certain Depressed Areas' in 1934 drew attention most vividly to the need for action in these districts. The report led to the passing of the *Special Areas (Development and Improvement) Act* of 1934, by which four areas — West Cumberland, Durham and Tyneside, South Wales, and the Scottish Lowlands — were designated as areas deemed to call for special aids to recovery. Loans were made available to local authorities in these areas to provide additional employment in new public works, schemes for the settlement of the unemployed on agricultural small-holdings were encouraged, centres for training workers in new skills were set up, and *Trading Estates* were established. On these, modern factories were built and special facilities like loans, tax and rent exemptions offered to entice firms to move into the estates. In all, the Special Area policy achieved very little before the second World War, but with the change of name of the Special Areas to *Development Areas* after the war, and their extension into many new districts, a new weapon has been forged for the regulation of industrial location.

The second class of government measures for industrial recovery in the 'thirties concerned particular industries. This assistance took two forms — of subsidies and of support for reorganization. Subsidies were used widely in many branches of agriculture. In the sphere of industry, a temporary subsidy was granted, for example, in 1925–6 to permit the existing level of wages to be maintained in the coal industry while the Samuel Commission made its enquiries (see Chapter 18, section 2). In the 'thirties there were loans to the shipbuilding industry by the *North Atlantic Shipping Act*, 1934: the main purpose of this act was to permit the completion of the partly-built 'Cunarder 534' (the *Queen Mary*) on which work had been abandoned two years earlier. Tramp shipping was aided by subsidies in the *British Shipping Assistance Act*, 1935.

Re-organization, however, was more attractive to the government, since it did not involve the government in much expenditure. Acts of 1926 and 1930 had tried to encourage amalgamations in the coal industry, but the Coal Mines Reorganization Commission set up by the latter act achieved very little, since it proved in practice to lack powers of enforcement. More was achieved in the cotton industry: an act of 1936 had established the *Spindles Board* which scrapped and compensated the owners of about one-eighth of all spindles before 1939, financing the compensation by a levy on output. A more comprehensive measure — the *Cotton Industry Reorganization Act* of 1939 — set up machinery for price control and other forms of regulation, but was shelved on the outbreak of war.

4. THE CHANGING ECONOMY OF THE 1930's

In the light of the techniques of economic policy subsequently made available, the expedients applied in the 1930's both by industry itself and by the government appear often mis-directed or at best ineffective; but the government had to act within the limits of existing techniques and without the assistance of any effective form of international co-operation. Economic theory learned much from the depression of the early 'thirties; in particular, John Maynard Keynes's *General Theory of Employment, Interest and Money* of 1936 has revolutionized the approach of governments to problems arising from economic fluctuations. The steps taken in the mid-thirties, and outlined in the preceding section, contributed in greater or lesser degree to recovery, but the general recovery of other countries in the world probably helped at least as much. Some of these countries had been worse hit by the depression than had Britain; the United States, with 15 million unemployed at the lowest point of the depression, and countries dependent upon one or two main products like Brazil, India and Australia, suffered even greater shrinkages of output and employment. But these countries were applying their own remedies as vigorously as Britain, and slowly world trade began to climb upwards. Once the worst was over, in 1932–3, every advance proved a stimulus to further advances; greater world trade meant greater exports, and greater exports meant higher outputs and a reduction of unemployment.

After 1936 a new, purely fortuitous element entered the scene. Adolf Hitler secured absolute power in Germany in 1933, and from that moment the peace of Europe was endangered. The startling rapidity with which the German armed forces were rebuilt by Hitler left the other European powers no option but to follow suit. In 1936 the British government inaugurated a programme of extensive re-equipment and expansion of the armed services. Steps were taken to assist the expansion of firms manufacturing armaments. The dramatic increase in the number of warships under construction gave an unexpected but wholly welcome stimulus to the still depressed shipbuilding industry. The young motor and aircraft industries benefited similarly. As these industries expanded to meet the urgent demand for arms, new life flowed back to the steel industry and through it to the coal industry. But lest readers should think that re-armament is the answer to any depression, they should recall that ordinary people cannot enjoy consuming armaments, that productive capacity employed in this way cannot increase the flow of goods they do want, and that the extra taxation to meet the bill for re-armament reduces everybody's purchasing power. Nevertheless, the re-armament programme remained a valuable aid to industrial recovery in the late 'thirties.

In spite of the seriousness of the decline in the older industries, some of the newer industries offered a welcome contrast. The continued growth of the motor industry throughout the 1920's and 1930's has already been mentioned (Chapter 18, section 5), while several branches of the chemical and electrical engineering industries also contrived to show increases of output in even the blackest of years. Even in the stricken textile industries, the relatively new rayon industry failed to succumb to the depression. Above all, the building industry, one of the largest employers of labour in all periods of history, enjoyed throughout the later 1920's and 1930's a boom whose roots lay in the courageous, if belated, municipal housing programmes of these decades. The building labour force increased by one quarter between 1929 and 1937.

The struggle for markets induced manufacturers in all industries to examine their costs very closely. An important result of much of the re-organization and re-equipment was a marked improvement in the productivity of labour. In its turn this led to more goods, often at lower prices. For those in employment, the 1930's, curiously enough, were years of rising real incomes; that is to say, though money incomes remained fairly steady, the fall in prices, particularly during the period 1929–33, enabled people to buy more with their money. With the acceleration in the middle and later 'thirties of the rate of industrial growth, the increasing flow of goods and service ensured the continuance of this rise in real incomes. Between 1931 and 1938, average real incomes rose by 20%. Set against the background of better housing, the increasing flow of luxury goods like motors and domestic electrical equipment, the new pleasures of the radio and the spread of paid annual holidays, for the fortunate majority the 1930's was not such a bad decade. In sharp contrast, however, the wretchedness of the unprecedented millions of families whose breadwinners were out of work has stamped the decade as the blackest of the last century.

INDEX